Renai LeMay

Renai LeMay spent a decade from 2005 as one of Australia's most influential technology writers; reporting and commenting on the intersection between the murky world of politics and the glittering potential of technology policy. This was capped off by a year locked away deep in the bowels of Parliament House as a policy advisor to a Federal Senator; and then another year in the same building as part of the Press Gallery.

At times he was a thorn in the side of those in power; at times he was seen as a laughing stock even by his most loyal supporters.

The most common thing people said about Renai's writing was that they didn't always agree with it; but that it was worth reading anyway.

The Frustrated State

How terrible tech policy is
deterring digital Australia

Renai LeMay

The Frustrated State

How terrible tech policy is deterring digital Australia

Renai LeMay

Cover design by **JC Negretti B**

Cover photograph (Parliament House) by **J. J. Harrison**[1]
Photograph licensed under the Creative Commons Attribution Share Alike 3.0 Unported licence[2]. This licence applies to this image only and not to any other material in this book.

Cover Matrix code image by **TheDigitalArtist**[3]
Image licensed under the CC0 Creative Commons Licence[4]. This licence applies to this image only and not to any other material in this book.

Book template design by **Themzy**

ISBN-13: 978-0-6482595-0-3 (Print)
ISBN-13: 978-0-6482595-1-0 (eBook)
ISBN: 9781724062482 (KDP Publishing)

*Dedicated to
the Delimiter community
– a wild and motley crew,
with hearts of gold.*

*And to my family
– for their great patience.*

Key Supporters

The publication of The Frustrated State would not have been possible without the following individuals and organisations, who directly contributed $75 or more each to the book during its successful Kickstarter campaign.

Many of these individuals were already known to Renai through his journalist work and his prior career. Others came out of the woodwork to support Renai when he needed it most. Renai thanks them all for their support. They are:

Josh Stewart, John Dalton, Joseph Miller, Aaron Theodore, William James Boakes Murphy, Samuel Wittwer, Mark White, Rhys, Nick Bannon, Amit Kuckreja, Chris Knight, Dom Stevens, Jeff Petre, Ray Herring, Stephen Collins, Owen Kelly, Lachlan McEachran, Jodi Blackmore, Andrew Donnellan, Voltagex, Andrew Bishop, Kalanyr, Catherine, Nick Coghlan, Brendan Forster, Paris Buttfield-Addison, Cuinn Wylie, Michael Bowe, Liam Svenson, Erin Turner, Guy Thomas, Peter Sandilands, Anthony Eales, Travis Winters, Peter, Alan Jones, Ian Fletcher, Simo, Craig Thomler, Paul D, Trevor Speering, Sean Bodor, Warren Schaeche, Nick Ross, Charles Gutjahr, Morgan Elliott-Smith, Stephen Dredge, Steph Hinds, John Slee, Hilary Cinis, Andrew, David Peterson, Steven Clark, Michael Devey, Charlie Somerville, Warwick, Christopher Angus, Mike Smith, Natali Vlatko, RocK_M, David Cooper, Sura Novi, Jethro, Alex Roberts, Andy Bright, Pru Quinlan, Jacob Kelly, Samuel Lowrey, Ethan, NPSF3000, Michael Harris, James Eunson, Duncan, Mark, Katherine Sainty, Donna Benjamin, MickeyP, Brent Varischetti, Daniel Beilin, Richard W, Mark Turnbull, Charles Gregory, Ian Birks, Wayne Suffield, Rob, Chris Adamson, Munksaway, Steve Bittinger, Alexander Mossman, Arjan Roseboom, Shaun Ewing, Colin Jacobs, Kieran Simpson, Indra Talip, Brenda Moon, Alex Brak, Paul Brooks, Hourann Bosci, Paul Crawford, Peter, David, Beck Stuart, David Austin, Daniel Myles, Robert, Gary McLaren, Gary Barber, Alan Perkins, Bill Robertson, Elizabeth Stark, Josh, Cassandra Scott, Rohan Latimer, Vlad Lasky and the Systems Administrators' Guild of Australia.

Thank you one and all.

Contents

INTRODUCTION BY MATT BARRIE

A House of Cards

Matt Barrie is widely regarded as one of the most influential figures in Australia's technology sector. A computer scientist and electrical engineer by training, Barrie went on to become a successful venture capitalist and entrepreneur. He is best known for founding online freelancing and crowdsourcing marketplace Freelancer.com, which listed on the Australian Securities Exchange in November 2013 at a market capitalisation of $1.1 billion.

I recently watched the Federal Treasurer, Scott Morrison, proudly proclaim that Australia was in "surprisingly good shape"[5].

I was pretty shocked at the complacency. Despite the fact that Australia has gone through twenty six years of economic expansion, at a fundamental level we really have very little to show for it.

The truth is that for over a quarter of a century, our economy has mostly grown because of dumb luck. Luck because our country is relatively large and abundant in natural resources — resources that have been in huge demand from our Chinese neighbours.

As a whole, the Australian economy has grown through a property bubble inflating on top of a mining bubble, built on top of a commodities bubble, driven by a China bubble.

Unfortunately for Australia, that "lucky" free ride will inevitably end, with China's economy undergoing structural change and the world in general buying less of our two top exports — iron ore and coal.

A hard landing for China would be a catastrophic landing for Australia, with horrific consequences to this country's delusions of economic grandeur.

But despite these facts, our Federal Government is actually doubling down.

Australia's Former Deputy Prime Minister Barnaby Joyce wants Australian taxpayers to be the lenders of last resort to Adani[6], an Indian miner, for $900 million to build a rail line from their proposed Carmichael Thermal Coal Mine[7] to the port at Abbot Point, where our coal would be shipped to India.

Adani is looking for a handout because, unsurprisingly, the banks knocked the company back as the project was too risky[8] and the public backlash[9] against the project overwhelming.

What makes the Adani project so absurd is that India has recently cancelled more than 500 gigawatts[10] of planned coal projects, noting that it intends to phase out thermal coal imports — precisely the type of coal Carmichael produces — entirely by 2020[11].

It's even more perplexing when you consider that 2016 was the year that solar became cheaper than coal[12], with some countries generating electricity from sunshine[13] for less than 3 cents per kilowatt-hour (which is half the average global cost of coal power) and by October 2017, wind power is now cheaper than coal in India[14].

Joyce is trying to take Australia in precisely the wrong direction — forcing us to swim against the tide. But this is hardly an unusual event in Australian politics.

These events are also ocurring in the context of the decline of other important sectors in Australia's economy.

Australia's last two remaining car manufacturers, Toyota and Holden, both shut up shop in 2017[15]. Ford closed the year before. In Australia in 2017, manufacturing as a share of Gross Domestic Product is on par with a financial haven like Luxembourg[16]. Australia just doesn't make anything anymore.

With an economy that is 68 percent services, as I believe John Hewson put it, the entire country is basically sitting around serving each other cups of coffee or, as the Chief Scientist of Australia would prefer, smashed avocado[17].

There is, of course, one area of the economy that is growing — property.

Successive Australian governments have achieved economic growth by inflating a property bubble on a scale like no other[18]. In 2016, 67 percent of Australia's GDP growth came from the cities of Sydney and Melbourne[19], where both State and Federal governments have done everything they can to fuel a runaway housing market. The small area from the Sydney CBD to Macquarie Park is in the middle of an apartment building frenzy which can only described as completely "insane".

That was the exact word used by Jonathan Tepper[20], one of the world's top experts in housing bubbles, to describe "one of the biggest housing bubbles in history". *"Australia"*, he added, *"is the only country we know of where middle-class houses are auctioned like paintings"*[21].

Unfortunately, the astronomical rise in house prices certainly isn't supported by employment data. Wage growth was at a record low of just 1.9 percent year on year in the second quarter of 2017[22], the lowest figure since 1988. The average

Australian weekly income has gone up $27 to $1,009 since 2008[23] — that's about $3 a year.

In short, Australia is building a lot of property that its residents can't afford to buy or sometimes even live in. Much of this growth is being spurred by offshore investment.

So why are governments so keen to inflate housing prices?

The government loves Australians buying up houses, particularly new apartments, because in the short term it stimulates growth — in fact it's the only thing really stimulating GDP growth.

If you look at all of this as a total sum, combined with our lack of future proof industries and exports, what is clear is that our economy is complete stuffed. And it's only going to get worse unless we undertake a major transformation.

What we do need is serious structural change to the composition of our GDP that's substantially more sophisticated in terms of the industries that contribute to it.

One crazy idea is to bolster wage growth by strongly supporting higher education in key areas such as science and engineering, which lead to better jobs with higher wages.

Instead the Government has proposed the biggest cuts to university funding in 20 years with a new "efficiency dividend" cutting funding by $1.2 billion[24], increasing student fees by 7.5 percent and slashing the HECS repayment threshold.

We should be encouraging more people into engineering, not discouraging them by making their degrees ridiculously expensive. In my book, the expected net present value of future income tax receipts alone from that person pursuing a career in technology would far outweigh the short-sighted sugar hit from making such a degree more costly — let alone the expected net present value of wealth creation if that person decides to start a company.

The technology industry is inherently entrepreneurial, because technology companies create new products and services.

Speaking of companies, how about as a country we start having a good think about what sorts of industries we want to have a meaningful contribution to GDP in the coming decades?

For a start, we need to elaborately transform the commodities we produce into higher end, higher margin products. Manufacturing contributes 5 percent to GDP. In the last ten years, we have lost 100,000 jobs in manufacturing.

Part of the problem is that the manufacturing we do has largely become commoditised while our labour force remains one of the most expensive in the world. This cost is further exacerbated by our trade unions — in the case of the car industry, the government had to subsidise the cost of union work practices[25], which ultimately failed to keep the industry alive.

So, if our people are going to cost a lot, we better be manufacturing high end products or using advanced manufacturing techniques; otherwise other countries will do it cheaper and naturally the industry will leave our shores.

However, the thinking at the top of government is all wrong.

I recently heard a speech by the Chief Scientist of Australia where he held up a smashed avocado on toast as a prime example of Australian innovation[26]. Yes, smashed avocado on toast. I am not sure which Australian company has the patent on smashed avocados on toast — it's too surreal to even think about.

In the same speech, he said that an Australian iron ore mine is every bit as innovative as a semiconductor fabrication plant. My mind was seriously blown.

You can throw as much automation, AI and robotics at an iron ore mine as technologically possible, but it doesn't change the fact that mines are, and always will be wasting assets that output a commodity for which we are a price taker, not a price maker, into what is currently an oversupplied global market. An iron ore mine, not matter how advanced, is not a long term scalable productivity multiplier; it is a resource to be extracted with finite supply. Once it's gone, the robots will be dormant.

A semiconductor fabrication plant on the other hand, makes automation of the mine possible. It powers the robotics, the AI and the software — not just for the iron ore mine, but factories and businesses all over the world. It's the real productivity and wealth multiplier. It's a long term sustainable, competitive advantage. Smart and efficient resource extraction is just an application of this technology.

That's why we shouldn't get confused about what is a technology company, because there is no other industry that can create such immense wealth, with such capital efficiency and long term benefit to the world, as the technology industry.

Today, the largest public company in the world, Apple, is a technology company. Apple's market capitalisation of $810 billion[27] is bigger than the entire US retail market sector. Its revenue of over $215 billion generates over US$2 million dollars per employee per year. And that's just the company directly. Think of all the business, jobs, wealth creation and benefits to society that have come indirectly from using the company's computers, mobile devices, software, services and products.

The largest four companies by market capitalisation globally as of the end of Q2 2017 globally were Apple, Alphabet, Microsoft and Amazon. Facebook is eight. Together, these five companies generate over half a trillion dollars in revenue per annum. That's equivalent to about half of Australia's entire GDP. And many of these companies are still growing revenue at rates of 30 percent or more per annum.

These are exactly the sorts of companies that we need to be building.

With our population of 24 million and labour force of 12 million, there's no other industry that can deliver long term productivity and wealth multipliers like technology. But today Australia's economy is in the stone age. Literally.

By comparison, Australia's top 10 companies are a bank, a bank, a bank, a mine, a bank, a biotechnology company (yay!), a conglomerate of mines and supermarkets, a monopoly telephone company, a supermarket and a bank.

We live in a monumental time in history where technology is remapping and reshaping industry after industry — as Marc Andreessen said, *"Software is eating the world!"* — many people would be well aware we are in a technology gold rush.

And they would be also well aware that Australia is completely missing out.

Most worrying to me, the number of students studying information technology in Australia has fallen by between 40 and 60 percent in the last decade depending on whose numbers you look at. Likewise, enrollments in other hard sciences and STEM subjects such as maths, physics and chemistry are falling too. Enrolments in engineering have been rising, but way too slowly.

This is all while we have had a 40 percent increase in new undergraduate students as a whole.

Women once made up 25 percent of students commencing a technology degree. But the figures are now closer to 10 percent.

All this in the middle of a historic boom in technology.

A while ago, I was writing some suggestions for the incoming Prime Minister on technology policy. I had a good think about why we are fundamentally held back in Australia from major structural change to our economy to drive innovation. And unfortunately, I came to the conclusion that it's all too hard to fix.

I kept coming back to the same points.

The problems we face in terraforming Australia to be innovative are systemic, and there is something seriously wrong with how we govern this country. There are problems throughout the system, from how we choose the Prime Minister, how we govern ourselves, how we make decisions, all the way through. This is a large part of why the message about how to form good technology policy is not getting through — the system itself is dysfunctional.

As such, we can't keep on just coming up with great ideas and suggesting them to governments which aren't listening. Instead, we need to think at a deeper level and deal with our structural political problems. Otherwise our politicians will keep on ignoring the difficult, long-term issues around the structure of our economy, as they chase short-term, unsustainable growth.

I'll leave you now with one final thought.

Harvard University created something called the Economic Complexity Index[28]. This measure ranks countries based upon their economic diversity — how many different products a country can produce- and economic ubiquity — how many countries are able to make those products.

Where does Australia rank on the global scale? Worse than Mauritius, Macedonia, Oman, Moldova, Vietnam, Egypt and Botswana. Worse than Georgia, Kuwait, Colombia, Saudi Arabia, Lebanon and El Salvador. Sitting embarrassingly and awkwardly between Kazakhstan and Jamaica, and worse than the Dominican Republic at 74 and Guatemala at 75, Australia ranks off the deep end of the scale at 77th place.

Thirty years ago, a time when our Economic Complexity ranked substantially higher, these words rocked the nation[29]:

"We took the view in the 1970s—it's the old cargo cult mentality of Australia that she'll be right. This is the lucky country, we can dig up another mound of rock and someone will buy it from us, or we can sell a bit of wheat and bit of wool and we will just sort of muddle through ... In the 1970's ... we became a third world economy selling raw materials and food and we let the sophisticated industrial side

fall apart ... If in the final analysis Australia is so undisciplined, so disinterested in its salvation and its economic well being, that it doesn't deal with these fundamental problems ... Then you are gone. You are a banana republic."

Looks like Paul Keating was right.

The national conversation needs to change, now.

The issues which I have mentioned in this introduction are large, intractable problems which Australia has grappled with for decades now — and will grapple with for decades more to come. It will take a colossal effort over many years for our nation to meaningfully move forward in the right direction.

The Frustrated State is part of that effort. This is because it offers more than just a bitter complaint about Australia's problems. In this deep dive, Renai has taken the time to analyse what went wrong across nine major technology policy areas in our recent past and highlight how to avoid the mistakes of the past in the future.

The Frustrated State is more than an academic exercise. It represents a practical tool to place in the hands of our politicians and policymakers as they struggle with future technology policy issues.

I commend it to you.

INTRODUCTION BY RENAI LEMAY

A Chaotic Mess

I remember very clearly the exact moment when it dawned on me that Australia's political class may not have the greatest grasp on technology policy.

It was February 2006, and I'd been a full-time journalist for a little over a year. For most of that year I hadn't had much to do with politics. Like most young people, I barely noticed the existence of Australia's political leaders. It seemed like John Howard was a permanent fixture in the Prime Minister's office, while Labor seemed like a formless mess of frustrated ambition led by a revolving door of faceless men.

At the time I was focused on writing about technology for technologists. I had written many popular stories about Microsoft's latest operating system, Windows Vista. And I had started reporting on Linus Torvalds' comments about the latest Linux kernel developments. But then my editor moved me onto the telecommunications beat, and my world underwent a seismic shift.

I had thought reporting on telecommunications meant detailing the latest broadband speed upgrades — routers, cables, all the usual speeds and feeds. But I soon discovered that everything to do with telecommunications was also deeply enmeshed in the mire of politics.

At the time, Telstra was the biggest game in town. But everything the company did caused outrage on the part of its small band of angry and energetic rivals. There was regular legal action, often involving the Australian Competition and Consumer Commission. The Government and the Opposition were fighting a long, drawn-out war over broadband funding and legislative reform, which frequently spilled over into shouting matches in Parliamentary Question Time. Things were a chaotic mess.

The language was different, too. Even Torvalds — known for his periodic outbursts — was usually quite polite and calm in his responses to my questions. But Australia's telco sector was peppered with huge personalities. It wasn't uncommon for people like Exetel chief executive John Linton to label ideas emanating from Canberra as *"totally insane"* and link them to to the Third Reich, while his counterpart at Internode, Simon Hackett, had gotten into the habit of regularly ripping Telstra a new one up one side and down the other.

One of the first people I interviewed, as I came to grips with this dynamic, was the then Shadow Communications Minister, Stephen Conroy.

In February 2006, in the midst of a steamy Sydney summer, I sat in a tiny cafe in Macquarie Street just down from Labor's state headquarters, and peppered the Labor Senator with questions, as he sat flanked by his advisor, the friendly future Labor MP Tim Watts.

Conroy was on top of his game: Passionate, confident in his knowledge of the issues, and with a deft skill at engaging that impressed me strongly. He was clearly a capable operator and answered my questions with aplomb.

But when I pushed him on technical details, a little doubt started to creep into my mind.

It was clear the Labor Senator could speak adroitly about technology policy issues. But did he really, fundamentally understand the technology which sat at the heart of the fraught policy debates he was engaging in? And what lay behind his sweeping pronouncements about the solutions to the industry's problems? What was the source of his views on broadband competition? How deeply did the historical context figure into his future plans? What evidence did he have for his predictions about the future of the industry?

As I became a more experienced journalist, these types of questions kept on coming up again and again, about politicians from every party.

During the debate over Labor's mandatory Internet filter policy, for example, it became clear that few of the politicians discussing the plan understood that it was technically unworkable. In another example, every year on Budget night, Ministers allocated hundreds of millions of dollars to large technology projects with what appeared to be little understanding of why such projects continually failed.

I distinctly recall a contact of mine commenting that perhaps one reason that few politicians seemed to understand anything about video games was that they — unlike almost the entirety of the rest of the population — didn't play them. In all of Parliament House — a building containing thousands of offices — it appeared that there was not one video game console. At another point, I recall a politician referring to iiNet — by then a billion dollar rival to Telstra — as a 'startup'.

The height of this trend came during the debate over the National Broadband Network, when it became commonplace for total technical falsehoods to be presented as fact.

In one sense, this situation is completely understandable. After all — and I cannot emphasise this enough — politicians do not specialise in knowing things about technology. They are specialists in a completely different set of skills, which revolve around sensing the needs of communities and helping to solve those needs. They are negotiators, networkers, marketers, and above all, communicators and consensus-builders. The best of them are leaders, and even the worst of them will display leadership qualities on occasion. Each has their own distinct personal interests. For some, like Conroy and Watts, this does include a personal interest in technology.

But it also means that they will never have the time or the freedom to investigate those personal interests as deeply as, say, an IT professional who works with technology on a daily basis, or even a professional from another field who dabbles in technology projects after hours.

Politicians also know that they will be frequently called upon to manage portfolios that they may know nothing about — and abruptly switched between portfolios. Today's Minister for Industry may be tomorrow's Attorney-General, and frequently is. This means that politicians must constantly rely on information and opinion supplied by other experts to make decisions. It would be impractical for all of this knowledge to come from their own experience.

I recently went back and read the interview which I conducted with Conroy in 2006. It's still online[30]. Two things are clear to me from that reading, eleven years later.

The first is that Conroy was doing the best that he could at the time. He was a passionate politician who had taken the time to educate himself about his policy area, to think through the issues, and to engage with all of the key stakeholders. This is what politicians are supposed to do: Engage with all pertinent stakeholder groups, collect information, and take an informed policy position that will push the country forward.

But the second thing is a lot more disturbing.

If we look back on Conroy's career making and influencing key decisions about technology policy, what is apparent is that he still got a lot of things wrong despite his best efforts

After all, Conroy is reviled by many as the Minister who tried to foist a mandatory Internet filtering scheme on Australia. And while his National Broadband Network project was a hugely positive initiative, the Labor Senator still made some mistakes that hampered its development.

In short, what we see is that even though Conroy did his best, his best was not good enough for many of us in the technology sector.

If you look back over the past several decades of technology policy in Australia, we see this trend repeated again and again.

Yes, there are many examples of politicians who did not have the best interests of Australia at heart when they made key decisions. Sometimes they've looked out for the interests of a limited set of stakeholders (for example — large corporations, or, on the other end of the scale, specific classes of workers).

But in my career as a journalist and then as a policy advisor, I've seen these people up close and behind the scenes, away from the cameras. By and large, Australia's politicians generally try to do the right thing by the nation — according to their own principles and beliefs — when they make major decisions. Their intent is not usually the problem.

The problem is that they often simply do not have the tools to make the right decision. They frequently lack the necessary resources, the context, the history and the frameworks to make the right decision. And so they make the wrong decision time and time again.

This is particularly an issue when it comes to technology policy, because technology is developing so rapidly, and changing so many areas of human endeavour simultaneously, that politicians have a hard time just keeping up with new developments — let alone correctly setting policy frameworks to deal with them.

The Frustrated State aims to contribute to this lack of resources.

Taken individually, technological developments are difficult to understand. But when you take a step back, it is definitely possible to identify trends in discrete areas that provide a guide for how future developments should be correctly handled, for the good of the whole community.

Each chapter in The Frustrated State consists of a case study detailing how things have gone wrong in the past in a specific policy area. More importantly, each chapter also traces how politicians and policymakers can use this context to make better decisions in the future.

Of course, The Frustrated State is but a tiny drop in the ocean. It will not be possible to convince every Australian politician with influence over technology policy to read it and internalise its lessons.

But if I have learnt anything about politics, it is that sometimes tiny drops can make all the difference.

Parliament House in Canberra — and this is also true of the State Parliaments — is a funny place, because these places sit right at the heart of our society. The right stone, dropped in that deep pool, often creates ripples everywhere else.

It is my hope that The Frustrated State will be one of those stones.

CHAPTER 1

Refused Classification

"I'm not into opting into child porn."

*– Communications Minister
Stephen Conroy*

It's a wintry grey day in Sydney and Stephen Conroy is visibly irritated.

The Victorian Labor Senator is two and a half years into his role as Australia's 53rd Communications Minister, and he has a job of work to do.

It's been barely a month since Julia Gillard ousted Kevin Rudd from the precarious position of Prime Minister. Unlike some of his colleagues, Conroy was fortunate enough to retain his Cabinet position through the Labor turmoil. It's not certain whether his conspicuous appearance on a TV soccer talk show while the leadership change was under way[31] had much to do with his seemingly ability to have a foot in both camps.

But Conroy does love soccer.

Now that's all over, and it's the Senator's job to get out and press the flesh as much as possibly, leveraging his name, his profile and the billions of dollars of cold hard cash which Labor has allocated towards its flagship National Broadband Network project to pimp the Government as hard as he can before the upcoming Federal election.

And today Conroy is pimping hard.

This afternoon's event is at Neuroscience Research Australia, a small non-profit research group based at the Prince of Wales Hospital in the Sydney suburb of Randwick.

And Conroy has a good news story to sell today: Something sexy and in the public interest.

NeuRA hit the media recently when the founding chief executive of the NBN company, Mike Quigley, donated his first years' salary to the institute. Today Conroy's back at the organisation to announce a proposal to use Nintendo's hit Wii video gaming system as a remote rehabilitation system via that same NBN network.

There's just one problem: The media isn't biting.

The real issue the cynical gaggle of journalists surrounding Conroy want to ask about is Labor's controversial mandatory Internet filter policy.

"We've seen a change in Prime Minister, are we going to see a change in the Internet web filter policy?" is the first question the Minister fields.

Conroy laughs it off, but the questions keep on coming. When will Labor's Internet filter legislation hit the Parliament? What does Gillard think of the policy? What does Conroy make of comments by the Greens Senator Scott Ludlam that the filter is effectively dead in the water?

Eventually the veteran Labor Senator cracks.

As his press secretary Suzie Brady watches on, Conroy finally loses his temper and reacts angrily to a question about Internet filter amendments proposed by his Labor stablemate, Senator Kate Lundy. The amendments would effectively make Labor's Internet filter policy optional.

"I'm not into opting into child porn," Conroy tells the journalists surrounding him[32]. He spits the words out contemptuously. He is annoyed.

This is not the first time that Conroy has publicly linked opponents of Labor's Internet filter with support for child pornography. Indeed, he has been making similar comments for years.

"If people equate freedom of speech with watching child pornography, then the Rudd Labor Government is going to disagree," the Labor Senator said in December 2007[33], shortly after taking up his Ministerial role.

And Conroy also blasted digital rights group Electronic Frontiers Australia on the issue in March 2010[34], labelling the group's campaign to defeat the filter policy as *"disgraceful"*. Conroy's comments at the time came in response to a question from Liberal Senator Sue Boyce, who had invited Conroy to respond to the allegation that he was stifling debate on the topic by *"branding critics as child pornography advocates"*.

But it was Conroy's comments about Lundy's amendments at the NeuRA press conference that really cemented his attitude on the Internet filter issue in the minds of the public.

Years later, when Conroy resigned, I labelled the Labor Senator Australia's *"greatest ever Communications Minister"*, for his visionary work on the National Broadband Network[35].

Many of my readers agreed.

Yet many more recalled Conroy's reaction to Lundy as a low mark in his career. They never forgave Conroy for foisting the

Internet filter policy on a largely unwilling Australian public. They never forgave Conroy for the long and bitter campaign the Senator waged to get the filter enacted.

And they never forgave him for the personal attacks he waged on the policy's opponents.

In the pages of The Frustrated State will be contained many stories about bad technology policies which well-meaning politicians have attempted to foist upon the Australian public.

Internet filter policies are probably not the most damaging technology policies which a politician has successfully promulgated Down Under. That title most likely goes to the mess which our political leaders have made of the National Broadband Network.

But, viewed with the benefit of hindsight, there is no doubt that the Internet filter policies have been some of the stupidest.

The tragedy of Labor's Internet filter initiative is that it was never necessary for Conroy to fight the battle that he did to enact it.

The policy was never supported by anything more than a tiny but vocal percentage of the Australian population. It would have been instantly defeated by trivial technical workarounds if it had ever been enacted. And even a cursory glance at the history of the policy makes it clear that it was poorly thought out from the start.

In this chapter of The Frustrated State, we'll examine how the policy came to be, how it failed, and what policymakers and legislators can learn from the exercise.

A dangerous new medium

Labor's mandatory Internet filtering policy published in 2007 has probably been the most high-profile attempt by an Australian Government to comprehensively control the Australian public's access to the Internet. But it was hardly the first. And both sides of politics have played this game over the several decades since the World Wide Web gained popularity in Australia in the late 1990's.

The web browser Netscape had barely graduated into the public consciousness in 1995 before the then-Keating Labor administration kicked off its inquiries into regulating access to Internet content, as part of a wider examination of classification laws.

Various state government initiatives — by Coalition Governments as well as by Labor — quickly followed. Many of these actually passed into law, and by 2003, the national debate over the issue was in full swing. Mainstream think tanks such as the Australia Institute were conducting research into the easy availability of pornography online. In 2018, this most likely seems a little silly to many people, but in 2003 it was a real issue.

The high watermark of this hysteria probably came in March that year, when then-Prime Minister John Howard and his Communications Minister, Richard Alston, acknowledged they were looking at the very same kind of Internet filtering scheme that would led Conroy astray four years later[36].

Alston confirmed at the time that one option was to force Internet service providers to supply their customers with Internet filtering software; another was to force all Internet material making its way to Australian computer screens to pass through a *"nationwide filter"*.

It is instructive at this point to identify where this idea originated, because it will be possible to trace the thread of mandatory Internet filtering from this point forward through the Conroy years and beyond.

The truth of the matter is that Howard's Coalition Government had already passed laws which aimed to protect the Australian public from the supposed evils of Internet pornography. The laws, which established a government NetAlert agency (now defunct) as well as an Internet censorship regime for material hosted in Australia, were passed in 1999 at the urging of Brian Harradine[37], the long-serving independent Senator who shared the balance of power in the Senate for five years from 1994.

The passage of the bills was viewed as part of Harradine's price for passing legislation to partially privatise Telstra.

Harradine may have been satisfied in 1999, but by the time 2003 rolled around, he had realised that the 1999 legislation was terminally ineffective, and was having little impact on the availability of Internet pornography to Australians. It appears to have been in response to Harradine's complaints and the ensuing public debate that Howard and Alston canvassed the issue publicly once more.

There was little real opposition to this kind of broad-brush Internet filtering scheme in 2003. Lobby groups such as Electronic Frontiers Australia, while aware of the issue, appeared to be primarily focusing on the then-higher profile issue of Internet piracy, and the broad alliance of Australian civil liberties, privacy, libertarian and even free market groups that is active on digital rights issues today had barely begun to stir in 2003.

The main rivals to the dominance which the Coalition and Labor enjoyed over Australia's political landscape were at that point the Democrats and the Greens. But the first was already well advanced into its decline and had little attention to spare for minor issues such as Internet filtering, while the Greens had not yet achieved the kind of focus on digital and privacy issues that they would with the election of former web designer and anti-nuclear activist Scott Ludlam to the Senate in 2007.

Perhaps the main voice being raised in opposition to the Government's move to placate Senator Harradine was that of left-wing Labor Senator Kate Lundy.

Lundy — who had built much of her parliamentary career on advocacy on technology-based issues — commented on the topic so frequently that Alston told the Senate on 4 March that the ACT Senator *"put out a press release every week which says, effectively, that it is all too hard, you cannot do anything about it, and the solution is user education"*.

Lundy felt so passionately about the issue at the time that she gave a major speech on Internet filtering at 11:17PM in the Senate two weeks later, blasting NetAlert and the Coalition's new filtering plans, as well as bundling in criticism of a wide range of other related areas, including what she saw as the Government's inaction in dealing with spam email.

"If one thing is to be learnt from the failure of the existing regulatory regime it is that ad hoc censorship and high-level filtering are not the answer," Lundy told the Senate. *"It is about time the Coalition Government concentrated on effective, realistic solutions and took a serious interest in helping parents to combat this problem."*

These were prophetic words indeed, and the truth of Lundy's commentary would be increasingly seen over the succeeding half-decade.

But while Lundy was railing on the topic from the sidelines, more pointed political moves were afoot.

At this time, Alston was facing questions about Internet filtering on an almost daily basis in the Senate from Harradine, who relished using research from groups such as the Australia Institute to tacitly link the growing popularity of the broadband services marketed by players such as Telstra to pornography; and not just pornography, but explicit images of *"sexual degradation"* and *"even rape"*.

Alston's typical response to such questions was to try to placate Harradine by highlighting the Government's existing projects on the top of Internet filtering, while pointing out Labor's *"lassez-faire"* approach to the issue.

"Clearly, you cannot just sit back and do nothing, as the Labor Party would do," Alston told Harradine in the Senate on the issue.

A political opportunist

Alston's pronouncement was pompous; but he also had a point.

If you read the Hansard transcripts from that period, what is apparent is that Lundy's position on Internet filtering as Labor's Shadow Minister for Information Technology — while technically correct and representing a sensible policy position — had left Labor open to the specific kind of political attack which Alston had started levelling at it.

While Labor had other spokespeople on the issue — including Shadow Communications Minister Lindsay Tanner — Lundy's strong views and her position in the Senate opposite Alston were colouring Labor's whole approach to policing the new online frontier.

What is also apparent is that one of Lundy's rivals from the opposite right-wing side of the Labor Party, Victorian Senator Stephen Conroy, had made careful note of this fact.

Conroy's position at the time as Shadow Minister for Finance, Small Business and Financial Services should not have given him much scope to get involved with Lundy's open war on Alston's Internet filtering plans. But his position as Deputy Leader of the Opposition in the Senate, as well as his own personal interest in the field, opened the door for him to eventually enter the Internet filtering arena.

There was also a personal element to this move. Conroy joined the Senate the same year as Lundy, 1996, and he has always shared an interest in the same portfolios as the ACT Senator — technology, telecommunications, the digital economy and even sport. The two have proclaimed friendship at various points during their parliamentary careers, but what is very plain is that they have also at times been bitter rivals.

A Shadow Cabinet reshuffle in October 2004 gave Conroy the Communications portfolio in his own right and the licence to close the gap in Labor's Internet filtering policy that Lundy had left open and that Tanner had not conclusively dealt with.

In June 2006, for example, Tanner publicly mocked then-Communications Minister Helen Coonan for the Government's plans to provide families with free, PC-based Internet filtering software.

"What the Government is proposing to do is half-baked, it's just an attempt to look like they're doing something, but it won't work," he said at the time[38].

Tanner's solution was an ISP-based Internet filter; a policy which mimicked the Coalition's own flirtation in the area directly. But he didn't ram the policy point home at the time.

That would be left up to Conroy in the years to come.

Special Interest Groups

Before we get too far into Labor's Internet filtering plans, it is instructive to pause for a moment to examine some of the other players involved in the situation at this time, as they will become critical to the debate later on.

One of the players with the most influence right from the start was an ISP industry lobby group named the Internet Industry Association. The IIA's mission was to be a leading body representing Australia's Internet industries, including not only ISPs and telcos, but also those concerned with digital content and other online platforms.

The IIA's ostensible approach to the Internet filter threat posed by Alston (and later, Conroy) was to argue that it would be expensive, ineffective and would slow Internet speeds, as well as backing better support for the existing NetAlert system.

But the group but would quickly make a name for itself by compromising with Government when it came to policy development in the area.

As some pundits pointed out in 2003, one of the only reasons that the Coalition was able to create a veneer of credibility for its original NetAlert platform was that the IIA had partnered with the Government to create a code of practice that would assist Internet providers in dealing with the legislation.

Other groups such as Electronic Frontiers Australia which were against the filter were much more strident in their opposition than the IIA. But by and large they lacked influence in Canberra.

On the other side of the fence were organisations such as The Australia Institute, a Canberra-based think tank, which had spurred much of the debate with an influential report on the access which Australian children had to online pornography, as well as the Australian Family Association, the Australian Christian Lobby, and later on, the political party Family First.

The quality of the positions and debating points emanating from all of these sources varied, but it appears clear that several underlying truths can be taken for certain about them.

The first is that there was a strong lack of technical understanding from groups opposing the filter about the viability of using technical measures to deal with such adult content online. At one point, Clive Hamilton, then-Executive Director of The Australia Institute, made the following statement[39], pontificating from the mount: *"For all of the hype, the information superhighway is principally a conduit for pornography."*

This lack of understanding about this emerging universal new media platform was matched on the other side of the fence by the lack of understanding which groups opposed to filtering had about how to engage with the political process.

The second was the disproportionate amount of influence that minority groups wielded on the policy-making process.

It's clear that conservative groups opposed to the filter enjoyed close links with the Coalition, but progressive groups such as GetUp! have also bemoaned the influence they enjoy with the more progressive Australian Labor Party.

One example of this 'inside track' in action was the report that the ACL was believed to have been briefed privately about Labor's July 2010 decision to delay its mandatory Internet filtering plans — ahead of other stakeholders.

It's difficult to get a picture of precisely who Labor spoke to about the development of its own mandatory Internet filtering policy in the mid-2000's. But it appears strongly likely that the ACL, to say the least, was on its list.

Laying the groundwork

It's important here to conduct a little analysis as to what the conditions were which led to the development of Labor's mandatory Internet filter. There are essentially three which acted in cohort to set the underlying environment which allowed the policy to be developed and promulgated.

The first is social pressure from a small number of outspoken interest groups.

It is clear that organisations with then-conservative views — ranging from the Australian Family Association to The Australia Institute were regularly injecting views into the public debate about the supposed corrupting influence of pornography. This constituted open pressure on both the Government and the Opposition to do something about the topic.

The second factor was the lack of a strong and well-integrated movement to oppose these views.

When the Abbott administration introduced comprehensive data retention (Internet surveillance) legislation to Federal Parliament in October 2014, it faced opposition from a broad coalition of interest groups, including civil liberties, lawyers', digital rights, privacy, libertarian and even free market organisations. But in the years from 2003 through 2007, this broad alliance did not exist and was nowhere near as vocal as it is today.

Notably, there were few voices being raised in Federal Parliament in 2003 against the idea of mandatory Internet filtering.

In short, what we can see in the years that led up to the development of the Internet filter policy was an imbalance. One side of the debate clearly had a much stronger connection with insiders in Australia's political system at that time, as well as a unified and coherent message that was actively shaping debate in places like Parliament House.

It is, of course, still possible to create good policy in the midst of such forces. As Kate Lundy pointed out in 2003, a number of parliamentary inquiries had already realised what it would take the major parties more than half a decade to accept — that broad-based, ISP-level Internet filtering was a solution that just would not work the in practice the way that its proponents were arguing it would.

Key figures within the Howard administration eventually realised this — or maybe it was Brian Harradine's decision not to contest his Senate seat in 2004 which did the trick. Either way, by June 2006 the Coalition had backed away from the idea of filtering the whole Australian Internet and had returned to its original model of supplying free, PC-based filtering software to anyone who wanted it.

But this move did not resolve the policy imbalance.

Figures such as Conroy and Tanner appeared to believe that this imbalance opened up an avenue for the Opposition to attack the Government on the moral issue of protecting children from inappropriate content online — and went on to exploit this perceived policy vacuum mercilessly[40] .

One final factor — and this will prove to be an ongoing issue throughout the pages of The Frustrated State — is the amount of resources that Opposition or minor parties have to investigate policy proposals when they are not part of the Government.

An Opposition portfolio holder such as a Shadow Minister will have a small handful of staff to rely on when developing national policy proposals, as well as a minor amount of help from the Federal Parliamentary Library, in addition to external think tanks and lobbyists.

In this context, and with the public debate on Internet filtering being relatively immature at that point, it's not hard to understand why Labor opted to make mandatory ISP-based Internet filtering a key part of its new policy platform for the 2007 Federal Election.

Labor appeared to be poorly educated about the topic, despite Lundy's efforts, largely cut off from politically naive special interest groups opposing the filter, and the lure of pulling votes away from rival parties on morality issues has always been an irresistible one for politicians.

Labor in 2007 was not immune to its siren call.

Beginning five years of policy pain

The formal announcement of Labor's mandatory filtering policy emerged in March 2006, under the then-Beazley-led Opposition. Conroy had been Shadow Communications Minister for almost 18 months at that point, but it was Beazley himself who broke the actual news.

Labor's policy shared much — including its nickname, the 'clean feed' — from a similar policy which the UK Government had legislated in 2003 and implemented in 2004. However, while the UK policy merely aimed to block a list of sites containing child abuse material, Labor's effort went substantially further, promising to block all sites contained material *"prohibited"* in Australia. Beazley labelled this category as containing *"child pornography, acts of extreme violence or cruelty, and X-rated material"*.

Later this would be codified to mean all material which the Australian Communications and Media Authority could not formally classify under the nation's admittedly restrictive classification system. Such 'Refused Classification' content was already illegal to be hosted on websites geographically located in Australia, with the ACMA having powers to order it be removed. The Clean Feed proposal would see a mechanism put in place for content located overseas to be blocked as well.

Some muted voices were raised in objection to this proposal, but what was far more interesting was the way that minority groups such as conservative family organisations and even law enforcement were already swinging in behind it.

When Beazley made the initial Internet filtering announcement, among the voices raised in support were Tasmanian Liberal Senator Guy Barnett, the NSW Police Child Protection and Sex Crimes Commander, and of course the Australian Family Association[41].

What was completely missed in much of the discussion about the filter at this point — especially from the political sector — was any semblance of technical debate about whether an Internet filter could feasibly be implemented and whether it would function as intended.

Most Australian technologists, at this early stage, viewed the feasibility of actually implementing a mandatory Internet filtering scheme about as remote ... of the chances of Beazley becoming Prime Minister. So the community outcry over the scheme was limited.

The electric factor that changed both situations was the ascension of Kevin Rudd to lead the Opposition from December 2006.

By mid-2007 it was apparent that Rudd's strategy of appearing as a younger, more energetic and progressive version of Howard was giving Labor a substantial electoral boost.

Behind the scenes, Conroy's office rewrote Labor's existing Internet filtering policy, codifying it and expanding it into a concrete policy that Labor took to the November 2007 Federal Election.

It was really only in the month after the election that Australians at large realised that this little-known document was one of the policy barnacles that they would have to put up with in a Rudd Labor administration. Rudd's progressive approach to environmental policy, foreign policy, broadband policy and indigenous policy was being applauded at that stage as having broken through barriers which Howard had kept up for years.

However, the Internet filter policy was hardly progressive; in fact it was a throwback policy which even the Coalition had rejected at that point, but which family-oriented Labor rightwingers such as Conroy[42] and Rudd[43] — who both had a background linked with the Catholic church — saw a benefit in.

The growing uproar in December 2007, when the nation truly realised the implications of Labor's Internet filtering policy, forced Conroy to publicly confirm the new Government was still committed to its plan.

It was at this point that Conroy's combativeness — even contemptuousness for — with opponents of the Internet filtering idea first became truly apparent. The new Communications Minister, with the ink still wet on his commission, made it clear that he was simply not going to hear the gradually rising voices of dissent against the Internet filter policy.

On 1 January the New South Wales Council for Civil Liberties described Labor's filter policy as a *"gimmick"* that any computer-savvy Australian would be able to circumvent in *"about two minutes maximum"*[44].

"Labor makes no apologies to those that argue that any regulation of the internet is like going down the Chinese road," Conroy fired back immediately, referring to the Asian country's infamous

tight control of its online environment. *"If people equate freedom of speech with watching child pornography, then the Rudd-Labor Government is going to disagree."*[45]

Burying the lead

It is instructive to pause here and to examine the situation which Conroy found himself in, in addition to consider the broader position of the Australian Labor Party at this time.

Like his colleague Kate Lundy, Conroy had won his Senate seat in 1996, shortly after John Howard put an end to the extremely long-running Hawke and Keating administration that had won Labor so many battles throughout the 1980's and 90's.

Howard went on to enjoy a reign of a similar length, before being deposed ignominiously by Rudd in late 1997.

What this meant for new Labor Ministers like Conroy is a great deal. Eleven years in Opposition — with minimal resources and minimal ability to affect the national agenda — is likely to engender a great enthusiasm in new Ministers. Suddenly thrust into the driver's seat of a large department, and sitting at the great Cabinet table, influential in making the great decisions of the day, is something that is likely to go to anyone's head — even the head of a veteran Senator, as Conroy was in 1997, ten years after he ascended to the Upper House.

And the filter was hardly the greatest policy effort which Conroy had promised the Australian people — and Rudd — that he would deliver.

That honour would go to another significant policy that we will examine in The Frustrated State's second and third chapters — the National Broadband Network.

As the greatest infrastructure project of its time — valued in 2007 at the price of $4.3 billion — the NBN was to be Conroy's signature policy as Communications Minister, the effort which would vault him into the history books and over the heads of his predecessors — broadband skeptics such as Helen Coonan and Richard Alston.

The Internet filter was merely an also-ran.

So Conroy did what any good Minister would do with an unpopular policy — what Sir Humphrey Appleby, the consummate bureaucrat from the BBC's *Yes Minister* TV show, would have advised him to do — he sent the policy off to be examined by the appropriate bureaucracy. This would have the effect of defusing the public concern and giving the appearance of action.

While Conroy and his team focused on the overwhelming challenges of wrestling Telstra into submission and getting the NBN policy off the ground, the Internet filter policy went back to the drawing board, to be poked and prodded by various experts.

The Australian Communications and Media Authority had a stab at the policy, noting international support for the idea in the progressive Nordic states. A "Cyber-Safety Consultative Working Group" was set up to improve online safety, featuring reprsentatives from children's organisations, Internet giants such as Google, and even the Australian Federal Police.

And the Government even launched a school program dubbed "Cybersmart Detectives" in order to educate children about the dangers to be found online.

Meanwhile and behind the scenes, Conroy had tasked the ACMA with commencing trials of mandatory Internet filtering technology to determine how feasible it would actually be to block the Refused Classification blacklist.

What is striking about all of these efforts is that they had all the hallmarks of a Government struggling to come to terms with the fact that it was trying to enact an unworkable policy.

The most successful legislation passed through the Federal Parliament generally either removes roadblocks which are in the way for private industry or citizens to carry out a desired and useful activity — for profit or social good — or puts controls in the hands of a regulator or law enforcement organisation which is able to enforce punishment on organisations which do not comply with legislation aimed at minimising harmful activities. These style of policies help to effectively structure societal behaviour.

Labor's Internet filter policy — which had not yet even made it into the Parliament — did neither.

Instead, it tasked a small regulator with limited resources — the ACMA — with trying to push a technically unworkable scheme onto a massive ecosystem — Internet access — in which hundreds of small companies were operating complex technical infrastructure.

The limitations of the idea became readily apparent in late July 2008 when the ACMA's report into its early trials of filtering confirmed what the industry already knew — that Labor's filter policy would cause broadband slowdowns, coupled with accuracy problems[46].

Then the situation went from bad to worse for Conroy.

The ACMA attempted to cover for its own technical failings by bringing in an outside firm — Melbourne's ENEX Testlab — to conduct a second set of trials with a limited set of ISP partners.

The trial overcame the technical difficulties and showed that Internet filtering was technically possible, although it was unwieldy and could be defeated[47].

But it also broadened the net of organisations which had access to the ACMA's controversial list of blocked Internet addresses.

The result was that in March 2009, infamous disclosure site WikiLeaks published what appeared to be a leaked copy of the Refused Classification list used in the trials. Among the list of 2,300 site addresses were innocuous sites such as the website of a Queensland dentist, a tour operator and a school tuckshop consultant[48].

Civil liberties advocates were aghast to find that the list also contained YouTube videos, pages about fringe religions, mainstream pornography destinations, Wikipedia entries and more.

The list appeared to show that Labor's intentions to protect Australians from harmful information went far beyond merely stopping the country from accessing harmful material … censorship of completely legal pornography and political speech was indeed on the cards.

The leaking of the list confirmed what digital rights advocates such as Electronic Frontiers Australia chair Colin Jacobs had been stating for some time — the use of a secret list of blocked sites for the Internet filter was not sustainable. At the very least, a transparent approach was needed.

But again, Conroy doubled down under the criticism, noting that those who had leaked the list could face police investigation if caught, and denying the list's veracity. *"This is not the ACMA blacklist,"* said Conroy[49], although he was later forced to admit that the later publication of a second list by Wikileaks bore a great deal of resemblance to it[50].

Insight

One high — or low — point in the great Internet filter debate which was increasingly enveloping Labor came in late March 2009. By that stage, the Australian public had had more than enough chances to digest Labor's mandatory filtering plan — and much of the population didn't like what it saw.

SBS saw a chance to expose a hot button issue and invited Conroy onto its Insight program[51], to debate the issue with a live audience and fellow panellists consisting of opinionated voices from both sides of the conversation — conservatives like Lyle Shelton from the Australian Christian Lobby, Jacobs from the EFA, and Tom Wood, a teenager from Melbourne who had infamously cracked the previous Howard Government's more limited, PC-based Internet filtering scheme in as little as 30 minutes[52].

At this stage there is little doubt that Conroy must have seen the Internet filter policy as a millstone around his neck. The controversy around it was doing a fantastic job of siphoning off public attention from Labor's flagship NBN plan, which had its own problems. But Conroy couldn't simply dump the proposal without alienating some of the conservative forces who had helped put Rudd in power.

There is evidence, too, that Conroy may not have fully understood why Australians so objected to the filter.

At most, after all, it would only see a few thousand sites blocked from the Internet. It was already illegal to host that material within Australia's Internet space; the filter would merely block it from reaching our shores. What, Conroy must have thought, was so wrong with that?

The ACMA's blacklist, Conroy told SBS host Jenny Brockie, was based on a list that had been generated during the Howard years; all Labor wanted to do was test a broad-based filter using that list.

"What are people afraid of?" Conroy asked. *"If the critics are right - the test will show it can't work. If the critics are wrong - the test will show it can work."*

It seemed at the time that Conroy thought the public had overreacted to Labor's filter policy — a response driven primarily by fringe groups such as the EFA. *"There's been, unfortunately a lot of misinformation spread about what our intent actually is,"* he said.

But yet again Conroy underestimated the strength and clarity of the opposition lined up against Labor's filter.

The Minister watched, aghast, as Mark Newton, a network engineer from independent ISP Internode — which had been a staunch force opposing the Internet filter — used all the technical gravitas of his profession to baldly proclaim that he could break through Conroy's filter in 30 seconds, that the ACMA list had been overextended to block websites which essentially contained political commentary about topics such as abortion, and that the whole scheme would not be effective in its aims.

"Does filtering work? Can you make it work?" Brockie asked Newton. *"No,"* he fired back.

At several points, the fiery Conroy allowed himself to be drawn into direct confrontation with the outspoken Newton. His disgust at the engineer's clear-cut, black and white response to his attempt at a nuanced policy discussion was apparent, as the Victorian Senator rolled his eyes on national television.

It probably wasn't apparent to Conroy at the time. But this episode probably marked the beginning of the end for Labor's filter policy. If the Communications Minister — with his decade of experience in political rhetoric in the Senate — couldn't win an argument on the topic with a lowly network engineer, then he had probably already lost the public debate.

False Endgame

Over the next year, opponents of the Internet filter policy had much to celebrate, as the movement against the policy contined to gain steam. As its potential for overreach became apparent, stakeholder group after stakeholder group — from librarians to family associations and more — came out of the woodwork to protest what many saw as the first step on a slippery slide to censorship.

Minority parties in Federal Parliament — ever eager to take up policy causes ignored by Labor and the Coalition — weighed in on the issue with a veangeance. A young Greens Senator, elected for the first time in 2007, made a name for himself with his vehement opposition to the policy. Scott Ludlam — a former web designer and graphic designer — was one of the first true digital natives to enter the Parliament.

Throughout early to mid-2010 — as Labor leadership tensions broke out in the wake of Kevin Rudd's downward spiral in the polls — the issue also percolated within the Opposition. A number of backbenchers saw the Internet filter as being fundamentally against core Liberal values, and made a habit of saying so in their party rooms.

Eventually, comparative progressives such as Shadow Treasurer Joe Hockey were convinced the issue was worth taking a stand on. Hockey's August pronouncement[53] that the Coalition would not support the policy was effectively the filter's death knell. Days later, Malcolm Turnbull held a public forum in his electorate to lay the issue to rest.

"It's dead, buried and cremated, and if it shows any signs of revival it will then be exorcised," a jovial Turnbull told the crowd, schooner of beer in hand[54].

And, for a while, it was.

For some months, the leadership squabble between Rudd and Gillard and the subsequent election shoved the filter issue to the bottom of the news pile. Conroy retained his seat as Communications Minister in Gillard's new cabinet — and the filter policy remained on Labor's books. But it appeared his department wasn't actively pursuing the policy. This was not a surprising development. At the very least, Labor would have struggled to get the policy legislated in the very dicey Parliament which its internal struggles had returned.

But something more disturbing was going on behind the scenes.

As it became obvious that the filter would not be easily legislated, Conroy had — prior to the election — asked Australia's largest ISPs to voluntarily implement most of the filter[55] , while passing the policy itself off to yet another review.

As the ramifications of this request became apparent over the second half of 2010, the ingenious nature of Conroy's request became clear.

By phrasing the call to arms as a request, Conroy was able to escape the need to directly legislate the filter. A convenient section of the Telecommunications Act — Section 313 — was dredged up to allow the request to be formalised as the Government, in the form of the Australian Federal Police, requesting reasonable assistance from the telecommunciations sector.

And the actual content to be blocked? Eventually it came to be restricted to a list of child abuse sites as supplied by Interpol, lending the policy the veneer of international support and respectability which it had already achieved in the UK — a jurisdiction which had successfully enacted a filter with that reduced blacklist years ago.

As with virtually every policy idea that had led to the creation of Labor's Internet filter initiative — and had evolved it over the years that it had been a live policy — the idea to thrust the filter as a voluntary project on the nation's telecommunications sector came from a minor outside interest group.

The Section 313 brainwave and the reduced nature of the Interpol child abuse list that Conroy proposed the nation's ISPs filter block originated with the Internet Industry Association, the ISP industry group mentioned earlier in this chapter.

With the broader political situation having shifted and the filter policy left hanging in the wind, the IIA sensed a chance to put the issue to bed once and for all — by compromising on a reduced scheme that most Australians could put up with, tied to existing legislation.

At first the scheme seemed innocuous enough, compared to Labor's much broader and more threatening mandatory scheme. After all, who could object to child pornography being blocked online? And even if the scheme did block a few legitimate sites, it's not as though it would be hard to circumvent.

So the idea went ahead, with several major telcos — Telstra and Optus — implementing it rapidly.

Pause for reflection

Again, it is instructive to pause for a second and examine what really happened here, in terms of the policy development process. around the Internet filter.

In the earlier pages of this chapter, we have attempted to demonstrate that the policy development process around the development of Labor's mandatory Internet filtering policy was hardly something that could be described as robust. Factors such as the lack of resources that Opposition parties are able to access, in addition to the disproportionate influence that small yet loud special interest groups often wield, tend to distort the policy development process; as does the requirements of political opportunism.

In this latter stage of the policy lifecycle of Labor's Internet filter policy, what we see is another factor.

What is often forgotten about the political process in Western democracies in countries such as Australia is that it is largely based on solving problems.

Politicians need to garner the support of as many individuals and groups as possible in order to be elected to parliaments. Once elected, most of them tend to try to solve their backers' problems to some degree. This can often mean a legislative or regulatory solution, or, when a politician is elected as part of a Government, the initiation of a program by the public sector.

This problem-solving mode applies even to issues which don't actually require a solution.

By the time 2010 came around, the policy debate around Labor's Internet filter policy could be regarded as substantially mature. The issue had been examined from every direction by every affected stakeholder group, and considered at length by the parliamentary committee process.

A substantial amount of evidence had amassed by this time that any mandatory Internet filter scheme that the Government could enact would be ineffective. As Mark Newton had so baldly stated to Minister Conroy's face on national television, it would be a matter of seconds to work around the block it placed on the Australian Internet.

Its potential for overreach was substantial, and to add insult to injury, the policy was unlikely to put much of a dent in the real Internet bad guys — those trafficking in abuse material online, or using the Net to organise sales of illegal drugs, for example.

Yet, because the issue had entered Australia's Federal political ecosystem, there was a natural inclination for the Government of the day to do something about it. Labor, having raised the issue at the 2007 Federal Election, could hardly abandon it wholesale. Doing so would be tantamount to admitting it had gotten its policy vision wrong in the first place, to say nothing of inviting invective from some of the conservative groups influential in keeping it in power.

The IIA's Section 313 scheme — ineffective though it would be — offered the Rudd and Gillard administrations the opportunity to reasonably appear to be doing something about the issue.

The same principle would come to apply to dozens of other technology policies passed through Federal Parliament in the past several decades.

Time and time again, in the pages of this book, this issue will come up as policies enter the latter stage of their development cycle before becoming enacted.

Even though the evidence thrown up during policy development will often show that the end result of that process will be a policy which may effectively do ... nothing to address the issue it was created to handle — and even though most of the Australian population may not want that issue even addressed it at all, or even see it as an issue — the trend continues to be that once policy issues enter the political arena, they end up being resolved through being enacted in one form or another.

As we'll see with relation to technology, this compromise process often leads to the opposite of good policy: It leads to terrible tech policy.

From bad to nightmare

Unfortunately — and despite repeated and constant warnings — this is precisely what happened with Labor's mandatory Internet filter policy.

Some sections of Australia's telecommunications industry were initially suspicious about the Government's use of so-called 'Section 313' notices to request that ISPs block a blacklist of child abuse sites sourced from Interpol.

But by 2013, the practice had become well-established enough that it was being taken for granted within Federal Government circles. Most of Australia's major broadband providers had implemented this milder version of Labor's original policy.

The IIA — who had originally proposed the model — had by then been integrated with a much stronger industry lobby group — the Communications Alliance.

At this stage, Conroy — still Communications Minister, six years after ascending to the role, and six years into the Internet filter saga — must have felt as though the Internet filter controversy had ground to a halt. Finally, the Labor Senator must have felt — and without any need to enact direct legislation to support it — a workable version of the filter was in place.

But it took only months after the filter was largely operational that things began to go wrong.

In May that year, it was revealed that the dreaded 'scope creep' which opponents of the filter had been predicting since the policy was first aired had already kicked off. Minor government agencies such as the Australian Securities and Investments Commission had noted the Section 313 usage and had started piggybacking their own censorship requests onto the Interpol child abuse blacklist[56] which was all that Conroy had planned for the filter to cover.

It was bad enough that ASIC and other agencies had started this practice without any transparency to the public.

What was worse was that their requests to major telcos such as Telstra and Optus were demonstrably technically illiterate.

On April 12, Melbourne publication the Melbourne Times Weekly reported that more than 1,200 websites, including one belonging to independent learning organisation Melbourne Free University, might have been blocked by *"the Australian Government"*. It shortly became apparent that this mass blockade of largely innocent sites could be laid at ASIC's door.

In June ASIC revealed the figure had arisen to around 250,000, due the regulator's careless blockade of a whole range of IP addresses — rather than just a simple URL locator.

Conroy responded quickly — calling for guidelines to be placed around the use of the so-called new Section 313 power — but those guidelines were late in arriving, and never really delivered the transparency and accountability — to say nothing of any ability for appeal — which could be expected from a nationwide Internet filtering scheme.

Four years later, it is not clear precisely what websites the Australian Government's new filter blocks, nor what Federal or State Government agencies are requesting the blocking, or what an innocent party could do if their website was unilaterally blocked by the Government.

The filtering approach is easily evaded through the use of consumer-grade virtual private networking software.

But that will come as no consolation to the many public opponents of Labor's filter.

So what about Malcolm Turnbull's 2010 statement that the Internet filter was *"dead, buried and cremated, and if it shows any signs of revival it will then be exorcised"*?

Upon taking up the role of Communications Minister in September 2013 himself, Turnbull hardly exorcised the new Section 313 filter. In point of fact, he presided over its expansion, facilitating its use by film, TV and music studios and copyright holders to block websites accused of hosting pirated material.

Lessons Learnt

When we look back upon the saga of Labor's mandatory Internet filter policy, it is possible to draw a number of key conclusions in terms of what this lengthy episode tells us about how all sides of politics deal with technology policy.

Firstly, it is clear that small, minority lobby groups wield a level of influence on the policy development process which is completely disproportionate to their size — and despite the fact that their views may only represent a tiny minority of the Australian population, even running counter to mainstream opinion.

Secondly, it is clear that the effectiveness of any specific technology policy is often not considered as important by political operators, as is the political capital they can gain by supporting — or opposing it.

And lastly, it is clear that once a policy idea supported by lobby groups with loud voices enters the political ecosystem, it will prove hard to eradicate — no matter how unworkable the policy may be in practice.

Labor's mandatory Internet filter policy was always unpopular and impractical. Furthermore, it was eventually opposed by everyone from senior Labor figures to the leading lights of the Coalition, and by interest groups ranging across the entire political spectrum.

But because the idea had political traction, and was supported by a small number of determined supporters, it eventually came to fruition.

It's a story which will be repeated again and again throughout the pages of The Frustrated State. The intent of this book is to ensure that future legislators make sure the mistakes of the past — so damnably visible during the Internet filter saga — are never repeated again.

SUMMARY

Policy Details

In November 2007, Labor proposed to impose a mandatory Internet filter on Australian Internet users. The filter was to block content deemed 'Refused Classification' — extreme material which could not be classified under Australia's existing classification regime.

What Went Wrong

1. The policy was technically unworkable and trivial to circumvent. It relied on a secret 'blacklist' of banned Internet addresses, which would be likely to throw up false positives. The burden for implementing the scheme would have fallen on industry, which was largely against it.

2. The scheme most likely represented an attempt by Labor to build political capital by meeting the demands of a small number of influential lobby groups.

3. But the policy was not thought through in depth during the policy development phase. In addition, there was little demand from mainstream Australia for a mandatory Internet filter scheme. Labor faced very strong opposition from a broad cross-section of groups when it tried to implement the policy.

Avoiding This Situation in Future

Policymakers could avoid this situation occurring again in future by consulting early, broadly, and in a transparent manner in the development phase of any controversial policy. In addition, there needs to be recognition that minority lobby groups may not argue for the views of society as a whole.

CHAPTER 2

Nation Building

"It's like watching a B-grade slasher movie but, in this film, the knives are out for millions of Telstra customers and shareholders."

Telstra executive Phil Burgess on Labor's National Broadband Network policy

It's breakfast time on a weekday morning and Sol Trujillo is just starting to warm up to his audience.

The Wyoming-born businessman has been recently appointed chief executive of Telstra, and he has a lot to talk about. His soft, comforting American drawl booms out across the major conference room of one of Sydney's most prestigious hotels, packed with people who have risen early to hear him speak.

Youthful, uniformed waiters hover around many tables offering orange juice and pouring coffee refills.

Each table has a small placard announcing the company which has paid for its seats. The nitty gritty details are lost to history, but Alcatel is most likely here, as well as Ericsson —

both key suppliers vying for lucrative Telstra network equipment contracts.

Filling adjacent tables are a bevy of top legal brands. Telstra has more in-house lawyers than most law firms to help it defend its operations from what it sees as onerous regulation, but it still farms a great deal of work out to top players like Mallesons.

Telstra's rivals are also represented. Optus is definitely here, in addition to smaller competitors such as Macquarie Telecom. Industry associations eye each other off across the room. And there's also seats for soberly dressed, clean-cut government bureaucrats, who eye Trujillo's thick, furry, flamboyant moustache with a little discomfort.

The executive's just getting started outlining his vision for transforming Telstra, when a discordant note enters the air. Suddenly, a loud ringing noise is heard from a table positioned right at the back of the room. It's a sharp interruption.

At the table, a cluster of journalists from major media outlets — invited by Telstra to hear its CEO speak — watch, aghast, as their host, Telstra's bombastic public affairs chief Phil Burgess, frantically fishes through his voluminous pockets to find the offending device causing the racket.

After a substantial search, Burgess finally finds his phone and switches it off. Silence returns to a slightly irritated room. Trujillo moves on. Back on message.

This discordant note continues at another media event that same year.

Telstra continues its charm offensive on the media by flying many of its favourite journalists down to Melbourne for a day trip. The purpose is to spruik the progress the telco has made on delivering Trujillo's corporate transformation plan.

The bus pulls up at Telstra's central exchange facility in the Melbourne CBD and the media is disgorged with a chaotic air. The host this time is Telstra's chief operations officer Greg

Winn. The executive — like Burgess — has been imported from the US by Trujillo. The media has dubbed these executives and others 'the amigos', referring to Trujillo's Mexican heritage[57].

During a brief Q&A session, held deep amongst the quietly whirring electronic circuits on the telephone exchange floor, Winn explains that, like rivals such as iiNet, Internode and Netspace have been doing for some years, Telstra has recently begun upgrading its telephone exchanges with high-speed ADSL2+ broadband. This is huge news for Australia's broadband-starved population.

But then Winn makes a jarring comment which throws the media session into uproar.

Telstra won't actually switch on the higher speeds to customers because, Winn says, because it's worried it will have to open up its network to its rivals[58]. *"We don't have it turned on, for all the obvious reasons,"* he says.

The statement appears to make sense to Winn, but the stupefied media looking on has dropped its jaw again. Why would you deploy fast broadband around Australia and then not switch it on? Winn never loses his confident smile.

Welcome to 2006: Ground zero for the development of Australia's first National Broadband Network policy.

The arrival of Sol Trujillo and his 'amigos' into Australia heralded the start of a clean, fresh new debate about Australia's broadband future.

It should have been a chance for politicians to come together with private industry and form a cohesive vision to unlock Australia's digital future and co-invest in positive outcomes for all.

But instead, as the years rolled on from 2006 through to 2009, those discordant notes evident early in Trujillo's tenure developed into a horrible symphony of back and forth verbal vitriol linked to broadband policy failure.

By the time Trujillo exited Australia in early 2009, the nation's broadband policy arena had been transformed into a fraught battleground inhabited by feuding factions. Logic and common sense in the field — to say nothing of sustainable, bipartisan policy solutions — had been sacrificed at the alter of political necessity.

Trujillo and his team weren't largely responsible for that policy failure. As executives, their principal role was to look out for the interests of the company they governed. But the discordant tone they injected into the public debate on broadband policy endured. And their aggressive attitude towards working with others also left its mark.

"The reason you kick pollies around is so that you can be nice to dogs," Burgess said of the nation's political sector at one point[59]. He later labelled the nation's competition regulator as being like *"maggots"*, always trying to 'eat up all the wealth'. As for Telstra's rivals?

"If Optus, Boptus, Moptus or Floptus wants to write a cheque for $4 billion or $8 billion or whatever, go right ahead. Do it. Don't talk about it, do it," Burgess said in late 2007[60].

As he departed in 2009, Trujillo fired a parting shot at Australia[61], labelling it racist, backward, and like *"stepping back in time"*.

"Adios," fired back then-Prime Minister Kevin Rudd at the time.

Trujillo and the Amigos

Labor Senator Stephen Conroy, who held the Communications portfolio for the party from October 2004 until Kevin Rudd re-took the Prime Ministership in July 2013, is the name that most Australians would associate with the development of Australia's National Broadband Network policy.

But the truth is that it was Trujillo and the cadre of Americans who the executive brought with him to help run Telstra from mid-2005 who truly set the framework for the development of what Australia knows as the NBN.

Under Telstra's previous leadership — Trujillo's predecessor, nuclear scientist Ziggy Switkowski, resigned from the role in December 2004 — the telco's strategic approach had largely still been dominated by its past role as a Federal Government department.

It was still majority owned by the Federal Government and tended to act in a somewhat quiescent manner in Australia's telecommunications marketplace. The sector was opened to competition in 1997 under the Howard administration, following directly from a number of other market reforms set in place by the pioneering team of Paul Keating and Bob Hawke, but it was still largely dominated by Telstra and its smaller sibling Optus. The telco's management appeared largely satisfied with the large profits it was continually making as a result of that fact, as did the political figures who still loomed large in influence over the company.

Trujillo's arrival in Australia in mid-2005 changed the situation dramatically. Suddenly, Telstra stopped playing nice and started playing high-stakes poker with its political masters.

With a significant amount of global telco experience in the US and Europe, Trujillo was no doubt highly aware of the fact that there was a high likelihood that a future Federal Government — and it could be the Coalition, or it could be Labor — would be likely to eventually carve the telco into separate chunks, splitting its operations up in order to accelerate the development of market competition from rapidly growing fixed and mobile telcos in the expanding Australian telecommunications sector.

This is precisely the fate suffered by Telstra's fellow incumbent telcos Telecom New Zealand and BT in the UK.

The new Telstra leader's mandate — given to the executive by Telstra's then-board, led by activist chair Donald McGauchie, who also appeared to be fed up with political interference in the company — was to help Telstra avoid this fate and ensure it continued to make fat profits for its shareholders.

In the process, Trujillo and McGauchie would need to force Telstra into the difficult transition from government department to fully privatised telco, while also entrenching its monopolistic position in Australia's telecommunications market.

There were a number of key planks to the strategy which Trujillo rapidly put in place after his appointment in mid-2005, outlined in detail during a marathon all-day briefing session in mid-November, six months after the American executive's ascension to the Telstra throne[62].

A number of these were aimed at positioning Telstra for the eventual third tranche of its share sale. Trujillo proposed slashing the telco's overweight workforce by between 10,000 and 12,000 jobs over five years, a move which would dramatically cut its expenses and lift profits. It would also modernise its network core and dramatically rationalise its IT platforms.

But it was the approach that Trujillo took with Telstra's mobile and fixed networks which represented the executive's truly strategic moves.

On the mobile side, Trujillo planned to steal a march upon Telstra's rivals by rapidly deploying a brand new 3G mobile network. Australia's other three mobile players — Optus, Vodafone and Hutchison — had gradually been encroaching on Telstra's mobile territory over the past half-decade, with Hutchison in particular making strides with its 3G technology while Telstra itself suffered a series of unfortunate adventures with poor mobile formats such as Japan's i-mode.

No other telco in Australia has the sheer scale of Telstra, nor its access to capital. Trujillo pushed supplier Ericsson to the absolute limit — forcing the Swedish vendor to work 24 hours a day, seven days a week, to get the new mobile network built in only a year. At times, he would call Ericsson chief executive Carl-Henric Svanberg at odd hours to demand updates. And at other times he pressured Telstra's internal staff relentlessly to ensure the pace was kept.

"I can certainly tell you that there hasn't been a project that we have been involved in ever in Ericsson that has been this demanding and this fast," Svanberg said at the launch of 'Next G' in October 2006[63]. Key to Trujillo's plans for Next G was a strategy of keeping its Next G infrastructure to itself. Telstra had been badly burnt in past mobile network rollouts, which it had at times been forced to open to competitive wholesale access by its biggest rival, Optus. Trujillo did not want the same situation to occur with Next G, and he would end up getting his way.

With relation to its fixed broadband networks, Trujillo had few plans for the HFC cable network Switkowski had built in competition with his old company, Optus, throughout the late 1990's and early 2000's. The technology — originally envisioned to deliver pay TV — was, in 2006, seen largely as legacy, although this has changed somewhat with the development of the DOCSIS 3 generation of technologies.

The copper gambit

However, Trujillo knew that he was facing the mother of all fights with respect to Telstra's copper network.

That network — built progressively throughout the past century when Telstra was known as the Postmaster-General's Department — was the brightest jewel in Telstra's crown. In 2006, and for many years to come, Telstra still made most of its revenue and a huge amount of its eventual profit from telephone calls and broadband services over the copper.

The 1990's entrance of Optus into the market allowed Australians to choose who they placed their long-distance phone calls with. The calls were largely still routed by Telstra but billed by Optus, with some integration with Optus' network.

But by the mid-2000's, as Trujillo entered the scene, Telstra's dominance of its copper network was under full-scale threat. A number of smaller and more nimble rivals — the aforementioned iiNet, Internode, Netspace and others — had started deploying their own hardware in Telstra's telephone exchanges and were cutting further and further into Telstra's margins.

This process had been aided by a constant series of favourable decisions by the ACCC designed to restrain Telstra and further develop a competitive local broadband market, based largely on allowing other telcos to gain fair wholesale access to Telstra's own network, undercutting Telstra's own retail operations in the process.

The challenge to Telstra was also based on the foundation of the Government's 1997 telecommunications industry reforms, which further opened the industry up to competition, following the initial regulatory efforts of the early 1990's.

We delve into this history not to give a detailed corporate history of Telstra — but to illustrate how the first NBN policy devised by the Labor Party and formally launched in 2007 came to be formed.

Trujillo's decision on what to do about the unfolding situation with its copper network was a momentous one that would shape the next decade of telecommunications policy in Australia and ultimately lead to the NBN project.

It took only a month or two after Trujillo took up the reins at Telstra in mid-2005 for the executive to propose to Prime Minister John Howard and other Cabinet Ministers that about $5 billion would be spent — either of Telstra's money or from the Federal Budget — upgrading its copper telephony network to support high-speed broadband through Fibre to the Node infrastructure. This plan wasn't wholly developed by Trujillo's team — at least part of it was in existence before the Americans arrived — but Trujillo and the Amigos were enthusiastic in promoting it to Government[64].

This proposal — which Trujillo formalised in November 2005 when he publicly presented his strategic approach to the media and Telstra shareholders — was a genuine one in the sense that FTTN was legitimately the technology which much of the global telecommunications sector was focused on, and which Trujillo believed would be an effective way to upgrade Telstra's copper network.

FTTN was viewed as cost-effective because it would see part of Telstra's existing copper network upgraded to fibre, while maintaining the bit which connects to each customer's premises. Significantly improved speeds, at a lower cost than a full Fibre to the Premises replacement, which would do away with the copper entirely.

Trujillo had worked in France — where France Telecom (now Orange) has deployed FTTN in its network, and French company Alcatel was a leading supplier of FTTN gear. The move towards FTTN was also gathering steam in other European countries such as the UK and Germany and is being used extensively by telcos such as AT&T in the US.

But the executive's FTTN proposal for Telstra's copper network was also a gambit.

In November 2005, the slide deck presented by Trujillo detailing his transformation plan to the media contained an infamous asterisk with respect to the FTTN plan, stipulating that the plan was subject to *"favourable regulatory conditions"*.

FTTN sounded great on paper — who wouldn't want higher speed broadband than was offered by Telstra ADSL at that point? Trujillo was offering 12Mbps speeds at a time when Australia was just getting used to offerings of 1.5Mbps. But in practice Trujillo was making an ambit claim.

Telstra, Trujillo had effectively told the Government, might not roll out the FTTN network at all if it was forced to open up the new infrastructure for wholesale access by its competitors. And even if it still progressed with the plan, it would need to receive a guarantee of favourable regulatory conditions from the Government so that it could continue to make fat profits from the planned network.

Setting the terms

Trujillo and the 'amigos' were loud, crude and sometimes bumbling. Burgess once famously remarked that he wouldn't recommend Telstra shares to his mother[65] and demonstrated his lack of political awareness by referring to then-Federal Opposition Leader Brendan Nelson in 2008 as *"what's his face, the guy with the funny hair"*[66].

And yet the group was not stupid. By merely proposing a model for Telstra to upgrade its copper telephony network to support high-speed broadband, the Americans were able to set the ongoing terms under which the debate on the need for an NBN policy would proceed.

Asked at one stage what his favourite movie was, Burgess said it was the Rob Sitch classic The Castle[67]. Asked why, he stated: *"What is there not to like about The Castle? Here, Darryl Kerrigan beats the government in the takings case."*

In Australia it was, and is, common for large corporations to play relatively nice in terms of their relationship with the Government of the day. Australia's historic industry structure based on a series of duopolies has meant that usually the political and corporate sectors have enjoyed cozy relationships based on mutual benefit. But Trujillo, Burgess and their colleagues imported from the US a very different and highly combative approach to government relations. They tried to push the Government of the day around.

But the savvy Prime Minister John Howard and his then-Communications Minister, Senator Helen Coonan rebuffed Trujillo's advances on regulatory certainty for a FTTN network and tried to focus the Telstra leadership on the third tranche of the Telstra share sale. This move eventually paid off handsomely for the Government, which netted billions from the T3 share sale in 2006. Howard was able to claim the mantle of the newest reformer of Australia's telecommunications industry, even if not much had actually changed for consumers.

However, while the 'T3' share sale captured the attention of Australia's financial markets, Trujillo's FTTN proposal simultaneously succeeded in capturing the imagination of the rest of the public, which had started to understand the benefits that they could access through universal high-speed broadband.

Attempting to leverage the hype to break Telstra's long-term market power, Optus CEO Paul O'Sullivan publicly wrote to Trujillo, proposing a joint project to build a National Broadband Network, and Optus also built a consortium of rebel telcos known as the G9 to propose a NBN be built with the support of the Government[68].

Still, the Government refused to act on the issue. Coonan — who had little background in telecommunications — focused instead on what appeared at the time to be a bizarre and undercooked plan to work with Optus and rural consortium Elders to build out a fixed broadband and wireless network to serve rural and remote Australia[69].

But the Coalition had seriously underestimated the mood of the electorate, whose imagination had been captured by Trujillo's proposal. For the first time, a viable path had opened up to achieving really high-speed broadband in Australia, replacing much of Telstra's ageing copper network. Trujillo's plan also had the potential to resolve some of the long-running 'blackspot' issues which had locked hundreds of thousands of premises out of acceptable levels of broadband for many years.

One man who didn't underestimate the mood of the electorate at the time was Stephen Conroy.

The Labor Senator had inherited the Communications portfolio from frontbencher Lindsay Tanner in October 2004, but had made little headway against the Howard Government on telecommunications issues over his first couple of years looking after the portfolio for Labor.

On one infamous occasion the Labor Senator presented at a telecommunications conference in Sydney, following on after Minister Coonan. At the time, Conroy's speech was so unappealing to the audience that nobody in the crowd had any interest in asking questions of Conroy, and the Shadow Minister was forced to make an ignominious exit at the end of his speech, while the TV cameras followed Coonan outside.

For all his strengths within political circles in Canberra and Victoria, where Conroy had emerged as a key player in Labor's right-wing faction, the Senator spent much of his first year on the margins of the industry's debate.

And yet, within only a few short months, things would change substantially as Conroy grabbed hold of Trujillo's copper gambit by the reins and rode it all the way to the 2007 Federal Election. In less than a year, the Telstra FTTN proposal would taken on a public policy life of its own.

Enter Rudd

It's not well-remembered, but the first glimmer of what would become Labor's National Broadband Network policy was laid out in May 2006, when then-Opposition Leader Kim Beazley mentioned — prompted by Conroy — in his Budget reply speech that year that Labor telecommunications policy featured a national, open access broadband network that would deliver speeds of 6Mbps, which Beazley described at the time as being *"25 times faster than the current broadband benchmark of 256 kilobits per second"*.

However, it wasn't until December 2006, when the power team of Kevin Rudd and Julia Gillard sealed a deal to take over leadership of the Labor Party, that the policy accelerated into a serious matter for Labor.

It's true that Stephen Conroy was always the driving policy force behind Labor's National Broadband Network vision. He had to be; he held the portfolio for Labor, and it was up to him to develop a credible broadband policy in Opposition that could help Labor win an election over John Howard.

However, it's also true that Rudd was the first Labor leader since Keating fully appreciate what Australia's telecommunications industry could become, given the right policy settings.

This was very apparent when, as Prime Minister, Rudd stood up in front of the Australian people in April 2009[70] and bravely announced that the Government would spend $43 billion on a universal Fibre to the Premises network. No Australian Government had ever spent anything like that on any kind of technology; none had embarked on an infrastructure project of such scale and complexity.

Labor's announcement of its initial, Fibre to the Node-based network on 21 March, 2007[71], might well be viewed as a rehearsal for that later, much grander announcement.

As with the 2009 announcement, Rudd made the 2007 announcement in Canberra. Flanked by Conroy and then-Shadow Finance Minister Lindsay Tanner, Rudd was very clear about what he wanted from Labor's nascent National Broadband Network policy.

"We regard this as an important part of nation building for the future," the Opposition Leader said. *"Nation building in the 19th century was about building a new national railway network for*

Australia. Nation building for the 21st century lies in building a new national broadband network. It's part of our pathway to the future."

These were words that the Australian population — starved of high-speed broadband as it was — had not heard from an Australian politician before. And they dramatically fuelled the growing fire of interest in broadband amongst the public. Howard's Coalition Government was not acting on this issue. Rudd had clearly signalled that Labor would.

Less clear was how Labor would achieve its aim. Rudd had stipulated that the policy would see $4.7 billion invested over five years to deliver, *"for 98 percent of Australians, a broadband service which is up to 40 times faster than they currently enjoy"*.

Rudd did detail where the funding was to come from — the Government's existing Communications Fund, as well as the Future Fund's 17 percent (at that time) stake in Telstra. But many of the details were unknown.

What was to be the relationship between Telstra and the Government over the plan? What about the relationship with the G9 group of rival telcos? What specific technology was to be used? How would the network be set up as an open access platform? Many of these questions were left dangling, and from the transcript of the press conference, it appears apparent that some of the Press Gallery journalists attending were not across the technical details either.

The reason for this was clear: In developing the policy, Conroy appeared to have assimilated chunks from existing NBN policy options already put forward by Telstra and the G9 group of companies led by Optus. This was not a fully developed plan, but merely the outline of one.

The cost of Labor's policy was about the same amount that Telstra and the G9 had proposed; the open access model was the one proposed by the G9; the model appeared likely to be the same Fibre to the Node upgrade of Telstra's existing copper network that Trujillo had originally pitched to Howard, and as for the speed claims — 12Mbps were the same speeds being talked about by the industry as the next step for the copper upgrade.

Conroy's initial, $4.7 billion NBN plan was not quite a copy and paste job from the models that industry had already proposed. The Senator and his staff had clearly done a substantial amount of research to work out how those models could work for Labor. And no doubt Rudd had an influence on the process as well; the vision of a glorious economic future underlaid by fast broadband appears to come substantially from Rudd's own view of what Australia's next generation should look like.

But it was close enough. It's clear that the model proposed by Trujillo — picked up and modified again by the G9 — had set the policy background for Labor's new model.

Pausing for a lesson

It's important at this stage to take a step back and look at how Labor's policy came together and what we can take away as lessons from this period of the NBN's genesis.

The reason for this is that it became apparent in 2008 and 2009, as the new Rudd Government elected in November 2007 attempted to actually implement the policy outlined by Rudd, Conroy and Tanner in March 2007, that the flaws which inevitably brought the policy unstuck were contained in it right from the beginning.

The first thing to very clearly realise about Labor's policy development process is that it appears to have been directly informed by the model that industry conveniently supplied Labor with, rather than by a broader and more organic policy development process undertaken over a protracted period.

Many seasoned watchers of Federal Parliament most likely feel that they have a relatively good understanding of how much of the nitty gritty of policy is developed and formed. The

Parliament — especially the Senate — frequently holds public inquiries into certain issues. Submissions into given topics are invited from industry, other key stakeholders and the public at large, hearings are held, questions are asked, and overall a great deal of resources poured into analysis that eventually hopes to come to conclusions about public issues and specific pieces of legislation or regulation.

Much of this process is mimicked by the Government of the day, when it wishes to decide policy. At the behest of their own interests or through Cabinet request, Ministers may request their departments to hold public or private consultations to develop the best way forward on a particular issue. There is a reason Australian Parliament House is designed with such a sweeping open front verandah — it was designed as a meeting place.

What is important to realise here is that in Opposition or as a minority party, political parties do not go through anywhere near such an exhaustive process in developing policy.

An Opposition portfolio holder such as a Shadow Minister will have only a small handful of staff to rely on when developing national policy proposals; typically only one dedicated policy advisor for a major portfolio. They may receive support from their party's head office, and from other parliamentarians. But usually it's their own small staff which bears the brunt of the policy development process in their own portfolio.

They will also be able to rely on, to a certain extent, the research skills of the Federal Parliamentary Library, which daily produces information dossiers on countless topics for Parliamentarians. Parliamentary Committees also conduct a great deal of research through the inquiry process into specific topics, which often throws up useful policy approaches.

And lastly, they will also be able to rely on external groups such as thinktanks aligned with their branch of politics for research material.

But at time he was developing Labor's first NBN policy, in Opposition, Conroy had very few resources to use to conduct policy analysis. As Shadow Minister in his turn, Malcolm Turnbull had a little more in the way of resources, but again there was only one principal telecommunications policy advisor, and some of Turnbull's extra resources are believed to have come from his own pocket.

There is little reason to believe that Conroy had much more than this when he held the same position from 2004.

One of the key influences in Conroy's office at the time is believed to have been his advisor Tim Watts, a Labor advisor who went on to work as a Telstra executive and then enter Parliament in his own right, replacing the retiring Julia Gillard in the Victorian seat of Gellibrand. Conroy is believed to have been influential in Watts' preselection[72].

Other influences on Conroy and the first NBN policy are believed to have come from the regulatory advisors at companies such as Macquarie Telecom and Optus, who were quite active in working with the Opposition on assisting with the development of mature telecommunications policy.

Further influence appears to have come from the lobby group the Competitive Carriers' Coalition — formed in 2001 to represent the interests of Telstra's rivals in Canberra, and closely aligned with Macquarie Telecom.

It is true that major parties such as Labor, the Liberal Party and the Nationals do have some policy resources that they can draw on from their central party offices. Even smaller parties such as the Greens may have a larger pool of resources in this vein. But the truth is that even these resources are spread quite thin, being forced to deal with many policy debates and development processes simultaneously.

In short, what we see here is a perfect example of an all-too-common situation where a poorly resourced Opposition party appeared to rely significantly on industry to propose workable models for future policy. No matter how flawed or poorly thought out that policy is, it then becomes the basis for formal Government policy in the event of a change in power, as occurred when Kevin Rudd kicked John Howard out of the Lodge in November 2007.

There is very little evidence that Labor had either the resources or the intention to conduct an exhaustive analysis of future models for Australia's telecommunications industry before its policy launch in March 2007.

If it had, it would have found that globally, comparable countries to Australia were wrestling with many of the same telecommunications policy issues as Australia: Key questions such as how to develop a competitive market, how to regulate the incumbent telco, and how to stimulate the upgrade of legacy networks to provide very high-speed broadband.

Globally, the approach eventually taken by each individual country varied largely according to the relationship which governments held with the incumbent telcos which they often still partly owned. In tightly controlled Singapore, the Government merely mandated that the monopoly telco, SingTel, would replace its copper network with FTTP, providing grudging access to a small cadre of approved retail players.

The UK went for a different approach, forcing incumbent BT to separate into retail and wholesale divisions and pushing — even directly funding, in rural areas — the telco to upgrade its network with a Fibre to the Node rollout.

It appears to be clear from the pattern of events that Labor's initial NBN policy was based somewhat on the model which Telstra had proposed. That fundamental proposal found in that model was that Telstra's copper telephony network would be upgraded with Fibre to the Node technology at a cost of around $5 billion. This is the model which Trujillo proposed to

Prime Minister John Howard in August 2005, and again to the Government in November of that same year. It's also, broadly, the model which the Optus-led G9 group separately proposed. Labor then appeared to integrate key elements of that model as its own policy.

Enacting the policy

The end result of Labor's NBN policy development process was that the party took to the 2007 Federal Election a national telecommunications policy which was highly attractive to the public, and which had its roots in proposals put forward by industry itself.

However, many of the details which would be necessary to actually enact the policy remained unclear; the policy platform as a whole was immature.

The Parliamentary Budget Office, whose job it is to cost political policies, was not established until four years later in mid-2012. Labor also still had few answers as to how the policy would be implemented, including crucial details of how it would force Telstra to open access to its copper network, how this first version of the NBN would stimulate a competitive marketplace and so on.

Because of this, it took only a very short time after Labor took power in November 2007 for the wheels to start to fall off the wagon.

Four days after being sworn in as Minister for Broadband, Communications and the Digital Economy, Stephen Conroy issued a terse media release about the Government's NBN plans — his first ever media release as Minister[73].

The release re-committed the new Rudd administration to the NBN policy and kicked off the race to find someone to build the actual network.

"We will hold an open and transparent process to determine who will build the network with our ambition being to complete the process by the end of June next year," said the new Communications Minister."

"We expect that there will be much public commentary, jockeying and lobbying from parties as they work to convince the Government that they are best placed to build the new network and seek the terms that are most favourable to them."

And Conroy did have a couple of early wins as Minister. For example, he quickly negotiated with Telstra to switch on its ADSL2+ broadband in 900 telephone exchanges nation-wide[74] — opening up higher broadband speeds to millions of Australians who had previously been suffering at the bottom of the rung. This was the infrastructure which Winn had publicly told journalists would not be switched on until Telstra could receive regulatory assurances from the Government.

But then things started to slow down. It took three months for Conroy's Department of Broadband, Communications and the Digital Economy to ask for public comment on the NBN proposal and to appoint a panel of experts to examine the proposals of those companies seeking to build the network[75]. Another month went by before the Government formally went to market asking for proposals.

Conroy had publicly stated four days after taking office that the Government wanted to complete the selection process for a NBN builder by the end of June 2008. But by September that year the process had barely begun, with the closing date for NBN proposals to be the end of November 2008. The NBN policy was six months late before it had even begun to be enacted.

The panel of experts appointed by the Government to examine the proposals to enact its NBN policy had something of a job of work in front of it when it started meeting from March 2008. The Government's tender process eventually received some six responses, from groups as varied as Optus, independent Canberra telco TransACT (which already had its own Fibre to the Node network covering much of the capital) and Canadian giant Axia Netmedia. A consortium named Acacia and led by the founder of Telstra's Countrywide division, Doug Campbell, also threw its hat into the ring, and the State Government of Tasmania also made its own pitch for local infrastructure (the island state has historically had some of the worst telecommunications infrastructure nationwide).

And of course, so did the Optus-led consortium, by then known as 'Terria'.

A late entrant to the process was Telstra, still led by Trujillo. The company at that stage viewed the NBN process as a hostile attack on its property, and its submission to the tender process was perfunctory.

Unsuitable

The Labor Federal Government never released the full text of the evaluation report which the NBN expert panel — staffed by venerable figures as varied as investment banker John Wylie and Treasury Secretary Ken Henry — supplied to the Federal Government in January 2009.

However, the two page report which the Government eventually published summarising the panel's findings with relation to the six groups which supplied responses to the Rudd Government's first NBN policy effort is revealing. It paints a picture of an inability of the private sector to meet the Government's request to build it a National Broadband Network.

At the heart of the panel's concerns were a series of fundamental issues which the Labor Government had not expected in some cases, or properly considered in others.

For starters, the volatility of capital markets associated with the Global Financial Crisis in 2008 had left most respondents to the Government's NBN tender process without the necessary capital to build their own National Broadband Network.

As Prime Minister — and with the assistance of figures such as Henry in the Treasury — Rudd had taken unprecedented measures to protect Australia from the GFC's fallout.

However, this still left the prospective NBN builders without enough resources to get the job done, without *"substantial support from the Commonwealth"*.

Furthermore, the complexity of the project meant that every proposal submitted was necessarily *"underdeveloped"*. *"No proposal, for example, provided a fully developed project plan,"* the NBN expert panel wrote. No proposal was able to meet the Government's demand that 98 percent of Australian homes and businesses could be connected to high-speed broadband with a Government contribution of just $4.7 billion.

Perhaps most crucially, the NBN expert panel found that every proposal was likely to require *"exclusive or near-exclusive access to Telstra's existing sub-loop customer access network — the so-called 'last mile'."*

"As well," the Panel added, *"providing such access to a party other than Telstra runs a risk of liability to pay compensation to Telstra. The Proposals have this risk remaining with the Commonwealth but they have not addressed the potential cost to the Commonwealth of any such compensation. In any event, the Panel considers that no Proponent could accept the cost risk and continue to have a viable business case."*

As it turned out, the only vaguely realistic proposal to be considered by the Expert Panel appeared to come from Telstra instead.

Telstra had access to a huge amount of capital, as one of Australia's largest and most profitable companies. It also had a huge amount of construction expertise, due to its ongoing activities of extending and maintaining its telecommunications infrastructure. And, most crucially, it already owned its copper network that would need to be upgraded under any proposal.

But again, the belligerence of the telco's American management got in the way.

Telstra had filed a perfunctory brief bid for the NBN process which the Expert Panel formally rejected, on the grounds that it was non-compliant with the Government's procurement process. Peter Hartcher chronicles in the Sydney Morning Herald[76] that the expert panel was aghast, at the prospect that Telstra would be so inept — or uncaring — as to have filed a non-complying bid to build the NBN. The panel took five separate pieces of legal advice on Telstra's response, but ended up believing that it was forced to eject Australia's incumbent telco from the process.

It is at this point that we can mark the failure point of the Rudd Labor Government's initial $4.7 billion National Broadband Network policy.

The policy had stood for only two years.

In March 2007, Rudd, Conroy and Tanner had stood up in front of the Australian people and had proudly announced their initial NBN policy. Two years later — with all the will in the world and holding the reins of power in Government — Conroy was forced to sit on the Prime Minister's private jet with Rudd during several flights between Australia's east coast cities[77] and explain that it was not possible to implement the policy that they had taken to the election a year and a half earlier.

So what went wrong?

The dissection

History will record that there were two key mistakes which the Rudd Labor Government made which led to the failure of the first NBN policy.

The first and most obvious gross mistake which Labor made in developing the policy was that it relied too heavily on private industry when attempting to set national telecommunications policy. Companies such as Optus, Macquarie Telecom, iiNet and others had proposed policy models to the political class from 2005 throughout 2009 which were simply not possible to enact.

As the NBN Expert Panel pointed out, the only way for Australia's broadband infrastructure to be upgraded on a national scale was to use the existing infrastructure — be it copper cables or be it pits and pipes where those cables flowed through — that was owned by the country's incumbent telco, the former government department, Telstra.

Rudd and Conroy believed they could use other companies and public funding to build an NBN, somehow either appropriating Telstra's networks or bringing the telco into the process at a later date. That was the message being passed to Labor by industry. Unfortunately this was simply not an easily workable model. Any NBN process would necessarily involve Telstra.

Trujillo and the 'amigos' knew this, having an intimate view of the scale of Telstra's operation, but it appears that Labor and Telstra's competition did not quite realise this essential truth of Australian telecommunications: Any really major initiative will require Telstra's participation to succeed; giving Telstra an edge in negotiations.

Shortly after the first NBN policy process failed, Rudd and Conroy attempted to correct this mistake through setting up a huge new telco — NBN Co — to rival Telstra and overbuild the telco's networks. However, even in this process, which involved a ten-fold expansion of the public funds Labor was throwing at the NBN project — Telstra has necessarily formed a core part of the process, selling its HFC cable and copper networks to NBN Co and even assisting in building much of its network.

Like it or not, Telstra was always going to have to be a huge part of the NBN.

Labor's gradually maturing understanding of this key role for Telstra is to some extent reflected in Cabinet documents leaked to the ABC in January 2018, which showed that Kevin Rudd's administration had carefully considered a nuanced strategy for dealing with Telstra on some fronts with respect to the NBN, while restraining it on others[78].

The second mistake Labor made was not to look globally and examine how smart — and cheap — regulatory options could solve the policy aim they were grappling with.

It is clear that Labor could have achieved many of its policy aims to upgrade Australia's telecommunications infrastructure by structurally separating Telstra's operations into retail and wholesale operations and incentivising or directly funding the newly separated wholesale branch of Telstra to upgrade its own broadband network. This would likely have been very costly and provoked a complex legal challenge from Telstra. But in the end it may still have been a far simpler and more natural path than the NBN policy provided.

This is precisely the path followed very successfully in countries such as the UK. The result has been an extremely rapid expansion in high-speed broadband infrastructure by the organisation most qualified to undertake it — the country's incumbent telco.

Additionally, Labor only needed to consider Australia's own history of telecommunications deregulation — especially the key reforms in the early and late 1990's — to find other examples of how setting a correct regulatory environment led to direct investment in next-generation telecommunications infrastructure, spurred by industry competition.

Another option would have been for Labor to have forced Telstra to divest its HFC cable network, which would have had the effect of creating a strong competitor for its copper network. Again, in the UK what we see is that HFC cable operator Virgin Media is a strong rival to incumbent telco BT.

It's true that Trujillo and his team took a belligerent attitude towards the Government, and at times appeared unwilling to work with Conroy and Rudd at all. However, it also remains true that separating Telstra and perhaps forcing it to divest its HFC network would have been a much quicker, more effective and likely even cheaper mechanism for Labor to have achieved its policy aims, than the complex process it has gone through with the NBN.

Telstra had a great deal of negotiating power in this process, but Labor — with the support of the Greens in the Senate — had more.

An understanding of many of these issues gradually made its way into Labor's second, much more ambitious $43 billion Fibre to the Premises-based NBN project, which turned out to be a much more viable policy to enact than the original $4.7 billion FTTN model.

Ultimately, what the failure of Labor's initial, $4.7 billion FTTN-based NBN policy in 2009 reflects is the failure of the policy development process in Opposition.

Labor did not have the resources or the broader understanding necessary as an Opposition Party in 2007 to form a workable National Broadband Network policy that could be enacted in Government. And it does not appear that it sought to deeply investigate how such a policy could be developed, drawing on global experience. This lack of resources drove it into the arms of industry, which itself did not have the necessary answers to resolve the situation.

Labor successfully capitalised on the Coalition's lack of ambition in broadband as part of its rationale for forming Government. Rudd and Conroy's initial NBN vision was an ambitious one which truly filled a gap which the public had been frustrated with.

The policy was popular. But ultimately the policy was poorly considered and unwieldly. Most likely, in the end, it was simply unworkable.

The lesson for future Oppositions here is clear: Consult widely — including internationally — when seeking to develop policy in Opposition that you might have to enact in Government. You will have scarce resources, so try and get a feel for the overall structure of the next several decades, rather than trying to form policy which may be short-sighted. And don't forget that the role of Government is more often to set the correct policy framework than it is to directly intervene in industry with public funding.

The alternative is that you may find yourself 18 months into your first term of Government and having to start the policy development process all over again from scratch — as Kevin Rudd and Stephen Conroy did with the NBN.

SUMMARY

Policy Details

In the years leading up to its 2007 election victory in the 2007 Federal Election, Federal Labor developed a policy to build a National Broadband Network using Fibre to the Node technology, at a cost of $4.7 billion. This project would have upgraded the existing copper network owned by Telstra.

What Went Wrong

Labor's initial NBN policy was operationally unworkable.

The idea of upgrading Telstra's copper network to FTTN was a good one and had been proposed by Telstra itself, following moves by similar telcos such as BT in the UK. However, Labor did not realise that Telstra was the only party reasonably capable of upgrading its network. Telstra's refusal to participate in the resulting tender process left the policy dead in the water.

Labor relied too heavily on ideas from industry when developing the policy. Rival telcos believed that a consortium would be capable of upgrading Telstra's network. Labor also failed to study international developments and realise that best practice would have been to incentivise Telstra to upgrade its own network, structurally separating its wholesale operations from its retail division if necessary.

Avoiding This Situation in Future

Where at all possible, policymakers should avoid taking a heavy-handed approach to reform that will fundamentally restructure an industry, despite the fact that this is often the approach which non-dominant industry players will argue for.

Learning from international best practice and determining what the minimal level of government intervention would be to ensure an effective outcome will serve policymakers well.

CHAPTER 3

Paradise Lost

"Who better to hold the government to account here than Malcolm Turnbull ... who has the technical expertise and business experience to entirely demolish the government on this issue."
–Opposition Leader Tony Abbott

The date is September 24, 2010, and Malcolm Turnbull is feeling right on top of his game.

The Liberal MP, multi-millionaire and former high-flying lawyer and investment banker is just days into his triumphant return to the pinnacle of Liberal party politics, re-entering the Federal Shadow Cabinet as the nation's newly minted Shadow Communications Minister[79].

It's been a tough eight months for the man dubbed the 'Silver Fox'[80] by many admiring women in Sydney's affluent Eastern Suburbs, where Turnbull's electorate of Wentworth is located. Ousted to the back bench by Tony Abbott after the Member for Warringah's successful Liberal leadership challenge in December

2009, Turnbull had initially planned to leave politics following his ignomious defeat.

But that time on the backbench proved fruitful for Turnbull. He re-grouped, renewed his famous charisma, built up his confidence and ate a great deal of humble pie to make up for the leadership arrogance which had alienated so many of his colleagues.

Now the man some like to dub the 'Earl of Wentworth' is back on the front pages of the nation's newspapers, and with good reason. Seizing the Communications portfolio from his colleague Tony Smith, Turnbull has perfectly positioned himself to grab attention for holding the Government to account for what many Liberals believe to be a giant 'boondoggle': Labor's $43 billion National Broadband Network policy.

The Liberal MP has been seeding the field for his ascension well. Just a month earlier, Turnbull caused a media splash by publicly describing the NBN project as *"a gigantic torching of taxpayers' money"* and a *"colossal white elephant"*. The occasion was an appearance by the Liberal MP at the Paddington RSL in his Sydney electorate, clothed in his infamous black leather jacket[81].

"The reality is, there simply isn't demand at the household and every small business level for internet at that speed, at a price which would make it even remotely financially viable," Turnbull opined at the time, nonchalantly waving a schooner of beer for emphasis. *"You'll spend $40 billion plus dollars, and you'll get an asset that's worth $10 billion."* No wonder the 'Duke of Double Bay' is feeling on top of the world.

But there's one audience that just isn't buying Turnbull's rhetoric on the NBN: The media.

And they're really not buying it.

The date is September 24, 2010, and Malcolm Turnbull is engaging with a group which often fawns all over him: Journalists.

But this time, Turnbull might have bitten off more than he expected to have to chew.

Days after Turnbull was appointed Shadow Communications Minister, the Liberal MP has invited a dozen or so of Australia's prominent technology journalists to an intimate gathering at his electorate office in the Sydney suburb of Edgecliff.

No doubt Turnbull expects the tech press to be a little over-awed by his presence, and more than a little compliant. It's not often, after all, that reporters who usually focus on the 'speeds and feeds' of the latest technology gadgets get access to a man who many expect will one day become Prime Minister.

Then too, first briefings with new Shadow Ministers usually have a cautious tone. Politicians new to a portfolio often use such briefings to test the temperature of the media (and hence the public) about key issues.

But as we engage with Turnbull in his office, in his first real outing as Shadow Communications Minister, it rapidly becomes apparent that the future Prime Minister is rubbing some of us the wrong way.

The problem is that Turnbull appears determined to take the same 'No Compromises' approach to his new portfolio that he has taken to so many other issues in the past: The argument for an Australian Republic, his preselection battle for the seat of Wentworth, Climate Change in his previous role as Leader of the Opposition, and more. Turnbull always wants to win. Now he wants to win on the NBN, and win big.

After only a few minutes, it appears that the Liberal MP's highly critical comments about the NBN at the Paddington RSL a few weeks earlier did not represent off the cuff thinking. Turnbull really does appear to fundamentally disagree with the basic principles of the project. And his confident outlook is brooking no objections to his view.

Some in the room meekly write down his every view for faithful reportage to their audience.

But others push the Member for Wentworth with unexpectedly difficult questions.

A key issue is how Turnbull could reasonably take a position of opposition to the NBN project as a whole, when the infrastructure will effectively be locked in for much of Australia by the time the next Federal Election is slated to roll around three years later in 2013. And the Coalition has just (barely) lost an election, after all. Isn't it time for some bipartisan thinking on the NBN? Given that it will take a decade to finish the rollout?

One of Turnbull's key objections relates to the Fibre to the Premises (FTTP) technology at the heart of the NBN project. Labor chose the technology for most of Australia because it was the best possible option for meeting Australia's broadband needs over the extreme long-term. It will also completely replace Telstra's legacy copper network, which still provides for most of Australia's telecommunications needs.

It's slow to deploy and costly compared with alternative options, but nevertheless, the FTTP rollout is technically superior and is going ahead. Changing the NBN's model after several years is viewed by almost every expert in the field as being nigh-on impossible — a huge risk for the Commonwealth and technically and financially destructive for the NBN project as a whole.

But Turnbull doesn't hesitate to respond in the strongest possible terms when confronted with this quandary. He does not back down at all. In fact, he goes on the attack.

"The idea that we should just wave it through, because it's politicially expedient, I mean — I wasn't elected to Parliament to just look the other way when billions of dollars are potentially being wasted," he fires back at the media[82].

Turnbull's immediate approach to the FTTP model is to argue that no in-depth financial analysis had ever been conducted into its details. In addition, he argues that Australians may not need the high speeds which it will deliver. 12Mbps may be enough for most people, he says, instead of the 100Mbps that the FTTP model would provide. If this is true, it could mean that the FTTP option is over the top for what Australians would actually use for their home broadband capacity.

"What are the applications that require bandwidth of this scale that's being proposed by NBN?" he asks the assembed media[83].

The truth is, there are plenty, and the NBN's financial underpinnings appear to be strong. But you wouldn't know it from the new Shadow Minister's 'take no prisoners' tone.

On the day, Turnbull also notes that he hasn't yet met with the earnest Labor-appointed chief executive of the NBN company, Mike Quigley. The highly respected former Alcatel-Lucent executive came out of retirement to lead the Labor initiative.

"I don't know him, don't have a relationship with him — looking forward to having one," the Member for Wentworth tells us[84].

Greens Communications Spokesperson Scott Ludlam — whose party has always supported Labor's fibre NBN policy — has previously warned the Coalition not to *"wreck it"*[85].

In his office that day, Turnbull rejects the Western Australian Senator's comments as he does most other criticisms.

"I'm not seeking to wreck or destroy ... my objective is to get some real transparency and accountability on this," he says. *"We need to have a more informed debate about it, the Government is talking about spending a really stupendous amount of money, and our job in the Opposition is to hold them account to that."*

And yet 'wreck' is precisely what Turnbull immediately proceeds to do to the NBN, first as Shadow Communications Minister, and then as Communications Minister in his own right.

And Mike Quigley will turn out to be his first target.

Playing the Man

It doesn't take long for Turnbull to crank up the war machine.

After only a few short weeks in his new position, The Australian newspaper — hostile to Labor's NBN project from the start — latches onto a series of reports out of the United States that the country's Securities and Exchange Commission has opened an investigation into allegedly corrupt practices at Quigley's former employer, network equipment manufacturer Alcatel-Lucent. The issue also touches Jean-Pascal Beaufret, the fellow Alcatel executive who Quigley has brought with him to help him run NBN Co as its first chief financial officer.

The claims have little to do with Quigley or Beaufret[86]. Although they relate to the Central American country of Costa Rica — technically under Quigley's remit when he led the North American operation of Alcatel-Lucent a decade previously — the US SEC has declined to interview either of the NBN Co executives, and there is never any suggestion either has done anything wrong.

"I was looking after North America," says Quigley at the time regarding the SEC. *"They weren't interested in us."*

Yet The Australian starts running story after story about the issue — effectively flogging a dead horse — and Turnbull latches onto the coverage with full vigour.

"NBN Co claims neither Mr Quigley nor Mr Beaufret were aware of these bribery schemes," thunders the Liberal MP at one point[87]. *"But both men owe the Australian public a far more detailed explanation."*

As the issue drags on day after day, with threadbare angle after threadbare angle, Turnbull begins to take every opportunity to raise it repeatedly — through the media, through his own posts on his website and on social media, and ultimately in parliamentary committees, which Quigley is obligated to attend as a witness.

There is a brief window where it appears that The Australian and Turnbull are raising legitimate questions which the public has a right to know more about. But as the weeks drag on, and Quigley continues to deny any involvement or, indeed, knowledge of the matters which the US SEC is investigating, it seems clear that Turnbull's interest in the case extends far beyond the available evidence.

At an indeterminable point, the pursuit of Quigley begins to take on all the flavour of a witch hunt.

It would have been one thing, after all, if Quigley had any personal involvement with the events in Costa Rica in question. It would have been a significant event if the US SEC had even wanted to interview the executive over any role he might have had in events in Costa Rica many years before.

But from the NBN CEO, in the early months of 2011, all the public sees is what Quigley actually is: A transparent, honest engineer turned hard-working executive who has done his best in his career — first for his long-term employer Alcatel, and then for NBN Co — to do the right thing. And the SEC continues to consider him of little interest.

This aligns with the image which emerged from industry research of Quigley shortly after he was appointed[88].

And now Turnbull is demonising him for daring to step out of retirement to lead Australia's greatest ever infrastructure project — a project which enjoys overwhelming public support.

The issue comes to a head during one particular parliamentary committee hearing in May 2011, during which it becomes clearly apparent to the public at large that Quigley really has no idea why he is being repeatedly targeted over an issue which had little to do with him.

"Nobody is making any allegations against you, least of all anybody here," Turnbull tells a somewhat flustered Quigley. But

that's not really the way the situation looks to many onlookers following the case. It feels as though Quigley is already on trial.

It dawns upon much of the media and public at that point just how determined Turnbull and elements of the conservative media are to tear the NBN down.

Turnbull's actions regarding Quigley appear to show that his issue with the NBN is not one of policy, or even one of personality. It appears to be political. For Turnbull to succeed as Shadow Communications Minister, he has to tear down the NBN. The destruction of Mike Quigley is just one stepping stone on the path that Turnbull seems determined to walk — stepping on heads all the way.

Quigley is eventually forced to admit that he should have proactively released more information about the Costa Rica issue, and even put forward his opinion that there were *"valid questions"* that needed to be asked[89]. However, the issue eventually died away as it became clear there had been no wrongdoing buy either Quigley or Beaufret.

In January 2011, then-Prime Minister Julia Gillard describes Turnbull's attack on Quigley as a *"personal smear"*, stating that Turnbull is *"scraping the bottom of the barrel"* to try and destroy the NBN[90]. Conroy describes Turnbull's approach as a *"witch hunt"*[91].

Depending on your own perspective, this might be Labor hyperbole, or fair criticism. But one thing is clear: Over the succeeding two years, Turnbull will not baulk at what he sees as the requirements to succeed in his mission of holding the NBN project to account.

The Member for Wentworth's war with NBN Co's chief executive eventually extends to the company's board as well[92], leading NBN Co's directors to seek their own legal advice as to their position being targeted by a high-profile MP who could be their main shareholder Minister just a few months down the track. Turnbull's criticism is based on the argument that Labor's NBN board lacked direct telecommunications infrastructure rollout experience. In return, the NBN board signals its concern that it could be investigated in the result of a change in Government.

"Non-executive Directors have been told directly and indirectly by members of the opposition that they can expect a Judicial Enquiry investigating their governance post-election," writes NBN Co chair Siobhan McKenna in a letter to Turnbull in July 2013[93].

These unprecedented attacks upon an executive team and board who were, after all, merely doing the jobs they had been appointed to do — carrying out responsibilities that they were legally bound to adhere to — set a dark tone for all of Turnbull's relationships with key NBN stakeholders.

At times, the Member for Wentworth appears determined to target every key NBN figure appointed under Labor.

Policy on the run

This dark tone also extends throughout Turnbull's approach to NBN policy during his time in Opposition.

The Member for Wentworth starts well enough in this field, filing legislation in his early days as Shadow Communications Minister designed to bring a heightened level of transparency to the NBN[94]. And it must be said that many welcome this push. As Communications Minister, Stephen Conroy has not always been forthcoming with the facts about the NBN project[95], even if Mike Quigley has done much to cover this lapse.

Yet Turnbull quickly turns away from this well-worn path for Shadow Ministers of enforcing accountability and transparency on the Government of the day, and towards a policy dialogue which will end up creating a complete distortion of the NBN playing field.

Initially this policy approach focuses on the idea that the HFC cable networks owned by Telstra and Optus could be incorporated into the NBN policy. In March 2011, Turnbull takes a trip to broadband-drenched South Korea and likes what he sees there. The idea of the HFC cable networks being maintained in competition with the Fibre to the Premises-based NBN appeals to Turnbull. Labor's plan would merely see the inferior HFC technology shut down.

"The way you get an affordable price is through competition so why seek to stamp out the competition from the HFC cable?" Turnbull asks[96].

To technical observers, this view does not make much sense. Why would anyone purchase HFC cable services over FTTP broadband, when the latter is far superior?

However, in many ways this is not a technical debate. And gradually Turnbull's view expands. By August that same year, the MP is openly talking about bringing Telstra in to play a large role in the NBN rollout. By October Turnbull's view has moved on again; this time to incorporate the Fibre to the Node approach which has been pilloried by commentators so many times as unworkable and archaic[97].

In 2005, when then-Telstra chief executive Sol Trujillo first proposed the FTTN model, it was seen as futuristic. It would push fibre further out into Telstra's broadband network, delivering higher broadband speeds by replacing the company's copper cable for some distance between telephone exchanges, while leaving the rest of the copper extending to customers' premises intact.

But by 2011, with Labor already having promised the more expensive but technically superior FTTP model to the electorate (featuring fibre all the way to each house and business premise), Turnbull's FTTN option is looking like a regression to the past.

In April 2012, Peter Cochrane, a former chief technology officer of British telco BT, which has been rolling out FTTN across the United Kingdom since 2009, tells the UK Parliament[98] the FTTN deployment is *"one of the biggest mistakes humanity has made"*, imposing huge bandwidth and unreliability problems on those who implement it. Turnbull has used the BT rollout as an exemplar of how FTTN could be successfully deployed in Australia.

Yet Turnbull ramps up his rhetoric and accelerates his push to support FTTN as an alternative to the current NBN FTTP approach. Again, his rationale is that Australians do not need the speeds which FTTP can provide. So we might as well settle for FTTN instead, given that it will be cheaper and faster to deploy.

"There's been no case made or evidence made that there is any benefit from having a speed higher than what we can get now in many of our cities, at least, from ADSL 2+," the Liberal MP tells radio station 2GB in Sydney in January 2011[99]. *"If I connect your house with one terabyte per second speeds – the sort of speed you might get over a transcontinental cable – it would be of no use to you. There's nothing you could do with it."*

When Turnbull gets fully involved in the NBN policy debate, he does so by immediately questioning the underpinnings of the NBN project — its Fibre technology, in addition to the Wireless and Satellite models planned for rural and regional areas; its business model, and the competitive framework which it would impose on the national telecommunications industry, ranging from behemoths like Telstra to loudmouth minnows like Exetel.

To a certain extent, this approach is legitimate. The role of the Opposition is to question the policies of the day, and to hold the Government accountable for them. All of this technology is relatively new ground for humanity and many countries are wrestling with how to correctly set regulatory frameworks that will support the mass deployment of high-speed broadband infrastructure. These technologies are very much up for debate.

But as that very policy debate proceeds, one trend becomes clear: Turnbull is personally refusing to accept the mountain of evidence that had begun to pile up regarding core aspects of the NBN project.

It's true that Labor's NBN policy has flaws. Indeed, from its earliest days both Quigley and Conroy have been constantly forced to face the fact that a number of mistakes were dogging the project. Some, such as the NBN's reliance on a wholly new, immature, startup company to guide the construction effort, are very much starting to make their presence felt. Quigley had been forced to build NBN Co around him from the ground up, and this brought with it challenges, as with the formation of any new organisation.

Others, such as the woeful decision to set a huge number of Points of Interconnect with the NBN network for retail telcos[100], would only make their dire impact felt much further down the track.

Yet other aspects continue to demonstrate the strengths of Labor's policy. The correctness of Labor's choice to fixate on a Fibre to the Premises model; the veracity of the choice to have NBN Co build and launch its own satellites, rather than renting capacity; and even the regulatory model for restraining Telstra from entrenching its market dominance; in all of these areas, evidence continues to pile up that Labor's model is the right one, for Australia and for Australians.

In one glaring example, Turnbull doggedly maintains that NBN Co has taken the wrong course of action by planning to build and deploy its own satellites to provide broadband access to rural and regional areas.

In February 2012, the Liberal MP claims there is enough satellite capacity available for rent on existing commercial satellites, and that NBN Co doesn't need to launch its own satellites in order to provide services to Australia.

"There is enough capacity on private satellites already in orbit or scheduled for launch for the NBN to deliver broadband to the 200,000 or so premises in remote Australia without building its own," Turnbull says[101].

However, an examination of the capacity available shows at the time that Turnbull's claims are simply incorrect, with NBN Co's satellite engineers demonstrating that they had already weighed the options available. And NewSat, one of the private satellite companies which Turnbull spruiks as being able to provide an alternative to the NBN, later goes bankrupt, its 'birds' unlaunched.

But despite the obviousness of the Labor argument, and as this evidence is thrust in Turnbull's face by a plethora of informed commentators, the Liberal MP simply refuses to accept it, buckling down on his own messaging instead. Turnbull often accuses the Labor Communications Minister of living in a fictional *"Conrovian"* dreamland when it comes to the NBN, but it appears that the Liberal is holding onto his own misconceptions.

In Turnbull-land, the evidence for HFC and Fibre to the Node technologies against FTTP, renting satellite access rather than buying it, and having the private sector build and operate telecommunications infrastructure, continues to be irrefutable.

Turnbull states repeatedly that he is agnostic when it comes to the technology being used in the NBN. In August 2012, he tells the Financial Review[102]: *"They try to paint me as a zealot, when in reality I am so unzealous on technology it is not funny; I am totally agnostic and in favour of whatever works. Whatever works and whatever is most cost-effective is what I want to pursue."* Yet Turnbull often appears to have already made a decision that the FTTP model is not the best option for the NBN, despite the very obvious technical and financial advantages that it offers over the long term.

Again, there is a point where the matter comes to a head.

ABC journalist Nick Ross, perhaps foolhardily so (given the ABC's strict policies on journalistic integrity), takes it upon himself to singlehandedly demonstrate the fallacy of Turnbull's policy arguments, building up through a series of strident articles to eventually pen a 13,000 tome of an argument[103] categorically refuting every aspect of the Liberal MP's views on NBN policy.

One of Ross's opening paragraphs states, with a categorical tone, what so many other lesser articles had been trying to say about the FTTN- and HFC-based model that Turnbull obviously preferred for the NBN.

Ross writes: *"The Coalition's NBN alternative is different by almost every measure. It uses different technologies to connect the bulk of the country; it has different uses and applications; it affects Australia's health service differently; it provides different levels of support in emergencies and natural disasters; it requires a different amount of power to operate; the cost of maintenance is different; the overall cost, the return on investment and the re-sale value are different; the management, ownership, governance, competition and monopoly factors will be different; it has a different life-span and upgradability issues; the effect on businesses (of all sizes) and GDP is different; the effects on television are different; the effect on Senior Citizens is different; the viability and potential for cost blowouts is different; the costs of buying broadband will be different; the reliability is different; the effect on property prices will be different; the timescale is different; the legacy is different.*

Ultimately, it has completely different aims.

In just about every case the Coalition's alternative compares unfavourably to the current plans - and usually in dramatic fashion. That's based upon the facts and the information currently available in the public domain."

The article earns Ross a leading role in The Australian's pantheon of ABC journalists who have stepped out of line, and howls of outrage from the Coalition side of politics.

But the article itself hits the mark with the public; and as with the previous episode involving Mike Quigley, it becomes apparent that Turnbull has gone too far in trying to knock something down which has obvious sound elements to it. Again, the public realises the Member for Wentworth is trying to sell them a lemon.

Turnbull's response is to fight back harder.

"Your relentless NBN propaganda is an embarrassment to the ABC," Turnbull tells Ross on Twitter[104]. *"Do you really work for the ABC or is it the NBN Co?"*

In another article, Ross sums up industry consensus that switching the NBN model to a FTTN approach would represent an *"expensive, time-consuming hindrance,"* given the efficiencies which NBN contractors have been able to achieve throughout the construction effort thus far[105].

"Well that is, with respect to whoever wrote that, complete and utter nonsense," Turnbull fires back[106].

Ross isn't the only one coming in for criticism. As a wave of public concern about the Coalition's NBN policy starts to gain traction, Turnbull finds himself under increasing pressure on the issue.

The Financial Review quotes Turnbull as blaming the tech press for what he perceives as biased journalists amongst its ranks[107]: *"He said specialist technology journalists were fanning a pro-NBN zealotry among tech-savvy citizens who wanted the ultimate broadband regardless of more feasible alternatives."*

And later in 2012, Turnbull tells a tech startup audience in Sydney[108]: *"We are so let down by the so-called technology media, here in Australia. The commentary about the NBN and the issues associated with it is just so unbelievably uninformed ... there is a sort of cheerleader approach to the NBN which is actively, actively misleading people."*

From a certain point of view, again Turnbull does have a point. Much of the media is extremely suspicious of the Coalition's rival NBN policy and takes every opportunity to pillory it, knowing that most of the readers in the technology sector are squarely on Labor's side on the issue, due to the superior FTTP technology Labor's NBN project focuses on. There is valuable web traffic to be gained through criticising Turnbull's alternative NBN vision.

In addition, it is also true that the FTTN model does indeed have merits that much of the media is overlooking. The BT rollout (among others) has shown that FTTN can be deployed rapidly into existing copper broadband networks. The technology is also cheaper to deploy than FTTP and can be upgraded to a full FTTP rollout in the long-term, even if this would be less efficient to implement than a 'pure' FTTP rollout.

In short, Turnbull isn't wrong to explore the idea of a FTTN model as an NBN alternative, or even HFC. The problem is that he appears to have become dogged about the idea, in a way that ignores much of the evidence pertaining to the strengths of the FTTP model. Worse, he has started to paint anyone who disagrees with him as a 'zealot' who would accept nothing less than broadband perfection, no matter the cost.

Labor has also made some questionable policy decisions on its own. The jury is still out on whether the model of building a giant new company — NBN Co — to roll out what is essentially a replacement for Telstra's copper network will actually work. Turnbull is correct in that the model has not been pursued in quite that fashion anywhere else globally.

But, as Howard's Communications Minister Helen Coonan did many years before, Turnbull appears to have underestimated the mood of the electorate on the issue. Articles by Ross and other tech journalists on the topic attract huge levels of attention, and the business media is also starting to get interested in weighing in.

Plus, there is the fundamental fact that the FTTN ship has probably already sailed. Had the Coalition pursued a FTTN policy in 2005, it likely would have achieved strong public support. But with many Australians already receiving FTTP services through Labor's NBN network, any lesser model looks anachronistic in the eyes of the public and technical commentators. Turnbull, in turn, looks like what the Greens Senator Scott Ludlam had warned the Coalition not to become — an NBN 'wrecker'.

Turnbull's antagonistic approach to the media also opens up a line of attack from Labor. *"... there now seems to be a policy of trying to intimidate ABC personnel,"* Conroy tells ABC Radio's Jon Faine at one point[109]. *"Malcolm Turnbull is constantly attacking and trying to bully some of your journalists."*

This, too, is a bad look for the tech-savvy, media-friendly Turnbull.

Abbott

Throughout this period of several years leading up to the Federal Election in September 2013, Opposition Leader Tony Abbott — who put Turnbull up to the task of dismantling the NBN policy from the start — also pops up occasionally to throw out what might best be described as 'thought bubbles' with respect to Labor's NBN policy. To put it mildly, the comments are even less helpful to the Coalition's broadband policy cause than many of Turnbull's have been.

The NBN, Abbott claims in December 2010[110], flanked by Turnbull in a Sydney press conference, won't amount to much more than a *"video entertainment system"* primarily used to delivery video games and high-end television programming.

"The question is, should the taxpayer be investing $50 billion in that, when there are so many other competing needs – roads, railways, ports, health, education and the mobile phone system, which still drops out frequently?" Abbott asks at the time.

And in May the next year, the Opposition Leader returns to the topic with a similar argument. At the time, Abbott describes the NBN investment as *"reckless"*, stating again that the capital could be re-allocated to serve other needs such as infrastructure and hospitals.

Abbott's comments open up further opportunities for Labor to lampoon the Coalition on the issue. *"The Opposition is determined to destroy the NBN,"* then-Prime Minister Julia Gillard says at a press conference in June 2011[111]. *"I anticipate the Opposition will go to the next election saying they'll dig the cables out of the ground."*

Gillard says Abbott has given Turnbull instructions to "destroy" the NBN. *"You destroy the NBN by ripping up this agreement, ripping the fibre out of the ground and keeping this nation in the past,"* she tells the media. *"Our intention is to build the project; you can talk to Tony Abbott about destroying [it]".*

Turnbull describes[112] Gillard's comments as *"ludicrous"* and *"false"*, and it's true the PM has gone a bit far with her criticism. It is unlikely a Coalition Government would rip any fibre out of the ground which NBN Co had deployed.

But again the comments strike a nerve with a public which is becoming increasingly concerned with the Coalition's approach to the NBN.

The Multi-Technology Mix

In April 2013 — a scant few months before the upcoming Federal Election — Turnbull finally launches the Coalition's alternative NBN policy. As many have long predicted, the platform is based on the same Fibre to the Node technology that

Telstra had unsuccessfully pitched to John Howard's Coalition administration back in 2005.

The policy is based on the core pledge that a Coalition Government would deliver download speeds of between 25Mbps and 100Mbps to most users by the end of 2016 — effectively the end of its first term in power — and 50Mbps to 100Mbps by the end of 2019 to a smaller set, effectively the end of its second term. These are lightweight speeds compared with the ultimate promise of Labor's NBN model, which offers theoretical speeds up to 1GBps. In addition, much of the financial estimates backing the Coalition's NBN model are questionable, to say nothing of Coalition estimates of Labor's own plan. And switching to FTTN would require a huge turnaround effort by NBN Co. This is a hugely risky and controversial plan, with dubious long-term benefits.

But the Coalition has bet on the public preferring a NBN model which would see broadband delivered to their premises quicker and at a cheaper overall cost. And the model is not unworkable. In point of fact, it reflects the Liberal focus on fiscal conservativism. But the truth is that it is a worse model than the one Labor aleady has in place.

Flanked by Tony Abbott and with a brief appearance by a holographic footballer, Turnbull launches the policy at a ritzy event in Sydney's Fox Studios[113].

The odd couple give a confident exposition of the policy. But again, much of the media doesn't appear to be buying the story. The questions come thick and fast about the expected lifespan of the Telstra copper network which would underpin the new Coalition policy. And Turnbull is forced to admit that no other government globally is pursuing quite the same model. This, he says, is something that has been forced on the Coalition by Labor.

"We are in the position of the guy that is going touring in Ireland and gets lost in one of those little country lanes and goes into the Irish pub and asks for directions and the barman with the generosity and helpfulness and kindness for which the Irish are famous says to him, "Well, sir if I were you I wouldn't be starting from here" and the truth is we wouldn't be starting from here either," he tells the media[114].

"Tony and I are inheriting the NBN Co but we're not about, you know, just moaning and groaning about the bad decisions made preceding it. What we are going to do is get this job done and we will bring very fast broadband to all Australians sooner, cheaper and more affordably."

Unfortunately for the Coalition, the policy is quickly panned by experts and the public alike, with one informal poll put by the ABC to its readers finding that 78 percent of the public is against Turnbull's model[115]. And the questions that continue to be asked are the same that were asked of Turnbull three years before: Why would a Coalition Government walk away from a FTTP model from the NBN, given that it was already being implemented and represented the best possible long-term platform for Australia's broadband needs? In April 2013, as in September 2010, Fibre to the Node is not a popular option with the Australian public, and continues to come with significant baggage attached.

What follows the launch is something of a feeding frenzy, as commentator after commentator launch attacks on the Coalition's rival NBN policy through every media platform imaginable.

The mood is perhaps best summed up by Mark Gregory, a senior lecturer in electrical and computer engineering at RMIT University, who is emerging as a frequent commentator on the NBN and critic of Turnbull's vision.

"The Coalition is taking a very short-term approach that ulti-mately is going to cost Australia far more in the long-run," Gregory

says at the time[116]. *"All the advice from people in the industry and from academia has been for the Coalition to not go down this path. So my question is, why have they decided to ignore all that advice?"*

The answer, of course, is that the Coalition — and Turnbull specifically — currently appears to see the NBN policy topic as a political issue, not an engineering problem.

As the September election gets closer, the debate gets even uglier.

Australia's technology blogosphere is exploding with strong opinions about the Coalition's NBN policy. One of the most strident — and, at times, one-sided — critics is Steve Jenkin, a long-time IT professional. On his blog, Jenkin has labelled the Coalition's approach a *"financial disaster"*. And unlike most online writers, he has engaged directly with Turnbull's office on the issue in an attempt to get some answers to his burning questions.

In August 2013, the frustration coming from Turnbull's office on the NBN issue explodes. In response to an email from Jenkin, one of Turnbull's senior staffers goes nuclear and swears at the blogger, labelling his writings *"psychotic rantings"* and worse[117].

In many ways Turnbull's staffer is not incorrect — Jenkin has been relentless in his criticism and has not been precisely objective. But again, it's the tone coming out of the Opposition that is off-balance. Turnbull's team has over-reacted.

After the Election

The date is 18 September 2013, and Malcolm Turnbull has been sworn in as Australia's 55th Communications Minister, in the new Federal Cabinet led by Tony Abbott as Prime Minister.

It doesn't take long for the new Minister to get out of the starter's gates.

One of Turnbull's first actions is to ask most of the NBN board to resign, which most of it does. A new chairman (former

Telstra and Optus CEO Ziggy Switkowski) is appointed[118]. The NBN's founding CEO, Mike Quigley, has already resigned[119]. Much of the NBN rollout is switched rapidly to a FTTN model, and much of the rest is later switched in December to a model based on upgrading the legacy HFC cable networks, based on a Strategic Review of the NBN model[120].

A further selection of new executives (some with connections to Turnbull personally[121]) rapidly take key positions within the NBN company, and executives with perceived links to Labor or who merely find themselves out of favour are unceremoniously let go. A number of the reviews into Labor's NBN model are conducted, with some of the reviewers having clear connections to the Liberal Party[122], and/or having been staunch critics of Labor's NBN policy.

Wider moves have substantial impacts on the broadband market as a whole. For example, changes to the NBN's regulatory structure allow major ISPs such as TPG to rapidly start rolling out their own infrastructure in direct competition with the NBN. This places Turnbull in something of a quandary: Should the Government continue to support the integrity of the NBN's financial model, or allow the market to pursue the market competition which the Coalition had been so insistent on during the election cycle?

The general picture painted is of a vengeful Coalition administration punishing the NBN for Labor's folly, and remaking its image as rapidly as possible according to Coalition and capitalist market principles.

This, in and of itself, is almost expected as a change of Government occurs. But here's the rub: As Turnbull's tenure as Communications Minister roll on, it rapidly becomes apparent that many of the criticisms made by commentators on the Coalition's alternative NBN policy have turned out to be, in fact, quite prescient.

Since its 2013 election victory, the Coalition has been forced to backtrack substantially on its use of the dated and problematic HFC cable networks as part of the NBN, for example[123]. And a series of leaks have appeared to show that the FTTN model which Turnbull had instigated has caused NBN Co significant headaches to implement[124].

Then too, in 2017 and 2018 the public's displeasure with FTTN as a broadband option continues to grow[125], based on poor real-world performance of the technology as deployed by the NBN company.

Meanwhile, other leaked NBN documents have shown that the cost and ease of implementing Labor's original FTTP model continues to be reduced[126] — as many experts predicted it would. Things are panning out very much as many commentators expected. Much of the criticism of Turnbull's model has been proven to be at least somewhat valid.

In November 2015, Turnbull — now the Prime Minister — says regarding the NBN that Labor had committed the Government to a *staggeringly ambitious project* with little research, describing it as *the craziest thing done by the Labor Party in six years of misgovernment*.

"Now, as is the lot of the Liberal and National parties, we've inherited this mess, and we've had to clean it up," Turnbull tells Federal Parliament[127].

But in 2018, it continues to appear as though the Coalition has much cleaning up of its own to do when it comes to the NBN.

The five years from Abbott's 2013 election have been turbulent for the NBN.

The departure from Labor's FTTP model for the NBN has caused havoc for the project as a whole. Many Australians are finding Turnbull's version of the NBN to be not much of an upgrade on their existing broadband infrastructure — if they can get it at all.

In some locations, such as Canberra, the NBN is overbuilding existing FTTN networks with more FTTN[128] … while leaving locations underserved by any high-speed broadband until latter stages of the rollout. Much of what is happening defies common sense and the public's expectations.

The HFC and copper infrastructure which Turnbull had been so keen on turns out to represent deep problems for the NBN company. NBN Co has especially been forced to reconsider much of its prior commitment to upgrading Optus' dilapidated HFC cable infrastructure.

In April 2018, the NBN chief executive, Bill Morrow, is forced to admit what many Australians already know — reusing the copper and HFC networks led to a faster and cheaper network build — but the tactic brought with it speed limitations, in addition to an increased fault rate[129].

Complaints from NBN customers keep on rising as they don't receive the speeds they have been paying for. Some retail Internet providers — iiNet and Internode amongst them — are even being forced to compensate their customers for slow NBN speeds[130]. And the 'nodes' which support the FTTN rollout are suffering their own problems — flooding[131] and being hit by cars[132] among other issues.

Many of these problems were predicted long ago by critics of the Coalition's NBN model.

In April 2018, Morrow resigns[133]. He's had a fair run and done his best with the company since taking its reins in December 2013. But it's hard to escape the feeling that more problems lie ahead for the NBN.

So how did all of this come to pass?

In order to understand the NBN as it currently stands, we must necessarily go back to where the current era of the NBN began: With an ambitious man named Malcolm Turnbull.

Initial Enthusiasm

It must be said that Turnbull's ascension to the role of Shadow Communications Minister back in 2010 had always been viewed as bittersweet tidings by many in Australia's technology sector.

There is no doubt that for many, Turnbull's appointment to the role brought somewhat of an initial sense of optimism with it. After all, the Member for Wentworth was, at that stage, perhaps the first true technophile to ever hold the Communications portfolio in Australia, in Government or out of it.

A decade of political ineptitude in the portfolio and even hostility towards some aspects of technological progress had taught Australia's technologists to expect that ambivalence towards tech policy was, perhaps the best that they could expect from our elected representatives.

On paper, at least, Turnbull offered the potential for something much greater: Understanding at last, if not compatriotism.

And it's true: the former Opposition Leader did bring with him to the portfolio a deep understanding of technology, both through his past as an investor in OzEmail, Australia's first major Internet service provider, as well as his personal interest in the potential that new consumer technology has to change the lives of all Australians.

In the three months before his appointment, the Member for Wentworth had emerged as something of a champion of the technology sector within Federal Parliament.

The ousted Opposition Leader was one of the first MPs to use an iPad in the House of Representatives[134]. He had taken to the new Twitter social media platform like a fish to water. And Turnbull had also emerged as one of the key forces in the Coalition which eventually consigned Labor's mandatory Internet filter policy to the dustheap where most in the sector felt it belonged.

"It was a really bad idea that could only have come up from people that didn't actually understand the Internet," a jovial Turnbull told an anti-filter forum in August that year at the Paddington RSL in his electorate in Sydney[135].

The audience applauded and Turnbull, a schooner of beer in hand, basked in their warm approval. The appearance of former OzEmail chief Justin Milne, who had himself been harshly critical of the Internet filter policy during his years leading Telstra's BigPond division, only reinforced Turnbull's tech-savvy nature for many in the room, and many who read about it afterwards.

Turnbull was also unlike most shadow ministers in that he was able to draw upon substantially greater personal resources during the NBN policy debate.

As we've discussed in previous chapters, most Shadow Ministers will spend their time in Opposition with only a couple of policy advisors to conduct research and assist them in honing policies which will deal meaningfully with significant issues in their portfolios, while also toeing the line of their respective party's general philosophy.

There is no doubt that Turnbull was able to bring more to the table during his own policy debate on the NBN.

The MP's substantial personal wealth meant that his office was more fully staffed than most of his colleagues; he had the resources to conduct deeper research into the local and international telecommunications landscape.

This too, drove tech sector positivity around Turnbull's appointment; Turnbull was not another lightweight in the communications portfolio.

But on that fateful day of Turnbull's appointment in September 2010, it only took Abbott minutes to dispel any enthusiasm which Turnbull's appointment may have garnered. His next comments left an incredibly bitter taste in the mouths of tech-savvy Australians which persisted for years to come.

The Opposition Leader made clear that Turnbull had not come to build Labor's NBN; but to destroy it.

Abbott's actual words on the day of the reshuffle which elevated Turnbull to the post of Shadow Communications Minister are often misquoted. There is little evidence that Abbott had asked Turnbull to *"demolish"* the NBN itself. In point of fact, Abbott's order was that Turnbull should *"demolish the Government on the issue"*[136]. This was a political command, not a technological one, although Abbott did later call for the NBN funding to be re-allocated towards what he saw as worthier causes.

"The National Broadband Network is a luxury that Australia cannot now afford. The one thing you don't do is redo your bathroom when your roof has just been blown off," the Member for Warringah said in January 2011, following the Queensland floods of that year[137].

Turnbull's personal views on technology policy

Turnbull's first demonstrated interest in Australia's technology sector came in 1994, when he purchased a half million dollar stake in OzEmail, which was, at the time, one of Australia's first real Internet service providers of any scale.

The deal has been well-chronicled over time by the Financial Review newspaper, and most recently, in Paddy Manning's unauthorised biography of Turnbull, *Born to Rule*[138]. Manning pinned the deal as having arrived on Turnbull's doorstop through Trevor Kennedy, who had worked with Turnbull during his time as a lawyer for media magnate Kerry Packer. At the time, Turnbull was emerging as a prominent investment banker in Sydney's burgeoning financial scene.

The brains behind the fledgling ISP business were contributed by Sean Howard, who had earlier founded Australian Personal Computer during the first big boom period of the PC revolution in Australia, eventually selling the magazine to Kerry Packer's Consolidated Press. OzEmail, itself then a minor part of the Packer empire, was doing poorly at the time — Howard had already burnt some $7 million on the project — so Kennedy brought his own funds and Turnbull's involvement to the rescue.

Shortly after, the business started flourishing alongside the rise of the Internet in general. Turnbull eventually played a pivotal role in selling OzEmail to WorldCom in 1999 for $520 million, making his fortune in the process. His share was approximately $57 million.

In 2004, Sean Howard made a number of comments to the Financial Review which were revealing about Turnbull's relationship with technology policy, as viewed through the lens of the OzEmail venture.

"I presented OzEmail to him and we cut a deal almost immediately," Howard said at the time[139]. *"Malcolm is a great user of technology and he 'got it', so to speak, straight away."* Turnbull also appeared to understand — years later — that the dial-up Internet market was commoditising, and it would be prudent for OzEmail's investors to get out of the company while the getting was good.

Howard's comments confirm one fact about Turnbull, and give us hints about another. They confirm, as many have opined, that Turnbull was, in effect, a digital 'native' ahead of his time. Although he grew up in the 50's and 60's, rather than the 80's and 90's, Turnbull appears to have that innate love for technology which drives Generation X and Y. He loves to play with new gadgets, and he has a gift for translating that interest into its impact on mass consumer and business markets that has strongly benefited him as an investor.

This interest would go on to drive later Turnbull family investments in next-generation companies such as WebCentral and Chaos.com, and it also prompted Turnbull's first major policy initiative as Prime Minister in 2015 and 2016: His attempt to prime Australia for the next wave of digital innovation through his landmark National Innovation and Science Agenda[140].

This enduring interest which Turnbull showed in Australia's technology and telecommunications industries also shows up in the maiden speech which the new Member for Wentworth gave to Federal Parliament a decade after his OzEmail investment, in November 2004.

However, the tenor of that speech also reveals the place that Turnbull personally believes technology has in Australian society and confirms the hint that we can glean from the Member for Wentworth's actions after the OzEmail sale.

For Rudd and Conroy, who would start launching successive versions of their NBN policy a year or so after Turnbull entered the House of Representatives, the NBN was a great leveller, a critical piece of infrastructure which would not only unlock the ability of every Australian to access important services, but also the ability of businesses to compete on a global stage.

Neither Rudd nor Conroy have displayed the same 'digital native' personal interest in technology that Turnbull has over the years — well, at least not to the same extent. But they have always held an idealistic view in the power of technology as a positive force in its own right.

In his maiden speech, Turnbull gave technology a particular twist that implied he believed technology to be a pragmatic tool rather than the key feature in the idealistic vision promulgated by those on the other side of the parliamentary benches.

He and his wife Lucy, Turnbull told the House, had found that much of their satisfaction in business had come from starting new businesses which created *"new jobs and new markets for Australian technology"[141]*.

In that speech, Turnbull also made comments foreshadowing the December 2015 launch of his Innovation and Science Agenda.

In his maiden speech Turnbull referred to the idea that Australia's economy and prosperity depended on a culture of initiative and enterprise. *"... the smaller, newer and more entrepreneurial businesses often feel disconnected or crowded out,"* he complained.

The new MP went on to discuss some aspects of the empowering nature that technology can gift its end users — such as its ability to unlock the ability of older Australians to continue to participate in the workforce.

But he never truly showed the idealistic enthusiasm for the enfranchising nature of technology that Conroy, fellow Labor Senator Kate Lundy, a technocrat like Rudd or former Greens Senator and ex-web designer Scott Ludlam have showed repeatedly in speech after speech over many years in public service.

Maiden speeches in Parliament often display the naked, honest views of the MPs who give them; they feel compelled to produce a transparent view of their plans for their parliamentary career because of the perceived significance of the occasion.

Turnbull's maiden speech, then, appeared to show the public what he really thought of technology; that it had its place, but that it was necessarily suboordinate — a tool — to serve economic, financial and societal needs, rather than something which was an inherent good on its own merits.

This facet of Turnbull's apparent beliefs is also somewhat evident in his approach to the tech sector after his OzEmail investment was so spectacularly successful.

Other Australian entrepreneurs who have seen similar capital gains from tech ventures have often become serial re-investors in that sector, either directly as angel investors or through venture capital funds. You can see this trend again and again if you look at the sector's history. Those who have built major tech-nology companies often want to help others build them too.

The launch of venture capital fund Blackbird Ventures in 2013[142] — backed by the founders of successful Australian technology companies such as Atlassian, Campaign Monitor and Aconex — is one of the greatest examples of this trend.

The Turnbulls did make some tech-related investments following the OzEmail windfall. But it became more common for their profits from that sale to make their way into other industries and capital instruments, rather than through the technology startup sector which so desperately needed cash injections in the lean years of the dot com bust in the early 2000's.

Some of this may be due to Turnbull's election to the House of Representatives in 2004. MPs usually eschew directly investing in companies, due to the vast potential for conflicts of interest.

However, Turnbull's ongoing roles outside the technology sector — such as his managing directorship of Goldman Sachs Australia from 1997 to 2001, or even his role leading the Australian Republican Movement from 1993 through 2000, also mediate against the idea of Turnbull being a technology sector champion.

Turnbull as NBN supporter?

Much has also been made of the theory that Turnbull was never personally partial to the idea of tearing down the NBN; and that the approach he took to the project was spurred by Abbott's command and Turnbull's desire to secure a Cabinet Ministership in a Coalition administration; not his organic policy beliefs. Many onlookers have long believed that Turnbull swung both ways regarding the NBN — against it in public, and for it in private.

Long-time Internode executive John Lindsay claimed as much in February 2011, telling South Australian radio that Turnbull secretly loved the project.

"Something that I find when I talk to Malcolm Turnbull about this is that he's got this kind of light in his eyes, he loves the NBN as a concept — because deep down he's a technocrat," Lindsay told listeners[143].

This idea has been advanced to me personally at times by almost every major figure in Australia's telecommunications sector. ISP chief executives, analysts, political insiders; the theory casting Turnbull as a closet NBN supporter is pervasive and widespread.

However, in 2018, with the benefit of hindsight and a view from behind the scenes inside Federal Parliament, it seems apparent that the NBN project was never something that Turnbull personally approved of.

It is clear that Turnbull likes the idea of Australia being covered by high-speed broadband; with all the benefits that such technology can unlock. He is a believer in the power of innovation; of fast-growing technology startups that turn into major companies; and of the benefits of universal connectivity. He knows that solid broadband infrastructure is a key enabler for Australia's future.

But it is also appears that Turnbull does not believe the Government should deploy that infrastructure itself.

"The NBN is not a public good, like a school or hospital, provided (essentially) free of charge to the public. It is a commercial business which will charge for its services," wrote Turnbull in September 2010[144], in response to an editorial by the Sydney Morning Herald.

The full knowledge of this fact puts a tragic slant on Abbott's comments.

Many Australians have viewed them primarily as an indicator of Abbott's ongoing personal inability to understand the potential that others see in the positive potential of technology; of his desire to tear down a landmark Labor project; and, even perhaps of his desire to cast Turnbull in the impossible political situation of having to take responsibility for a Labor initiative which many Coalition voters disapproved of from the start.

There is little doubt that these were all factors in Turnbull's appointment as Shadow Communications Minister. Abbott handed Turnbull a poisoned pill, and both of them appeared to know it. And it's also true that Abbott — as he made clear during the 2010 Federal Election campaign — is certainly *"no Bill Gates"*[145] — not a technical expert.

But in the wake of all that has happened since, we must necessarily see Abbott's comments as also being more reflective of Turnbull's personal views on the NBN than many would like to believe.

They are a clear harbinger of the wrecking ball which Turnbull would swing through Labor's utopian NBN policy, first in Opposition, and then — tragically — with the full force of a Coalition Government.

The key theme of this chapter is thus the understanding that the personal political philosophies of politicians – in this case, Turnbull's strong belief in Liberalism and the virtues of letting the private sector construct its own infrastructure building blocks – have a strong potential to poison the well of good technology policy, even if a politician may personally understand the tech sector and tech concepts well.

Turnbull versus Abbott

It is also instructive to contrast Turnbull's view of the Government's role in investing in and supporting the rollout of telecommunications infrastructure with Abbott's.

There is no doubt that Abbott has always been person-ally against the NBN; it's a policy which he would never have proceeded with. There is little evidence that Abbott ever really cared about broadband as a social or economic enabler or saw the validity of arguments supporting infrastructure develop-ment in this area. And the Liberal leader has never been a strong personal user of technology.

Like Abbott, Turnbull never agreed with the need for direct Government investment in the field. But at a fundamental level, Turnbull did appear to grok the arguments for broadband as an enabling force — and he understood the personal appeal of better technology.

Throughout the past decade, it appears to have been the two Liberal leaders' personal views on technology which has driven their differing approaches the issue.

Abbott was content to essentially ignore the NBN, viewing it as a project that the public did not care about and that he could be openly contemptuous of. But unlike Abbott, Turnbull appeared to understand that the NBN was indeed an electoral factor, and perhaps a major one.

There was a great deal of evidence around at the time to support this view.

A report by former Howard minister Peter Reith into the 2010 election had found the NBN policy to be influential in some areas, particularly the sensitive Tasmanian electorate, which was slated to receive the infrastructure first[146].

Turnbull appeared to be aware that the Coalition could not simply take a policy to the Election that would see the NBN project merely set aside. The immense popularity of the project — shown repeatedly through polling through the three year period leading up to the 2013 Federal Election — medi-ated against this idea, as did the fact that the Government had already in-vested multiple billions of dollars in it.

On paper, after all, the NBN project was slated to be a winner for every stakeholder. The Australian public would finally get the world-class broadband it had been demanding for many years, based on the best possible technology — Fibre to the Premises. The Australian telecommunications industry would receive massive government investment and competitive oppor-tunities stemming from the enforced separation of Telstra's retail division from its soon-to-be-defunct network infrastruc-ture.

And crucially, the NBN project was also slated to make money. A great deal of money.

Ultimately, if the project's finances panned out the way that Labor's modelling showed they would, NBN Co itself would make a significant long-term return on the Government's multi-billion-dollar investment in it.

And things would get even better down the track. Not only would NBN Co be able to pay back the billions the Government would invest in it to deploy fibre around Australia; the company itself could be privatised down the track to massive profit, as Telstra had been before it.

Many on the Labor side of the fence saw a future in ten years or so when NBN Co could, like Telstra before it, be floated on the Australian Securities Exchange, leading to a multi-billion-dollar once-off windfall for the Australian treasury. Far from creating further public debt, the NBN company was set to help pay it back.

However, for Turnbull the problem also went beyond policy and to his personal political fortunes.

The Earl of Wentworth needed a version of Labor's NBN policy that would both enshrine traditional Liberal values of market competition and accountability for public spending, as well as present a credible challenge to Labor's own model. It was only through this combination that Turnbull could ensure his own position on the national policy stage, within the election campaign, and within any future Coalition Federal Cabinet as a Min-ister.

To meet this challenge Turnbull needed a NBN policy which would retain some of the bones of Labor's original vision (enough to retain a vestige of credibility for the Coalition) but also one which would radically depart from the FTTP model which would cost the Government so much in terms of invested capital, and take so long to deploy. This was the so-called Multi-Technology Mix, which brought HFC and FTTN technology to the NBN.

Lessons learnt

In the previous chapter, we traced the failure of Labor's initial, $4.7 billion Fibre to the Node version of the NBN policy to two factors: A reliance on the private sector to help develop policy; and a failure to look globally for best practice policy models.

These two factors reflect the weakness of the policy-making process in Opposition, in which MPs have a severely limited set of resources in order to present a coherent policy alternative to policy developed by the ruling party, with all the resources of government behind it.

Yet Malcolm Turnbull did not suffer from these issues.

Compared with predecessors such as Stephen Conroy, Turnbull was able to muster significantly greater resources to the task of holding the office of Shadow Communications Minister, owing to his greater personal wealth and background in the technology sector.

So what went wrong?

The inescapable conclusion from this chapter is that two things went wrong with the reshaping of the NBN policy under Malcolm Turnbull.

The first might be politely termed 'personal ambition'.

It is no secret that Malcolm Bligh Turnbull has long desired to be Prime Minister of Australia. Turnbull had an initial chance to succeed at this goal, from the Opposition Leadership in 2008 and 2009. But it would take his long second tilt at the leadership to take the Prime Ministership from Tony Abbott.

This tilt started when Turnbull reneged on his decision to quit Parliament after losing the Liberal leadership to Abbott in 2009. But it wasn't until 2010, when the Member for Wentworth returned to the Shadow Cabinet and officially took on portfolio responsibilities, that the run gathered pace.

Without a credible framework for tackling the NBN, Turnbull could not remain a credible Shadow Communications Minister. And without a credible post in Cabinet, he could not be part of an Abbott-led administration. This would essentially leave him little platform to challenge for the leadership down the track.

In hindsight, it appears that that Turnbull sacrificed the success of Labor's NBN policy to his own personal ambition.

The second factor relates to a politicians' own personal experience.

When Turnbull reached out for a policy that would allow him to both oppose Labor's NBN policy, while still adopting and adapting the overall NBN project to be his own, he did not appear to reach much further than his own personal convictions.

The Member for Wentworth was able to successfully give the impression that he was open to differing policy options for the NBN — even, perhaps, Labor's own approach. But when it really came down to brass tacks — elucidating a definitive Coalition policy on the matter, and, as Communications Minister, enacting that policy, Turnbull drew primarily from his own entrenched opinions to guide his actions, appearing to ignore the available evidence about some of the strengths of Labor's approach.

In an ordinary citizen, this is a logical approach.

Even for a Shadow Minister or ordinary Opposition back-bencher, this is a valid approach. The Australian public tends to like 'conviction politicians' — elected representatives who faithfully follow their own personal values, sometimes despite the available evidence.

But in a Minister dealing with complex and fast-moving policy areas, it can be a terrible approach.

The reason for this is simple; convictions aid politicians well when they go to matters of personal integrity; ethics and human relations. But the dictates of complex economic and competition theory, amongst many other complex policy areas, mitigate against simple rationalisation.

The Federal Government's large up-front investment in a universal fibre NBN, for example, just feels wrong to a Liberal MP who believes technology should serve business interests rather than the public interest; to a Liberal MP who believes that existing infrastructure should not be ignored when considering the potential of new technology platforms.

But that doesn't mean it *is* wrong. At least in the absence of a better alternative.

Empirically, Labor's NBN policy made a great deal of sense. It would have broken, once and for all, Telstra's dominance over Australia's telecommunications industry; delivered Australians as a whole world-class broadband and set the nation up for the forthcoming digital economy.

Almost as a side note, the project would have made the Federal Government and the Australian taxpayer a lot of money — not only the initial, up to seven percent return on the Government's capital investment, but also many billions more, from the eventual privatisation of the NBN company itself — in a repeat of the Telstra privatisation that was so successful decades before.

There is no doubt that Labor's model had its problems. But those problems did not appear to lead to the conclusion that it was worth abandoning completely, or even substantially modifying it significantly, as the Coalition did.

A typical alternative approach from the Liberal Party would have been to abandon this policy and focus squarely on the development of capitalist-style competition in the telecommunications infrastructure market. This would have involved winding back government investment in the sector drastically.

Ultimately, however, neither of these approaches would prove useful to Turnbull's own political needs. As an ambitious politician, Turnbull could neither give his support to Labor's big-spending NBN vision, nor propose winding it back entirely. Supporting Labor's approach ran directly against Liberal Party ideals, while Turnbull appeared to be aware that taking the opposite minimalist approach would leave him bereft of a realistic platform to oppose Labor's plan.

So Turnbull chose the middle ground: An approach that would allow him to continue to utilise the bones of Labor's vision, while also aligning the model further towards Liberal Party values and his own personal philosophy. This had a distinct political advantage for Turnbull: Giving him a viable position to oppose Labor's approach, while not abandoning its populist roots wholesale.

What this tells us is something as disturbing as it has been dramatic.

The policy failings in the NBN's first chapter of The Frustrated State appeared to be driven by political process; especially the lack of resources which Opposition parties have available to assist them in policy formation.

But the policy failings in the NBN's second chapter appear to owe more to personality and personal ambition.

If Stephen Conroy had never been appointed Communications Minister, one suspects that as Prime Minister, Kevin Rudd would nonetheless not have ignored the potential of an

NBN-like policy. And other ambitious, tech-savvy figures such as Kate Lundy also waited in the wings. Such is the nature of Labor in general; it will tend to hear the complaints of Australians en-masse; and Australians have long been concerned about the general availability of fast broadband.

But we cannot say the same for the Coalition.

If almost any other Liberal or National politician had been appointed Shadow Communications Minister in 2010, the Coalition would have probably taken a similarly minimalist policy to the 2013 Federal Election that it had pitched to the public three years before[147].

Under standard Liberal policy, the NBN project would have probably been dismantled; handed back to Telstra; or even quickly split up and privatised. It is very hard to say that a Liberal Government would have allowed the NBN vehicle to continue, even heavily modified. Its core principles — overwhelming levels of government investment to restructure Australia's telecommunications industry — remain inimical to the Liberal platform, even cloaked as they were in the guise of better broadband for all.

But Malcolm Turnbull's ambition did not appear to allow this.

The key theme of this chapter is thus the understanding that the political ambitions and personal philosophies of politicians – in this case, Turnbull's need for a vehicle to oppose Labor from a Shadow Cabinet position, combined with a strong belief in Liberalism and the virtues of letting the private sector construct its own infrastructure building blocks – have a strong potential to poison the well of good technology policy, even if a politician may personally understand the tech sector and tech concepts well.

Legitimacy

It is worthwhile at this point to pause for a second and invite the question of whether Turnbull's actions as Shadow Communications Minister were what we might call 'legitimate'.

As mentioned earlier in this chapter, there are those who would cast Turnbull in a saving grace with respect to his actions with respect to the NBN project. Those who make this argument highlight the contrast between Abbott and Turnbull. Sometimes the pair — even from the same podium, at the same event — would make essentially different arguments with respect to the NBN policy, with Turnbull not excusing Abbott's antipathy to the project, but not condoning it either.

"I don't know how he did it, but Malcolm Turnbull has turned the Liberals under Tony Abbott into an NBN party. In the process, he has saved Abbott from a terrible mess if he had gone to the election still promising to dismantle the NBN," wrote seasoned business journalist Alan Kohler after the April 2013 launch of the Coalition's NBN policy[148].

It is also true that Turnbull went much deeper down the policy wormhole with respect to the NBN than most Shadow Ministers go. With the resources available to him, the Member for Wentworth produced a complex NBN policy for the 2013 Federal Election, and went so far as to distribute a separate costing document outlining the economics and rationale behind the Coalition's policy decisions[149].

It'll never be possible to completely disbunk this 'saving grace' theory without a degree of inside knowledge which would be very difficult to obtain.

However what is clear from a cold and dispassionate examination of Turnbull's many, many statements about the NBN project and telecommunications and technology policy in general over the past several decades is that the Member for Wentworth's position on these issues never appeared to fundamentally change.

Throughout his time in industry, in Parliament, as a Shadow Minister and then as a Minister and eventually Prime Minister, Turnbull has appeared to maintain a consistent personal policy position on issues such as the NBN.

Again and again, throughout his tenure as Shadow Communications Minister, Turnbull supported the view that existing telecommunications infrastructure owned by major players such as Telstra and Optus — such as HFC cable, copper and even satellite — had a role to play in a future NBN platform, and that the NBN should incorporate these platforms into its technology mix.

The 'Multi-Technology Mix' which the NBN ultimately adopted when the Coalition took power in September 2013 and Turnbull became Communications Minister deviated from the vision which Turnbull had espoused in April 2013, placing a higher emphasis on the utilisation of HFC cable technology than the FTTN-based vision which the Coalition had taken to the 2013 Federal Election[150].

But the fundamental concept at the heart of Coalition telecommunications policy under Malcolm Turnbull has always remained the same. Turnbull's view has always appeared to be that the NBN project should not exist; and that if it had to, it should not throw the baby out with the bathwater in terms of abandoning inferior telecommunications networks such as HFC cable and Telstra's copper network.

If you trace the history back, it is possible to see this clear connection over many years, and the fact that although Turnbull's thought processes appeared to become nuanced with respect to the NBN policy; and although they came to suit his personal and political agenda of the day; his original convictions never really appeared to change.

Without being able to get into details, this view is also consistent with the many conversations which I've had with close advisors to Malcolm Turnbull over the years. The passion with which Turnbull and his staff have put forth these views speaks further to their long-term consistency.

In this sense, Turnbull may be said to be a conviction politician when it comes to telecommunications policy. When it came to the Coalition's policy on the NBN which Turnbull developed in the years leading up to 2013, it may be said that Turnbull's policy beliefs appeared to align with his political needs.

Seasoned political journalist Paul Hartcher wrote in 2009[151] that former Prime Minister Paul Keating offered then-Prime Minister Kevin Rudd some advice when Turnbull took the Liberal leadership at that time. First, Keating told Rudd, Turnbull was brilliant. Secondly, he was utterly fearless. However, the new Liberal leader had one fatal flaw: He had no judgement.

As we learned from his dealings with the NBN in the years after 2010, Turnbull did indeed have some judgement when it came to matters of technology policy.

Just, tragically for Australians and the long-term future of the NBN, not enough.

SUMMARY

Policy Details

When the Abbott administration took power in September 2013, it radically overhauled the model for Labor's National Broadband Network project, introducing a mix of technologies to replace the near uniform rollout of Fibre to the Premises.

What Went Wrong

The Coalition's Multi-Technology Mix approach was a bad model. It destroyed the level playing field approach which Labor had taken to deploying broadband infrastructure, meaning that premises would receive different types of broadband.

This played havoc with the integrated regulatory model which Labor had deployed alongside the NBN infrastructure, and ensured the NBN project would be plagued with the need to maintain legacy technology into the future.

If Malcolm Turnbull had not been Communications Minister, many observers believe it likely that then-Prime Minister Tony Abbott would have cancelled the NBN project. Turnbull's ambition to remain within the Cabinet — and eventually become Prime Minister in his own right — appeared to led him to develop a complex model which saw the Coalition retain the NBN in some form.

In doing so, it appears Turnbull relied too heavily on his own opinion of the correct path forward for the NBN, rather than weighing the international and local evidence, which tended to support much of Labor's existing model.

Avoiding This Situation in Future

Large infrastructure projects must be undertaken on a bi-partisan basis if they are to be successful over a construction period of a decade or more.

CHAPTER 4

Abomination

"... it is an unholy disaster, a massive debacle. There is very little dispute that it will eventually cost double what the previous government told the public."

—Queensland Health
Minister Lawrence Springborg

The date is 7 June 2012, and the location is Queensland State Parliament.

Health Minister Lawrence Springborg should be a happy man. It's been three months since his Liberal National Party swept to power in the state. Springborg's fortunes have risen with those of the party leader, maverick former Brisbane Lord Mayor Campbell Newman, and Queensland is expanding rapidly on the back of the new LNP administration. Things are looking up.

But Springborg is not happy. Instead, he tells the Parliament[152], he is very angry. And he's not the only one.

"Queenslanders are angry," he says. *"As a parliamentarian I am angry at the consequences visited on Health employees and the taxpayers of Queensland."*

Springborg is having words to say about one of Australia's most infamous IT disasters, the ill-fated revamp of the payroll platform at Queensland Health. The Queensland Government has just released a scathing KPMG report finding that the new IT platform has cost the state some $417 million and will need another $837 million to fix over the next five years.

That would be bad enough. There is no State Government in Australia that would find it easy to justify spending $1.2 billion on any IT project, let alone one as mundane as payroll software.

But there is worse to come: Adding insult to injury, Queensland Health's new payroll platform still does not actually work, even in the most fundamental sense.

"KPMG links this abomination to Labor's centralised control and its lack of due diligence," the Health Minister tells his colleagues in Parliament. *"This is the system Labor commissioned, without so much as a business case, to pay every public servant in every department in Health in the state. It fell at the first hurdle and the implications continue to emerge."*

"Even today this fragile system cannot calculate the basic leave entitlements of the workers it was installed to serve."

He is livid and contemptuous. He spits the words into the air. It's easy for onlookers to tell that the new Health Minister wishes he could be rid of the whole sorry mess.

Unfortunately for Springborg — and for Queenslanders in general — this is one mess that is not going away any time soon.

Over the next several years, the saga of Queensland Health's botched payroll systems upgrade — already a significant factor helping Labor to lose the recent State Election — will continue to haunt Australia's entire IT industry.

It will haunt public sector chief information officers and IT project managers with the spectre that their own projects could become the next national debacle.

It will haunt Ministers and policy advisors with the potential for their decisions about major IT projects to become the same sort of political millstone around their necks that Queensland Health's IT payroll systems debacle turned into for Anna Bligh's doomed state Labor administration.

And most of all, it will haunt private sector IT companies, who fear the loss of revenue and reputation that comes from failing to deliver complex IT projects on time and on budget; a feat seemingly impossible in this day and age.

As the State Government lurches from one extreme approach to the project (walking away from it entirely) to another (trying desperately to remediate it within a reasonable cost envelope) the whole epic journey starts to take on the character of a farce.

A royal commission is called to get to the bottom of what went wrong with the project; the offices of the Queensland IT Minister and Queensland Health chief information officer become revolving doors in which no figure can hold their seat on anything like a permanent basis; bureaucrats and IBM executives alike are hung out in public to dry; drastic mitigation plans are put in place to avoid similar catastrophes in future.

And then the lawsuits begin.

IBM and the Queensland Government had their day in front of a royal commission; then they had their day in court.

Four years later, the saga still had not fully abated. The issue lives on in the collective unconscious of Australia's IT industry; a kind of general warning about the dangers of complex IT projects.

And yet, as bad as the failed Queensland Health payroll upgrade project was, as botched as it was, the fact that the project failed and strongly influenced nothing less than the ejection of a State Government administration; this was not the greatest tragedy of the saga.

The greatest tragedy of the Queensland Health payroll saga was that it was just one failed project among many.

A national state of emergency

Indeed, if you take a brief inventory of Australian Government IT projects and IT service delivery over the past 15 years, what you will find is that the Queensland Health payroll upgrade project is nothing if not standard. Bog standard.

At the time that Queensland Health was suffering so many issues with reforming its aged payroll IT systems, systemic issues were also gripping almost every aspect of the state government's business as usual IT operations.

In October 2012, an interim audit of the state's IT systems found that more than half were outdated, and that it would cost up to $6 billion to replace them[153].

Problems ranged from the fact that a vast amount of the state's IT platforms were so out of date that they could no longer be supported by their manufacturers, to a massive amount of duplication of basic IT platforms performing financial, document and case management — all basic functions for a normal state government.

The following year, the full version of that audit pegged the complete cost of IT system replacement at up to $7.4 billion[154].

It also noted that the situation was so urgent that it could lead to a basic failure for government to be able to deliver needed services — which the auditor at the time described as a *"Systemic Business Risk"*.

The report stated: *"The Audit revealed a number of systems that present a critical risk to government. These systems are typically long overdue for replacement, large and complex, and underpin critical activities. These systems will require urgent attention to avoid rendering key parts of government inoperable."*

In short, Queensland was collapsing under the weight of its ageing IT infrastructure. And funds were not forthcoming. As just the grossest among a series of glaring examples, the state admitted it could not even afford to get off Microsoft's Windows XP desktop platform[155], released more than a decade before.

Yet Queensland was not alone in this situation.

A cursory glance around Australia showed that most government jurisdictions were in a similar state.

In 2011, Victoria's Ombudsman handed down one of the most damning assessments of public sector IT project governance in Australia's history, noting total cost over-runs of $1.44 billion, extensive delays and a general failure to actually deliver on stated aims in 10 major IT projects carried out by the state over the previous half-decade[156].

Put simply, the report found that Victoria had virtually no capacity to carry out major IT projects. At all.

In New South Wales, the Coalition State Government was forced to admit in 2012 that its IT systems were stuck in *"the dark ages"*, as it launched an ambitious strategy to remediate them[157].

Eight years after it was begun and with its credibility in tatters, the Western Australian State Government in 2011 announced it would cancel its controversial plan to provide shared corporate services to its departments and agencies through a centralised IT platform, walking away from the initiative at a cost of many millions of dollars[158].

No jurisdiction — state or Federal, it appeared, was exempt.

In December 2013, Northern Territory Deputy Chief Minister and Minister for Corporate and Information Services David

Tollner stood up in Darwin's own Parliament and accused the previous Labor Government and technology giant Fujitsu of creating a *"diabolical mess"* and *"scandal of epic proportions"* for what he saw as the company's botched implementation of a new asset management system using software from German giant SAP[159].

(It is likely that the situation was not as black and white as Tollner had painted it[160], and Fujitsu noted at the time that it was working with the NT Government to resolve the issues.)

The Federal Government has also seen its share of IT project scandals.

In October 2005, supported by EDS, the Australian Customs Service went live with its Integrated Cargo System. The intention of the project to develop the platform was sound; to replace an existing solution that served users such as freight forwarders and importers for more than 20 years.

However, the launch quickly turned into a nightmare for Customs, with the application spectacularly failing and leaving cargo piled up at ports all around Australia[161].

Hardly a great look for the Federal Government — especially during the middle of a busy Christmas season.

"The management framework that Customs had in place to support this project lacked many of the basic fundamentals necessary to successfully implement a large ICT project," the Australian National Audit Office (ANAO) wrote in a report into the debacle released in February 2007[162].

Major efforts such as the Australian Taxation Office's Change Program, the Department of Immigration and Border Protection's Systems for Change initiative and others have shown that the Federal Government does have some capacity to deliver major IT programs of change[163].

However, it is also true that even these programs — widely lauded as being successful — nevertheless still ran over time, over budget, and caused numerous minor controversies during the periods in which they were implemented.

And it is far more common for Federal Government departments and agencies to suffer similar problems with budget and time overruns, aged IT infrastructure and even failed IT projects, as their State Government counterparts.

One of the most salient examples of this trend was Australian Parliament House itself. Most Australians probably think of the building as relatively modern, when they think of it at all. It was built in the 1980's at a cost of around $1.1 billion.

But in 2012 the Department of Parliamentary Services, which runs the IT infrastructure behind Parliament House, essentially found that its technology platforms were a complete shambles, releasing a landmark report noting that it had widespread problems with IT service delivery and infrastructure[164].

The issues appeared to stem from the fact that the Department had *"no parliament-wide IT strategic plan"* at the time and no mechanism for making strategic IT decisions, despite a decade of reports warning of the situation.

Some of the most basic issues included the lack of a Chief Information Officer; the poor speed of the broadband found in the offices of MPs and Senators, the lack of Wi-Fi access in those same offices, and many problems with the corporate IT apps used across the Parliament.

It's hard to believe these issues plagued even the chief decision-making body in Australia. But a cursory examination of recent history shows that they are everywhere in Australia's public sector. Federal Parliament is hardly immune: Indeed, it is typical in this regard.

At this point, it is clear that when it comes to the way that technology projects and are created and run inside government in Australia, there is something — or, more than likely, many things — which are fundamentally broken.

It is also clear that this problem extends beyond specific projects and into the realm of daily IT service delivery.

There is no doubt that the private sector has its own major problems in this field, both with IT project delivery, as well as in the provision of business as usual IT services.

However, the sheer reliability around the fact that public sector IT projects will go wrong on a predictable basis is something that is not as clear cut in private industry. In addition, private industry does not appear to suffer from the same problems at the same scale that the public sector does with legacy IT infrastructure.

In this chapter, we will explore why this is the case, in the hope of providing a perspective on breaking the cycle of failure in future.

Root causes

The evidence as a whole appears to show that the cycle of IT project and service delivery failure within Government starts with two sources.

The first case is where a Government enacts legislative or policy changes that require the application of technology to implement.

This stimulus will usually result in a Government allocating a discrete parcel of money, with the intent to spin up a project to implement a new IT platform that will allow a new type of service to be delivered. Sometimes the money is allocated towards modifying and expanding existing IT platforms instead.

A good example might be the Department of Immigration and Border Protection's Systems for People Project.

Systems for People was a project that was the result of a direct policy change stimulated by external circumstances which affected the Department at the time.

The project was first approved in the 2006 Federal Budget as a mammoth technology overhaul of the then Department of Immigration and Citizenship's IT systems.

The stimulus was the landmark Palmer and Comrie reports, which had documented the unlawful detention of a number of people by the Department, especially Cornelia Rau, a German citizen and Australian permanent resident who was unlawfully detained for ten months in 2004 and 2005.

The project was initially valued at a whopping $495 million. However, after its initiation it was awarded several budget increases. In later years, for example the project picked up a further $169.6 million over four years for *"ongoing maintenance funding"* of its operations[165].

Systems for People was spearheaded by primary contractor IBM and has also involved a number of other major IT firms. It was based on Oracle's Siebel software.

The second case is where technological change itself forces changes in the way that Government operates internally or provides services externally.

A good example of this is the impact that the creation of smartphones has had upon governments globally.

Prior to 2007, when the Apple iPhone was first released, the use of smartphones for work-related business was seen as a desirable, but not essential, service provided mainly to senior public servants.

However, as private enterprise and individual consumers rapidly took up the iPhone and similar Android-based devices in the years after 2007, the public service in Australia saw a strong need to adopt the technology itself, to gain the same benefits — such as instant communication and access to a rich amount of information — that had attracted the private sector and consumers to these platforms.

This necessitated a wholesale technological change in terms of the way that government delivered services to its internal users. And eventually, this also started to flow through into the way that services are provided to the public.

In 2007, for example, relatively few Australians interacted with Centrelink's welfare services through mobile devices of any kind, even if they used its website. But in 2018, most transactions which the Department of Human Services deals with, come through its various mobile and online platforms. And many in Government espouse a 'mobile-first' approach to service delivery, recognising that the smartphone is currently Australia's most popular computing device.

This style of technological change has also affected governments in multiple other areas. One need only think of the wide-reaching effects of the cloud computing, cyber-security or software as a service trends to see it in action.

What we see in both of these cases is that a fundamental driver for change exists.

In some cases, this driver for change is forced on departments and agencies by their political masters. The need to provide new services or modernise and refine old services causes a consequential demand for new technology platforms to be constructed.

In other cases, technology itself changes and develops. Systems become obsolete and unsupportable; they need to be replaced. Meanwhile, new functionality develops in other platforms that becomes desirable for government.

These are not unique problems to the public sector; in fact, they are extremely common challenges faced by organisations of every size worldwide.

In addition, government technologists are very well aware of these forces at work.

And it also extends beyond technology itself into process. The creation of the PRINCE2 and ITIL frameworks for project management and IT service management respectively had their roots in government, especially in the United Kingdom. They are commonly used in many other jurisdictions in order to develop new IT platforms and control the delivery of services.

The latest process framework trend to sweep government is Agile methodology; but it will surely not be the last.

The challenge of enacting change

Yet, when this change does occur, it immediately faces a number of challenges unique to government which stop it in its tracks.

The first is that the budget set aside for major Australian government departments and agencies to deal with technological change is not sufficient — in the remotest sense — to keep pace with that change, let alone deal with changes in the regulatory environment.

It was reported in March 2017 that the Federal Government would spend nearly $10 billion on IT-related goods and services that year, which appears to be a massive amount[166].

Yet that $10 billion is a tiny tiny fraction of a percent compared with the Federal Government's 2016 income of some $378 billion.

Recognising this, Digital Transformation Minister Angus Taylor referred to years of neglect and under-spending on IT[167]. *"Our IT infrastructure and services have been run down for many years, and we're re-investing,"* he noted. *"Too many governments have put this off — we can't keep putting it off."*

One glaring example is the ageing transaction platform used by the Department of Human Services to process Centrelink welfare payments. Then-Treasurer Joe Hockey admitted in April 2014 that the platform was *"in bad shape"* and *"run down"*. Its aged nature made implementing new policy at DHS extremely difficult[168].

This chronic underfunding — also strongly present in State Governments — means that when drivers for technological change do occur within government, they must normally be funded through extraordinary expenditure in the form of IT-focused projects.

Public servants making the case to a Minister to approve expenditure on an IT project usually do so through rolling up new functionality and required upgrades into major projects that can score political points through demonstrating value to voters.

For example, every year the Federal Government — Coalition or Labor — announces a number of new major IT projects in that year's Federal Budget. Each is billed as fundamentally improving the service delivery to Australians, and is accompanied by the release of a Ministerial press release breathlessly announcing the benefits of a new IT project.

But the reality is that each project is usually just as much focused on remediating legacy and unsupported IT infrastructure as it is about actually improving service delivery.

If we take the Centrelink example mentioned by Joe Hockey, what is clear is that not only is DHS' ageing payments platform making it hard to enact new policies, but even remaining on the platform at all entails a huge risk. The platform uses the Model 204 Software developed by Computer Corporation of America … technology which is so far out of date that only DHS and the US Pentagon using it any more. This is technology so old that it has been almost universally abandoned as totally irrelevant to the modern age.

The software is almost completely unsupportable due to the difficulty of getting updates for it and IT professionals with skills in dealing with it.

What is happening here is a clear indication that policy-makers are not providing sufficient ongoing funding to keep fundamental IT services up to date. So public servants are forced to seek extraordinary funding through project expenditure merely to keep up with technological progress.

Exacerbating this issue is the inability of government departments and agencies to access many of the services that assist the private sector in keeping its costs down.

It is commonplace, for example, within Australia's financial services and telecommunications industries, for call centres and basic IT break/fix services (help desks) to be outsourced to low cost centres in countries such as India, the Phillipines, South Africa and even Eastern Europe.

Australia's largest three telcos — Telstra, Optus and TPG — all routinely create and store extremely sensitive customer information similar to that stored by governments around the country. Yet they all operate substantial offshore call centres in order to deal with customer needs.

Australia's major banks do the same with software development. ANZ Bank, for example, has for years operated an IT hub in Bangalore, India. The IT services companies which support the Commonwealth Bank of Australia, Westpac and National Australia Bank all do the same, supplementing their high-end, expensive Australian workforce with cheap offshore labor where appropriate.

The Federal Department of Human Services has repeatedly come under fire in recent years for its inability to answer the phone when many of its many millions of clients call. Yet it remains politically unpalatable for the Department — which has as one of its many policy aims finding unemployed Australians work — to employ offshore human resources to take its calls.

The Department of Immigration and Border Protection is in a similar boat. Although it has extensive software development requirements, its nature as a security-conscious public entity means it is unable to follow Australia's banks and telcos and hire offshore developers to cut code.

Governance

The second in a series of issues affecting the public sector is a lack of good project management and governance associated with major IT projects.

In his landmark 2011 examination of public sector IT projects in his state, for example, Victorian Ombudsman George Brouwer wrote that none of the ten projects investigated were *"well-planned"*, especially when it came to business case development[169].

The PRINCE2 project management framework — freely available and widely mandated within the public sector — focuses strongly on continued business justification for IT projects as being one of its fundamental tenets. The clear allocation of roles and responsibilities is another.

Yet not only were many of the roles and responsibilities for those leading the Victorian projects Brouwer examined not clearly defined, but senior government officers often appeared reluctant to make critical decisions when they were needed — and project steering committees often did not have sufficient expertise in the areas concerned.

Business cases weren't updated as projects changed — or in some cases, even read by key figures involved. Agencies gave politicians no choice other than their preferred technology project option — and failed to give them adequate advice to make informed decisions about the initiatives.

"In some cases, optimism bias led to costs and timelines being based upon hope, rather than evidence or comparisons with similar projects and despite advice from experts and vendors," wrote Brouwer.

This would be laughable if it weren't so abjectly tragic.

In general, departments and agencies felt they needed to create *"big vision"* projects to capture politicians' attention — increasing project complexity and risk. However, in some cases the state Cabinet only partially funded projects, ignoring business case requirements and cost estimates. Despite this, agencies didn't revise the scope of their projects downwards to fit them within the allocated budgets.

A lack of leadership, a lack of accountability, a lack of governance, poor planning, inadequate funding, below standard probity controls and under-par project management. All of these were issues raised by the Victorian Ombudsman at the time. And in the extensive case studies which Brouwer published at the end of his report — detailing each project's history and issues — all of the same problems continually re-appeared.

Brouwer's report is not the only document in which these problems were highlighted.

In June 2010, for example, Queensland's Auditor-General found, in one of many reviews of Queensland Health's payroll IT systems upgrade, that the project's woefully inadequate governance structures were largely to blame for its problems[170].

Another issue highlighted by the auditor was the fact that all concerned with the project — ranging from its government overseers to prime contractor IBM — underestimated the scope required to make it work.

Even some of the basic fundamentals of project management — such as budgeting — were missing.

"... there was no one entity or officer monitoring and managing total project budget versus costs being incurred by all of the various stakeholders for the LATTICE payroll system replacement implementation," wrote the Auditor-General at the time.

A later report investigated the issue further[171]. The report's author, former Supreme Court Justice Richard Chesterman, wrote: *"I have identified two principal causes of the inadequacies which led to the increase in contract price, the serious shortcomings in contract and project management, and in the State's decision to settle with IBM."*

"Those causes were: unwarranted urgency and a lack of diligence on the part of State officials. That lack of diligence manifested itself in the poor decisions which those officials made in scoping the Interim Solution; in their governance of the Project; and in failing to hold IBM to account to deliver a functional payroll system."

What we see in both of these cases is that the most entry-level industry standard project management and governance structures — or even basic probity controls around awarding major IT contracts — were not being followed, despite the fact that the frameworks for doing so are freely available.

Bedevilled by Politics

Some of these problems are linked to the political process.

It's not hard to understand that Ministers who have announced new IT projects linked to service delivery improvements will be reluctant to back away from those projects when they exceed their boundaries in terms of cost or time to deliver.

If one of the foundational tenets of PRINCE2 is that of the need for a project to maintain continued business justification for it to progress, another one is that that justification is linked to an organisation being willing to continue funding a project only if its cost remains within a certain envelope. This is known by project managers as being 'within tolerance' — or in other words, within tolerable boundaries.

In the private sector, where costs are closely linked to profits and capital is strictly limited by what corporations can afford to spend, projects blowing their tolerances, especially in terms of their budget or delivery timeframes, brings real consequences for shareholders.

In the public sector, these consequences — and hence the risk involved in pursuing major projects — are spread across entire governments.

A certain department which loses hundreds of millions of dollars on a failed IT project will certainly feel the whiplash of disapproval from its responsible Minister — or even the leader of the Government of the day.

But that loss will not imperil the operation of that department as a whole as it would a corporation. The department's legislated function will continue, because walking away from the provision of essential public services would only compound a government's embarrassment and perhaps invite legal action.

Governments are therefore far more likely to approve further project expenditure — appearing to throw good money after bad — than they are to cancel failing IT projects wholesale.

This is particularly the case if it is actually a new Minister — or a whole new Government administration — calling the shots. Any past losses or problems can be expediently blamed on the previous office holder — while any future successes can be attributed to a renewed spirit of good management, applied alongside a judicious splash of new funding to push an ailing project across the line.

In the private sector such behaviour from corporations is punished by shareholders. In the public sector, it is often rewarded by citizens who value the continued delivery of essential services above cost control.

The cyclical nature of political fortunes ensures a steady progression of new leadership figures who can be blamed for project failure. Meanwhile, the same lack of strong project management controls and purchasing rigor continues to plague projects behind the scenes — no matter who is the public figurehead.

Worst case scenarios

In many cases, the factors which we've explored above lead to outcomes which are sub-optimal, but not necessarily disastrous for the departments and agencies concerned.

It is commonplace for public servants around Australia to complain about the inefficiencies rife within their workplaces[172].

Outdated desktop PCs and web browsers, phones which don't always work, green screen data entry systems which make it hard to transfer data round; these are all items which head the list of complaints which our public service has about their work environments.

But at the end of the day, these platforms are still facilitating the delivery of essential public services. They may do it in an inefficient way and be out of step with modern technology, but often they can still be broadly effective at getting the job done.

However, there are also 'worst case scenarios' where the factors above have led beyond mere inconveniences and to horrendous outcomes which have resulted in drastic consequences which reach far beyond the normal. Some of these include:

- The wrongful classification of a number of immigrants within the IT systems of the Department of Immigration and Border Protection, which led to their wrongful detention in immigration detention centres

- The failure of Victoria Police IT systems to pass along information about offenders between jurisdictions, which contributed to the death of Luke Batty at the hands of his violent father[173]

- The failure of a number of state-based IT systems to track children at risk and prevent them from coming to harm, over a prolonged period[174]

- The failure of systems at welfare giant the Department of Human Services to accurately track clients' entitlements, leading the wrongful billing of many clients for refund of payments[175]. This has had the potential to leave many clients financially destitute.

- The failure of the new Queensland Health payroll system to accurately pay medical workers across the state, leaving many without a salary for certain periods

The lack of strong governance and procurement controls has also opened the door to unethical practices at a number of departments and agencies.

Anti-corruption agencies such as the New South Wales Independent Commission Against Corruption have chronicled cases, for example, where IT firms engaged unethically with public officials for NSW authorities, receiving significant gifts for awarding contracts[176].

In 2012, the Victorian Ombudsman exposed a number of similarly suspect procurement activities being carried out at IT shared services agency CenITex[177].

At the time, Victorian Ombudsman George Brouwer wrote: *"In some instances, nepotism and favouritism influenced procurement and recruitment practices. Often, the companies or contractors were chosen because they were associates or friends of other contractors already working at CenITex."*

"Some appointments were made on the basis of fabricated or false documentation. Some engagements were initiated or overseen by individuals within CenITex who had a clear conflict of interest and stood to gain financially from the transactions. Such conflicts were often not declared, or declared late, inadequately or misleadingly. Even conflicts that were declared were ill-managed by CenITex. This led to opportunities for improper conduct."

Other Government departments have also been reprimanded for unethical practice in major IT contracts.

It's true that such improper practices are not exclusively found within the public sector — far from it.

However, it's also true that the systemic lack of strong governance, probity and project management controls in government does much to open the door for such activity to creep in.

How to solve the problem

If you've made it this far through this chapter, you will be clearly aware that the problem facing Australian Governments at all levels when it comes to IT project and service delivery is nothing short of gargantuan.

Put simply, many major Australian public sector organisations have little to no ability to deliver major IT projects. This means that they cannot take steps to improve their IT service delivery capabilities. This cycle of failure keeps them locked in the technological dark ages, as then NSW State Premier Barry O'Farrell put it in 2012, impeding their ability to deliver essential public services in a modern fashion.

Along the way, they're opening the door to injury, poverty and yes, in some cases, even death.

So what steps can policymakers take to resolve this mess?

Firstly, let's look at the structural problems.

Budgets

If politicians and policymakers want to resolve these problems in the organisations they help govern, their first and most important task is to start allocating something like the amount of funding actually required to deliver the IT services that keep those organisations functioning.

Ideally, this would mean allocating a higher proportion of government revenue to departments to explicitly keep IT services on a modern footing — strengthening the IT budget's top line.

This is no easy task. In and of itself, it will require public sector policymakers and politicians to recognise what the private sector already has — that IT is not only a necessary evil, but that it can actually enable improvements in fundamental service delivery.

Modern financial services organisations such as the Commonwealth Bank, when it comes down to it, are essentially large software houses that provide IT platforms which allow Australians to conduct financial transactions. The banks have recognised this fact and altered their IT spend accordingly. This allows them to better compete with their rivals.

Major government departments do not generally face competition from private sector rivals. Yet they still face the same pressure from the public to continually improve their services to keep up with a changing technological landscape. They are driven by social expectations and need to fund their IT operations accordingly.

At the very least, departments need to recognise that they need to maintain enough business as usual IT funding to stop their IT infrastructure from reaching end of life without a feasible path for continual service delivery.

Increasing the proportion of government income that goes towards funding IT infrastructure and services is one way to reach the aim of a more sustainable technology platform for Australian governments.

However, increasing the top line is not the only way that this goal can be reached. Another goal is for policymakers to allow the public sector to follow long-established best practice in the private sector and utilise offshore resources to meet the need for basic IT services.

"Governments have largely ignored the whole opportunity to leverage offshoring," said Longhaus managing director and long-time Australian IT analyst Peter Carr, in the wake of Victoria's highly publicised IT project woes[178]. *"They're the first to complain when they get charged $4,000 a day by IBM or Accenture to have project managers sitting around a meeting table three times a week. But the fact, is, IBM and Accenture will continue to charge $4,000 a day while there's a model for it."*

"Governments need to fundamentally change the underlying mechanism for it."

If you set aside government agencies that are legitimately concerned with issues of security, then it is clear that much of the more mundane public sector could benefit from shifting low risk services such as basic break/fix IT support, call centre and even many areas of data processing offshore.

Security issues can be worked around by requiring all data to continue to be stored in Australia and only accessed remotely under strict security; as well as by forming close partnerships with IT outsourcing companies with a long history of operating securely in multiple jurisdictions, such as IBM, HP, Accenture and more. This is standard practice with Australia's major banks.

If Governments place strong security controls around their IT offshoring agreements — and security controls are certainly one area that government technologists specialise in — then IT offshoring relationships could achieve the dual aim of allowing departments and agencies to both cut costs and increase the level of services they are receiving. This, in turn, will free up funds for better service delivery to Australians or to reinvest internally within departments and agencies — for example, to help keep basic IT infrastructure current.

There are many areas where offshoring basic essential IT services would be inappropriate for Government, especially when it comes to security-focused departments and agencies, or where it would represent a high risk to do so. But there are also a number of low risk areas where this issue could be handled a lot better. It's easy to imagine, for example, a situation where millions of car registration renewal forms could be processed in another country at a low cost, just as Telstra uses offshore facilities to assist customers with basic support services for its mobile network, or the banks offshore basic cheque processing.

Done correctly, IT services offshoring has the potential to create a win/win/win situation for every stakeholder involved in the cycle of failure within government technology circles.

One potential loser from the situation is the large number of Australians currently employed in the field of government IT. This group has the potential to see wage growth stall and some jobs lost as a result of government IT offshoring. However, there is also substantial evidence to suggest that such efforts would, for the most part, result in most of this group merely being redeployed into higher value — and sometimes higher paid — tasks. This appears to have already occurred to some extent in Australia's private sector.

There are also a range of other ways to cut costs out of government IT service provision that have not yet been fully explored at scale by many governments.

These range from the centralised purchase of all popular software and hardware platforms (to benefit from scale) to the use of cloud computing platforms at the Infrastructure-, Software- and even Platform-as-a-Service levels.

The private sector has long embraced these trends, for both the cost and flexibility benefits they bring. But they have not yet been comprehensively explored in the public sector.

Change Business Processes
before Customising Software

If you examine many of the major IT projects which have suffered substantial problems in Australia over the past decade especially, one of the most common attributes you will find is that they took the approach of attempting to customise a major software platform to fit business rules which were highly specific to an organisation's own operations.

This approach was very much in evidence during Queensland Health's botched payroll systems upgrade.

During the Commission of Inquiry which the State Government initiated into the project, it was noted that Queensland Health had around 300 different number of cases or business rules which the new platform would need to cater for.

In order to ensure that these business rules would be catered for, the project planned to heavily customise the software platform it was using. However, it turned out to be a struggle to customise the platform to enable this complex web of business rules to be implemented.

This is a situation which has played out repeatedly throughout the public sector over the past decade.

Western Australia's IT Shared Services initiative suffered from similar problems. The project used a different software platform. But again, the large number of business rules caused substantial problems during the project, with the state struggling to customise the platform sufficiently to cover all of its use cases.

A number of technology analysts have, over the years, wisely suggested an alternative: Why not customise the business rules first, before trying to customise software platforms?

Most of the major enterprise software houses originally built their software platforms to meet the most common needs that they were seeing in the market. The largest players do have a substantial number of software modules which aim to suit specific use cases for their software — but even in these cases, they still aim to meet the needs of specific industries.

For example, a vendor may offer payroll software which will meet the needs of any given department and agency. What the company would probably not offer is software that can be customised to do absolutely anything.

By customising business rules to match the existing setup of standardised software platforms, Australian departments and agencies are able to remove risk from implementing those platforms, because they are following standard practice which software vendors apply globally. But by forcing such platforms to conform to very specific business rules used by only one department, a substantial amount of risk, cost and time to implement is added to software-based projects.

The repeated failure of IT shared services schemes across Australia over the past decade demonstrates the pitfalls in not standardising business rules before attempting complex software customisation efforts. Western Australia, Queensland, Victoria and other jurisdictions have all attempted to force myriad small departments and agencies to adopt uniform, standardised IT platforms for functions such as payroll, finance, HR and so on.

In general, these schemes have comprehensively failed. Much of that failure can be traced back to the fact that each jurisdiction did not enforce standardised business rules on each department and agency before they attempted to integrate them into their standard platform. Instead, each organisation brought with them their own set of heterogeneous business rules.

With each new complex set of rules, the so-called standardised shared services platforms because ever more impossible to implement.

Accountability

Lastly, there are a number of rather obvious steps which would help correct fundamental problems with IT project and service delivery within Government.

It should be obvious by now that making free and widely available project and program management frameworks such as PRINCE2 and Managing Successful Programmes (MSP) mandatory within the public sector is necessary.

Training to understand the foundational tenets of such frameworks generally only takes about three days. Governments should make taking such training a basic requirement for anyone who will be working at the governance or project management layers for any IT project of scale. And they should insist upon the same qualifications being held by outside companies who conduct IT projects for government.

The transparency of data about in-flight projects should also be considered paramount, so that policymakers at all levels are able to gain visibility of the projects that they have ultimate oversight of.

Some countries, such as the United States, have started using public dashboards to track the progress of major projects. This isn't a bad idea — and a number of jurisdictions in Australia are following suit — but so far it hasn't gone anywhere near far enough. Only the largest IT projects are being covered by such approaches. When every project of scale is using a basic framework like PRINCE2, the population of such dashboards with current data should be trivial.

Such an approach would force a heightened degree of scrutiny on all IT projects of scale on a sustained basis, in a manner that would ensure they would necessarily focus on the concept of continual business justification on an ongoing basis. This would be likely to have the effect of weeding out projects that could not continue to justify their existence, in addition to forcing projects which are able to justify their existence to walk the tight line of staying within their tolerances for budget, timeframe, deliverables and so on.

Mandating at least certain aspects of agile methodologies such as SCRUM would also have a big impact on major IT projects, particularly those dealing with software development and customisation.

This is because such methodologies are often focused on rapid prototyping and feature development techniques aimed at taking a lot of the risk out of major IT projects. When risk is reduced, so is the potential for disaster.

Or, at the very least, those making key decisions about major IT projects will be able to see the inevitable disasters coming sooner than they would using traditional 'waterfall' frameworks.

Lessons from the private sector

When policymakers think about the problem of public sector IT project and service delivery, the most damning aspect to consider is probably that governments realistically have no choices about how they will tackle the issue.

Throughout this chapter, I have most likely at times made it appear as though politicians and the advisors who serve them have many decisions to make in this field.

The truth is that they do not.

The failure of government IT project and service delivery is so vast and so pervasive that positive forward progress will most likely only be made if all of the solutions that I have mentioned in this chapter are all pursued simultaneously.

Australia's public sector must realise what Australia's private sector realised many years ago.

IT budgets for business as usual IT service delivery must be dramatically expanded. At the same time, costs must be cut so that funding can be re-allocated to keeping critical IT platforms in a modern and supportable state.

Simultaneously, strong project and program management and governance controls must be imposed in the area of IT project delivery. This must include a widespread, broad upskilling of both executives and project managers on common frameworks such as PRINCE2 and MSP.

Transparency must be added into the mix so that projects are able to be weighed for their ability to continually justify their continued existence and funding status. And the new breed of agile frameworks must be integrated in a much-needed attempt to de-risk projects and provide early forward visibility of project failure.

These are all critical aspects of the way that IT projects and services are delivered in 2018, and they will only become more crucial as time goes on, and the delivery of government services further mirrors the private sector and becomes ever more dependent on strong technological underpinnings and strong process control.

Most competent IT professionals who've been around in Australia's private sector IT environment for some years take many of these necessary solutions for granted.

But as science fiction author William Gibson once said: *"The future is already here — it's just not very evenly distributed."*

It will take some time for all of these features to become standardised throughout Australia's public sector. One can only hope this happens sooner rather than later.

There are also other worthwhile suggestions on the table.

Paul Shetler was the founding leader of the Federal Government's Digital Transformation Agency, set up by Malcolm Turnbull in an attempt to solve many of the thorny issues mentioned in this chapter.

Upon leaving the agency in December 2016, Shetler was clear about what he saw as the issues the Government faced in getting its IT systems under control[179].

The Australian Public Service, he stated, needed to focus on re-skilling its staff so that better decisions could be made, without the need to rely on expertise from consultants and vendors.

"Too frequently, we actually ask vendors to tell us what they think we should buy," he said.

Other problems included *"institutional inertia"* and resistance to change. And the complexity of Government itself posed a challenge.

But still, Shetler was optimistic, pointing out that the private sector had already solved many of these same problems.

"When it comes to service delivery, the transaction volumes of government services are small compared to the wider world," Shetler said at the time.

"Government might think it's huge, but its daily transaction volume is equivalent to just a few minutes of Twitter – or even less on the NASDAQ."

SUMMARY

Policy Details

Federal and State Government Auditors and Ombudsmen in Australia have detailed a history of failures and budget blowouts in major IT projects over the past several decades. This cycle of failure also extends to the provision of basic IT services. Both of these failures have had real-world outcomes, including death and risk to vulnerable individuals such as children.

What Went Wrong

At the heart of this issue is a series of key misunderstandings by policymakers. Firstly, policymakers often do not appear to understand that technology-led services require continual adequate funding to keep up with new technological developments.

Secondly, policymakers do not appear to appreciate the key sources of project failure. These often relate to a failure to customise business processes to match standardised software platforms; as well as a lack of strong program/project management and governance. Another factor is a continual revolving door in the role of responsible ministers.

Avoiding This Situation in Future

Governments must provide adequate and continual funding for basic IT services, through expanding the top-line funding envelope, as well as cutting expenses through utilising offshore resources, centralised purchasing and cloud computing platforms.

To stem the tide of project failure, strong program and project management and governance controls must be introduced, and government should focus on customising business rules to fit standardised software platforms, rather than the other way around. The use of agile methodologies to de-risk project delivery may also assist.

CHAPTER 5

Game Over

"... the cut to Screen Australia and the Interactive Games Fund ... is an incredible blow to a burgeoning knowledge-based and creative arts industry.

What am I going to tell my students now? Why would anyone choose to stay in Australia to develop games after this? Why would I stay here to teach it?"

— Dr Adam Ruch
Department Coordinator
SAE Creative Media Institute

It didn't take Nick Smith long to realise he'd made the right decision in choosing to leave the United Kingdom and travel halfway around the world to join Australia's video game industry.

The graphic artist started his career in 2001 with Creative Assembly, an English video game development firm based in the West Sussex town of Horsham. But Australia's fast-growing video game scene soon attracted his interest, and it was only a few years later that he made the jump across the world to settle in Brisbane in the mid-2000's.

"Upon arriving in Brisbane to join Sega Studios Australia almost ten years ago, I was heartened to see the wealth of local video game studios," Smith wrote in a submission to the Australian Senate's inquiry into Australia's video game development industry[180], which ran over 2015 and 2016.

"It gave me a great confidence that I'd made the right choice emigrating from England, where I'd started my career some four years earlier. I had entered a vibrant, creative community, which, with studios like Pandemic, Krome and THQ, was on the up."

Others also noticed the strong levels of positive energy and investment flowing into what was then a rapidly growing local video game development scene.

A fellow developer, Dean Walshe, wrote in a similar submission to the same inquiry that he first started in Australia's video game development industry in the same period.

He recalls that at the time, the Australian industry was riding high, with large studios in Melbourne and Brisbane dominating the scene. *"Producing 'blockbuster' titles with high development budgets, commercial/critical success and large development teams attracting international talent, these studios were industry tent-poles and substantial employers,"* Walshe wrote.

It's true that Australia's video game developers had developed a strong reputation globally at the time with major multinational video game publishers.

A key aspect of this was our history as a 'safe pair of hands' to take responsibility for the development of the so-called Triple A ('AAA') titles which video game publishers such as Electronic Arts rely on to make billions of dollars in revenue each year.

Pandemic Studios, for instance, had been entrusted with a number of Star Wars titles throughout the early 2000's, for large platforms such as the Nintendo GameCube, Microsoft Xbox and PlayStation 2. Krome Studios was picking up accolades for its own TY the Tasmanian Tiger series, in addition to a number of branded AAA titles, while THQ Studio Australia enjoyed success with games based on the popular Nickelodeon TV franchise.

Other successful developers included Visceral Games, Team Bondi and KMM Brisbane, all of which were enjoying financial success and strong growth in staffing levels.

Yet even as the good times were rolling, with Australia's video game development industry employing thousands, and with millions and millions of dollars being ploughed into local innovation in the scene, there was a hint that things were shortly to become much tougher down the track.

One sour note at the time came from Jason Rubin, the co-founder of hyped US studio Naughty Dog, which had worked its way to eventual financial success through the 1980's and 90's, culminating in the hit title Crash Bandicoot.

Rubin controversially quit Naughty Dog in 2004, after helping to sell his company to Japanese giant Sony. The game developer told Australian media at the time that he was interested in setting up a studio Down Under to test innovative ideas. However, he also noted that the games industry as a whole was ripe for disruption.

"I'm not saying the industry is about to collapse - that's crazy. What I'm saying is the old way of doing things may collapse," he told the Sydney Morning Herald at the time[181].

"From a gamer's standpoint, they'll get better games and they'll buy more of them. "But behind the scenes there is going to be a lot of turmoil."

Walshe also remembers Rubin's comments, which many saw as outlandish at the time.

"I recall renowned industry leader Jason Rubin warning the Australian industry in 2005 of complacency," he told the Senate.

"At the time, the dominant structure created a lot of studio growth, but he predicted a readjustment to the market could have a huge impact on the industry if studios hadn't made themselves independently valuable outside of the very interchangeable contract-based work-for-hire model we had come to be known for."

Unfortunately for Australia's video game development scene, Rubin proved extremely prescient with his 'doom and gloom' view of the imminent collapse. And Australia's industry would prove to be amongst the hardest-hit geographies globally.

The Fall

It took a few years, but by the early stages of the following decade Australia's video game industry was in free fall, with no end in sight to the decline.

One of the first signs of the collapse came in 2009, just four years after Nick Smith had emigrated to take advantage of the local boom. The signal at the time was the closure of Pandemic Studios[182].

In some ways the move was not a surprise. Pandemic had been bought by Electronic Arts at the end of 2007. But with EA suffering much larger problems globally — in November that year it laid off some 1,500 staff[183] — there was little doubt that Australia was going to feel the heat from the broader financial problems the company was suffering, partially as a result of the Global Financial Crisis.

But the news still came as a shock to a local industry which had persistently seen itself as being on the way up — in some ways invincible — even as it was very much aware that the heady mix of creativity, technological change and the unfolding dynamic of a new medium could make for chaotic company fortunes.

The failure of Pandemic alone — important as it was to Brisbane's video game development scene — might have been taken as an outlier. But the hits kept on coming over the next few years, until they started to feel like body blows.

In 2010 Krome Studios let as many as 100 Australian staff go, and went into a state of dormancy, although it would later return with a number of titles from 2012.

Others would follow, with 2011 in particular being a year of devastation. The Australian industry lost a trio of major companies — Visceral Games, Team Bondi and KMM Brisbane — within that 12 month period alone.

When KMM Brisbane shut down, the studio's art director Jason Stark finally openly expressed what many in the industry had been thinking.

"The writing has been on the wall for a long time," he told the ABC at the time[184]. *"But it's maybe a little surprising the extent to which it has happened. We've all expected the industry to be shrinking - it's been bad times. It's gone from being a mild contraction to being pretty much obliterated."*

That term — *"obliterated"* — would be thrown around again and again in the media and in the industry — as thousands of Australians wondered what had happened to their livelihood and the companies that had seemed on the verge of conquering the world.

At the heart of the issue was one central question: How had companies which had been so financially successful, which had employed so many staff, which had acted as substantial 'hubs' in the local video game development ecosystem, failed so quickly?

And even if they did fail, what about the rest of the industry? Were these large video game development firms all that there was? What about the famed Australian 'ecosystem' that surrounded them? Where were the independent studios?

Part of the answer was readily apparent.

Naughty Dog's Rubin was dead on the mark in his original comments: Australian video game development companies had certainly relied too heavily on revenue from the big international game publishers, effectively acting as outsourcers to develop titles that wouldn't ultimately support the development of a sustainable and independent Australian industry. The link was too close; when those global publishers suffered, so did Australian companies.

The fact that so many Australian video game houses had failed to develop and market their own intellectual property — games which they controlled — meant that they were particularly vulnerable to rapid failure when the global contracts that were sustaining them dried up.

Major IT services outsourcers such as IBM, HP and CSC have long understood that they exist in cyclic 'boom and bust' phases. A major contract with a huge government department can mean hundreds or even thousands of jobs to such companies. But those jobs will be almost instantly lost when a rival nabs a key contract.

It was time for Australia's video game developers to learn the same harsh truth.

If this was the only factor behind the obliteration of Australia's video game industry over the past decade, then it would not have been worth chronicling in the pages of The Frustrated State. It would have been mere commercial folly.

But a closer examination shows us there were other subtleties of policy that also contributed to the fall; factors that were entirely within the control of the Federal Government at the time. This chapter of The Frustrated State will explore some of these factors.

Behind the Scenes

It may not have been immediately apparent to many individual game development professionals at the time, but behind the scenes, the Australian regulatory environment has always been almost proactively hostile to the development of this incredibly lucrative industry.

Sam Cartwright, a long-time video game developer and chair of the Gold Coast chapter of the International Game Developers Association (IGDA) wrote in the organisation's submission to the Senate's video game development industry inquiry that in 2010, he was tasked with expanding the operations of French video game company Gameloft into the Oceania region.

He noted that his employer had several criteria at the time which needed to be met before it would set up a local studio in a country in the Oceanic region: *"These included internet speed, proximity to an international airport, rental prices, proximity to public transport, the number of game schools in the area, and the presence of any tax breaks or advantageous regulatory frameworks."*

Cartwright continued: *"Gameloft was looking to grow the studio very quickly, anywhere up to 200 employees in around two years."*

But from a government support perspective, he struck out Down Under.

"Despite this I could not find anyone at any level of government in Australia willing to talk to me."

The situation across the ditch in New Zealand — a country much smaller than Australia — was very different.

The Kiwis arranged *"first class airfares"* for Cartwright and two other senior managers to travel to the country, tour local video game development studios, inspect office space and meet with local tax and legal professionals able to provide advice on how to set up local operations.

Given the support, Cartwright notes that it was *"unsurprising"* that Gameloft eventually chose to locate its new Oceanic studio in Auckland.

"Studio manager Patrick Wagner has been quoted as saying that one of the deciding factors for the company to set up in New Zealand was the assistance and advice in setting up the company provided by the government during its early stages," he told the Senate.

It was, in fact, apparent that other countries had been providing similar support for many years before the Global Financial Crisis hit Australia from 2009 onwards.

For example, in 2006 the Game Developers' Association of Australia (GDAA) made a submission to the Federal Government's review of its Film Funding Support. At the time, Adam Lancman, chief executive of successful local video game development studio Beam Software/Melbourne House specifically highlighted the fact that a number of other countries, such as Canada and many others, were putting in place incentive schemes which would attract video game development studios to their shores, to Australia's loss.

The submission further referred to comments by Evelyn Richardson of the GDAA. Richardson told the Government at the time:

"Rapidly emerging game development markets such as China, India, Russia and the Eastern Europe 'hot spots' (Prague and Zagreb) provide on average forty per cent cheaper production compared with Australia."

"At the same time, countries such as Singapore, China and Korea offer significant incentives to attract game production and establishment of studios in their territories. Singapore is right now trying to attract many of our major studios away from Australia and actively pursuing international publishers and developers."

"The global entertainment industry is changing rapidly and Australia needs to move quickly to ensure it is well positioned going forward to capture its potential share of the global market pie."

It was not hard for anyone in the past decade with their ear to the ground to notice that there was a rapid uptick in video game investment flowing to such locations. The same energy that was being seen in Australia at the time was also being seen in rival locations such as Canada and New Zealand.

But where in Australia the Federal Government was almost actively ignoring the development of the industry, in a number of other jurisdictions policymakers were deliberately supporting and magnifying the organic commercial growth.

Interactive Media Fund

The lobbying efforts by the major video game development studios and other associated media organisations eventually did hit the mark in Australia.

In November 2012, then-Federal Arts Minister Simon Crean — apparently convinced by the weight of evidence that this rapidly growing, lucrative export industry deserved support — threw the sector a small bone.

The Australian Interactive Games Fund (AIGF) commenced in 2012/13, delivering $5 million per annum in its first and second years, jumping to $10 million in 2014/15. The money was earmarked to help build a sustainable base for video game development firms to grow in a global market.

Crean billed the fund as recognising the international potential and originality of our local interactive entertainment by assisting Australian companies during a period of increased pressure following major shifts in the market — the shifts that Rubin had predicted many years before.

In point of fact the funds allocated were actually paltry — less than a rounding error for the Federal Government. They also represented a mere fraction of the expansive support doled out for years to similar creative industries such as film and television.

However, this $20 million funding allocation was still a watershed moment for an industry which had been ignored by the government for many years, even during its toughest times.

In its briefing notes associated with the program, Screen Australia — which was responsible for administering the funds — explicitly recognised the industry failure that had come before, especially the lack of AAA console titles being commissioned, the impact of the Global Financial Crisis, and the increased competition from low cost regions such as China, India and Russia.

This also had flow on effects.

"... the local talent pool has been severely diminished as a consequence of recent studio closures, which resulted in the loss of hundreds of jobs. As the local industry is too small to absorb the employees from defunct studios, many of them have moved overseas," wrote Screen Australia[185].

"The local industry was well positioned to take advantage of digital distribution platforms due to the skills development and training facilitated by local console development activity in the 2000's."

"But without a critical mass of talent and experience, the industry will not be able to rebuild in the future, even with the return of favourable trading conditions such as a more competitive Australian dollar and the forecast upturn in physical retail sales over the next five years."

Nevertheless, the funding had a dramatic impact.

Nick Smith noted in his Senate submission that, following the demise of much of Australia's video game development industry by 2013, he was *"lucky enough"* to join a local studio, Defiant Development. This afforded the developer the opportunity to witness the success of the Interactive Games Fund first hand.

"Defiant was the recipient of $550,000 from the Interactive Games Fund in 2013, and has gone on to create the critically acclaimed Hand of Fate," Smith told the Senate. *"This success has allowed the Brisbane developer to pay back the government money, and reinvest into the company to secure 17 jobs, and led to being selected as Developer of the Year at the 2014 IGDA awards."*

The Game Developers' Association of Australia, which worked closely with Crean and Screen Australia to create the AIGF, wrote in its own Senate submission that the fund had strongly demonstrated the success of its model, with several recipients of funding going on to achieve *"global success"*.

The fund's approach to ploughing returns back into its coffers for further future investments — a strategy proposed by the GDAA during the AIGF's establishment — was validated through this success, according to the GDAA.

Smith has since gone on to assist in the foundation of a new video game studio.

"As part of a three man start-up EarthWork Games, I am now acutely aware of the difference government financial incentives could make," he told the Senate.

"Programmer Tim Auld, Composer Jeff Van Dyck and myself as artist, are working on our first game Forts in our spare time. With no outside help, we have succeeded in getting our game green lit on Steam, Valve Entertainment's market leading online game store, in only a couple of weeks. In addition to this, we are exhibiting our game at PAX Australia in October, and hope to get the game over to GDC in San Francisco in the new year."

"While government financial assistance could aid hard-working devs like EarthWork Games to go full time and make Forts one of the growing list of internationally successful Australian games, such as Crossy Road, Fruit Ninja, and Hand of Fate, more broadly, it could help nurture, inspire and retain homegrown talent, as well as attract the best talent and investment from overseas."

Yet despite the rapid success of the AIGF, it would prove to be short-lived.

Cutting industry funding

It had taken Australia's video game development industry some time and protracted lobbying efforts by several groups to successfully convince even the Australian Labor Party to directly invest in the sector. And this was a party which, under Kevin Rudd as Prime Minister, was notably open to opportunities stemming from the growing Digital Economy.

Even then, the amount invested — $20 million — was merely a drop in the ocean compared to the capital being thrown at video games by governments globally. Yet, as Smith and many others have noted, it was a start which allowed independent developers to claw their way into a position where they could start to address global markets for their intellectual property.

But even this level of funding proved to be short-lived.

In September 2013, Tony Abbott's Coalition Opposition won power in Canberra, and it didn't take the new Prime Minister and his Cabinet much time to determine that the AIGF was not the kind of initiative that they wanted to fund. The money was quickly added to the list to be chopped in the May 2014 Budget.

This decision should not have come as a surprise.

During the years leading up to his 2013 victory, Abbott had made it clear that he had little affinity with Australia's technology sector, as we have explored in previous chapters. Abbott's 2010 denunciation of the National Broadband Network as a *"video entertainment system"*[186] should have particularly warned the video game sector as to how the Liberal MP viewed it.

In some senses, it's not hard to understand why the Abbott administration cut the AIGF as it did. Many of Australia's conservative politicians — some of whom are too old to have personally grown up with video games in their household as a child — believe video games to be at best a pointless indulgence and at worst a dangerous waste of time that stymies the potential of the nation's valuable youth.

Many of these same conservative forces had been behind the previous push to block the creation of an R18+ classification rating for video games in Australia. The introduction of this new rating — which ultimately succeeded — was merely slated to bring this new interactive medium up to par with other forms of media such as television, film, books and music. Yet many on the conservative side of the fence objected to the interactivity the new medium featured.

And yet the cuts in the 2014 Federal Budget still took the sector by surprise.

The GDAA issued a statement at the time noting that it was *"disappointed and mystified"* by the decision to cut the AIGF funding. Not only had the sector not been consulted on the issue, it had actively been rebuffed.

"It is concerning that the decision to end the Australian Interactive Games Fund was made with absolutely no consultation with industry," said Antony Reed, CEO of the GDAA[187].

"We made numerous attempts to contact the Attorney General's office in the months leading up to last night's announcement, including providing economic data and highlighting the successes the Australian game development sector has had on the global market. We have yet to receive a single response."

The move was universally condemned by the industry, with virtually every Australian video game studio of any size issuing statements condemning the cuts.

And their complaints turned out to be prescient.

Long-time video game developer Kieran Lord wrote in his submission to the Senate Inquiry that the Australian video game development industry had managed to survive the challenges posed by the Global Financial Crisis and the Australian dollar reaching parity with the US greenback. He noted at the time that investors and studio owners had tightened their belts and focused on their core development facilities in the United States.

"But the talent remained in Australia ... and Australian developers are pretty resourceful," he wrote.

This meant that many local developers turned to new mobile platforms such as Apple's iOS and Google's Android systems, where they could rapidly develop and self-publish relatively simple games that could still achieve global scale.

"Lots of people turned to the cheaper market of developing mobile games, and it's not a stretch to say that we are now the best in the world at it," wrote Lord. *"The list of hugely successful mobile games is disproportionately Australian: Flight Control, Fruit Ninja, Ski Safari, Crossy Road — to name a few."*

Although it disbursed relatively small amounts of money, the AIGF had still been disproportionately useful to the small studios which were successfully producing these games, as it gave local developers the ability to devote 100 percent of their time — instead of *"50 percent or 20 percent"* — to work on their own intellectual property.

Basing their operations on their own IP not only showed the industry had understood and outgrown its mistakes in the past — but also provided a much more sustainable platform for future growth.

The fund also wielded a disproportionate amount of influence due to the fact that Australia lacked the kind of alternative regulatory support mechanisms which were starting to pop up in other jurisdictions.

"I want to finally stress how little money it takes to make a difference," Lord told the Senate.

"The Screen Australia program was big enough to see real change within a single year, for the entire industry. That's less than one twenty-fourth the cost of the School Chaplains program. The govern-

ment already provides billions of industrial support to the mining, manufacturing and energy sectors, and those sectors are shrinking despite that investment."

"We were thriving when we had 10 million in support across 4 years."

During the Senate inquiry, the Chief Operating Officer of Screen Australia, which had administered the AIGF, spoke positively of its results, noting that of the 36 video game projects it had supported, the $3.7 million provided generated production budgets of $14 million. This figure is likely to increase further, with a number of the supported games still to be released.

The cancellation of the AIGF, then — and later signals by the Coalition administration that it would not support bringing support for the video game development sector up to parity with other mediums such as books, film and TV — meant that much of the sector lost its only support mechanism in one cut.

"The situation has been, in a word, troubling," Lord noted.

"There's a real feeling in the industry that the current administration doesn't just not understand our business but rather they are opposed to it. The immediate slashing of the games fund scuppered the plans of many small businesses, forcing them to find other work outside the games industry instead of doing what they do best."

"Recent proposed changes to arts & film funding have explicitly stated that new funding programs would not be available to our industry... a confusing and deeply worrying indication that our industry isn't valued."

Some of the gaps have been filled by funding initiatives from state governments, with the tech-savvy Victorian Government particularly coming to its rescue.

But at the same time, other countries had also started to drastically alter their policies to support their local video game industries, taking advantage of Australia's weakness.

The Canadian experience

Perhaps the most stark example of how much of a difference government policy can make in the development of an entire industry is that of Canada.

In many ways, Canada is not dissimilar to Australia, sharing extensive historical, cultural and economic links and with a population in the same order of magnitude (Canada has about 35 million residents, Australia 24 million).

Yet strong local support for the country's video game development sector has ensured a substantially different outcome for this specific industry.

According to numerous reports, Canada now ranks third in the world for developing video games, with only the US and Japan ahead of it in this field. Some 20,400 people are employed in the sector, with more than 470 studios operation across the country. The industry reportedly contributes about $3 billion to Canada's gross domestic product.

At the heart of this success is strong policy support.

Both the Canadian government, in addition to its provincial governments (similar to Australia's states) provide substantial incentives for video game development companies to set up and expand operations in the country.

Some of these which apply to game companies in the city of Toronto alone[188], for example, include:

- The Ontario Interactive Digital Media Tax Credit (a refundable tax credit of up to 40 percent for eligible labour and marketing expenses for video games, up to C$100k per product

- Grants up to C$50k for concept development and up to C$250k for production, with a 1:1 matched funding model

- Grants from the Ontario Media Development Corporation of up to 50 percent of a project, capped at $150k.

Similar tax credits and grants are also available in other cities such as Montreal. And federal support may include direct, upfront support for research and development, support from the Business Development Bank of Canada, which has a mandate to *"aggressively support video game start-ups within Canada"*, and direct support from the Canada Media Fund.

This type of support … even the language being used to describe it — is entirely alien to Australia.

Other countries which provide similar regulatory relief and financial support for video game companies include Finland (home to mobile game companies such as Rovio and Supercell), the United Kingdom (which has a dedicated Video Games Tax Relief program), France (which offers video game companies a 20 percent tax offset for production expenditure and the United States, where a number of states offer tax incentive programs for video game production.

Even New Zealand gets into the act, with the Grow Wellington program in particular kicking goals in supporting local video game development companies.

Policy options which could be explored

If you've read this far in this chapter, it should be rather obvious that there is a strong imbalance when it comes to Federal Government policy regarding Australia's video games development industry.

It's easy to argue, as many classical liberal political thinkers will, that national governments should not artificially support the development of certain industry vertical sectors over others. Many believe that it would be more beneficial in a macro sense for governments to instead create strong, underlying level playing fields for every sector to develop — fertile ground in which many seeds can take root.

This is a valid argument, and it's one which has been pursued internationally to great effect.

However, this is certainly not what is happening in Australia. When it comes to industry development policy down under, successive Federal administrations have directly prioritised specific industries over others. It's common to see major grants for the automotive manufacturing industry, for example, or the resources sector — while knowledge worker industries such as the IT startup sector or even online retailers receive little to no support for decades at a time.

Politicians tend to believe they can pick winners — and even better if the sectors they support aid in their own political fortunes.

This trend is even more visible when it comes to the media industry, which the video games development industry can be broadly included in.

In Australia, our Federal Government provides direct and indirect support for our film industry, our television industry, our book industry and our media industry.

And yet that support — with the exception of a couple of historical examples such as the AIGF — has never been extended to the local video games industry.

The evidence that support of the sector will drive economic and employment outcomes within Australia is, at this point, incontrovertible. This has especially become the case due to the onset of the global Internet; which has allowed a small clutch of small Australia video game developers to survive and even thrive in an almost hostile local regulatory environment.

The sheer fact of the matter is that the video game industry is an ideal sector for Australia to exploit. We have all of the elements that are required for it to shine — infrastructure, a strongly educated economy with many creative knowledge workers, and even a growing investment scene willing to take risks for potential high rewards. All we lack is government policy to support these factors and ensure Australia is competitive with other countries.

What this failure points to is an inherent bias on the part of Australia's political sector.

Within the closeted confines of Australian Parliament House, video games are still largely regarded as 'child's play' — a form of entertainment which may divert, but which does not represent a mainstream form of content which could assist in meeting the same political aims as its fellow travellers in the broader arts scene — creating jobs, creating profits, and meeting cultural aims, both mainstream and alternative.

So what is to be done about this situation?

The 'how' is difficult. If we're being honest about it, much of it has to do with time; letting politicians of older generations retire and be replaced by younger ones, who better understand the essential role video games now play in our personal and economic lives.

Much of the rest has to do with emphasising the role that some — but not all — video games play in becoming examples of high art, in addition to building stronger structures for industry representation in political spheres.

But the 'what' is much more clear and easy to define.

Policy Options

When it comes down to the nuts and bolts, virtually every significant player in Australia's video game development sector agrees on the fundamental policy levers which should be exercised in order to bring about a gradual but significant expansion in the size of the local industry.

The first — you will probably not be surprised to read — is a resurrection of the successful AIGF instrument which had already assisted in such local success.

As Black Lab Games — developer of the Battlestar Galactica: Deadlock game and a number of others — noted in its submission to the Senate inquiry, the AIGF was successful in growing the entire industry:

"Whilst each individual game is a relatively high-risk investment, the industry as a whole is of significant value, so the key to a successful investment is spreading the risk across multiple companies and projects," Black Lab wrote.

"This is why the ... AIGF, previously administered by Screen Australia until it was suddenly terminated in the May 2014 Budget, was an important initiative. By spreading a single fund across dozens of projects, it was far more likely to grow the industry as a whole, irrespective of the success or failure of each individual project. Reinstatement of the AIGF would be a good first step in growing the local industry."

The obvious counter-argument to this demand for direct government financial support for the Australian video game industry is that this extremely small level of investment — the AIGF, after all, only held a total of $20 million in funding — could easily be provided by the private sector, and is, in the case of other tech-related startups.

However, it is also true that private industry has not yet stepped up to the plate to provide the level of investment which local industry would require to support its continual growth.

That investment has come to Australia's broader technology startup sector, and it will inevitably arrive in the video game development industry as well. But until it does, there is still a strong argument that there is a role for government to play in filling the gaps which private sector investors have left.

The second policy lever which makes a great deal of sense for the Federal Government to pursue relates to a little-known item dubbed the 'producer tax offset'.

The producer tax offset is a refundable tax offset for Australian expenditure, which currently applies to Australian films. Its application essentially means that 40 percent of the cost of producing a 'feature film' in Australia — and 20 percent for a film that is not a 'feature film' — can be written off for taxation purposes.

There is no doubt that extending this tax offset to the video game development industry would lead to a gradual expansion of the sector.

As Black Lab Games noted during the Senate Inquiry:

"If a similar system was put in place for games, it would encourage investment in the sector, which would lead to more projects with substantial budgets getting off the ground, and in turn providing more employment and export opportunities."

The Internet Games and Entertainment Association — which largely represents the interests of large publishers in the Australian market — expressed similar sentiments, displaying evidence of broad support across the sector. The association stated that extending the producer offset:

"... has the capacity to assist studios in becoming more competitive internationally. It creates financial incentives for projects with significant commercial value, particularly high-end console games. Through attracting domestic and overseas investment, interactive games developers are more likely to build stable and sustainable studios which are critical to longer-term growth of the industry."

A number of the other levers which policymakers are able to apply to Australia's video game development industry should be quite familiar; because they have already been successfully applied to other industry verticals.

These include support for the early stage investment and venture capital sectors (which naturally have a strong interest in the high risk/high reward nature of the video game industry, particularly where original intellectual property is being developed); opening the doors further to crowdsourcing funding for video game development; supporting gaming conventions and trade missions and leveraging other financial instruments such as Export Market Development grants.

It's worth reiterating at this point that it is hardly unusual for a Government to apply such levers to support the development of an industry.

A plethora of other industries, notably in resources, agriculture and manufacturing, have enjoyed strong support from Australia's Federal Government through such mechanisms for many decades.

Nor is it uncommon globally for such support to be applied to the video game sector specifically. In fact, it is much more common for first-world countries particularly to target the development of this highly lucrative and successful industry within their own borders.

But it is unusual within Australia. And that lack of support has cost us dearly.

Waiting

In June 2017, Greens Senator Scott Ludlam, who had put forward the original motion calling for the Senate to investigate Australia's video game development industry, got to his feet in Parliament House to remind Australia's political sector of a very unfortunate fact.

Unusually in such divided political times, the committee which investigated the issue in 2015 and 2016 had published a unanimous report as the result of its inquiry.

This report — backed by Senators from parties as diverse as the Greens, Labor and the Coalition — strongly recommended the Government investigate using many of the same policy controls which we have discussed in this chapter to stimulate the growth of Australia's video game development industry.

Yet the Federal Government completely ignored that report for a protracted period, declining to respond to repeated requests from industry to do so.

When the response eventually came, in February 2018, Malcolm Turnbull's Coalition administration did little more than pay lip service to the report's recommendations. The only new initiative announced by the Government at the time was a paltry $17,000 in funding to assist the GDAA to attend one solitary international games conference.

In short, the Government continues to display the same lack of interest in this vibrant and lucrative sector that so many Governments have before it.

This is not a criticism of the current Coalition Government specifically. Administrations from both sides of the fence — as well as politicians from smaller party groups — have ignored Australia's video game sector for decades.

But it is an indication of policy failure, driven by negative, close-minded bias for certain industries, at the clear expense of others. And Australia deserves better.

As Ludlam told the Senate Chamber: *"This is an industry that is ready to get on its feet if the government is ready to listen."*

Meanwhile, that industry is getting on with business.

As John Kane, local developer of games such as *Killing Time at Lightspeed* and *Mallow Drops* wrote in the wake of the anaemic response from the Government to the inquiry's recommendations[189]:

"This was the response I expected, but it's still gutting to see such a dismissal of an entire industry like this. To be honest, the Australian

games industry exists despite the Federal Government, not because of it. We'll keep on making amazing work, just as we always have, even if we have to move elsewhere to do it."

SUMMARY

Policy Details

In the years leading up to 2011, most of Australia's major video game development studios suffered severe financial issues.

Successive Federal Governments did little to stem the tide, and Tony Abbott's Coalition administration actively contributed to the downhill slide by cancelling a major industry direct investment program, despite the fact that it had been succeeding.

What Went Wrong

The lack of action by successive Federal Governments to follow other jurisdictions with measures to directly support the industry meant that the nation's video game studios were not able to effectively compete internationally. It also meant startup development houses were not able to easily get off the ground.

Labor partially addressed this issue through the creation of the $20 million Australian Interactive Games Fund (AIGF). But the lack of bipartisan support for this scheme meant it was cancelled when the Coalition took power in September 2013.

The lack of support for Australia's video game development industry comparable to that of film, television, music and other creative arts can be attributed to the lack of understanding which policymakers have of the emerging video game medium.

Avoiding This Situation in Future

Governments must pick winners to actively support industries which will be most beneficial for the public interest. This support should be based on factors such as evidence of economic growth and ability to generate employment.

This involves continually reviewing new and developing industries. Government should also review industry support with a view to the global competitive environment.

CHAPTER 6

The Australia Tax

"It's simply staggering to see Apple make more money but manage to pay less tax in Australia. When you consider the massive overcharging that has occurred with some of their products, it seems both Australian consumers and taxpayers are shouldering a heavy load to fund Apple's bottom line."

—Labor MP Ed Husic

The date is 14 February 2013, and Adobe chief executive Shantanu Narayen has made a bad mistake: Inviting Australian journalists to a press conference.

Adobe's reason for holding the press conference is at once positive and obvious; a good news story. The company, one of the largest software houses globally, is celebrating the opening of its plush new Sydney office.

The event is attended by political luminaries such as NSW Premier Barry O'Farrell — whose State Government is openly trying to entice local investment from precisely the kind of multinational technology vendor that Adobe represents.

Federal Communications Minister Stephen Conroy is also in town. Like O'Farrell, he is at pains to associate his own Government with any occasion in which a major technology company can be said to be ploughing capital into the local market.

Everyone's been in a good mood all morning. Narayen is playing up the occasion as both guest and host. Conroy has plainly enjoyed being paraded around Adobe's new offices. And O'Farrell has been magnanimous in his praise for the company.

But as the official photo opportunities fade and the politicians discreetly exit the building for their next appointment, Narayen faces the Australian press in an open press conference for the first time. The gloves come off within seconds and it quickly becomes apparent that the veteran software executive is not going to have an easy time of it. The questions from journalists come thick and fast.

The key issue relates to Adobe's flagship Photoshop product.

Photoshop is the media industry's absolute gold standard for digital image editing. It's a comprehensive best in class product that does anything a graphic designer could ask. Over the years, its ubiquity has elevated it to monopoly status amongst the ranks of anyone who works in the visual medium.

There are alternatives, but none of them are as good as Photoshop. And it always seems pointless to try to use anything else, when the whole media sector has already standardised on Adobe products.

The only problem: Photoshop costs up to A$1,400 more in Australia than it does in countries such as Adobe's home market of the US.

Narayen's clearly been anticipating a question about this price hike, and he tries to deflect it, highlighting his company's new Creative Cloud product, which offers a subscription-based alternative to the usual flat Photoshop purchase price.

To a certain extent, the executive's point is valid. Adobe is moving away from 'single purchase' pricing on its products and towards ongoing subscription pricing. This pricing offers Australians a better deal than before, even if the subscription price is still more than our American cousins are paying.

But several journalists continue to press the Adobe leader about the issue with a relentlessness born of their readers' frustration with Adobe's pricing. As the minutes continue to run down, Narayen gets a little frustrated, even flustered. Why won't these Australian journalists just pipe down and accept his comments?

Eventually his language descends into a gabble of generic marketing messages and official corporate line, all run together[190].

"Again, the Creative Cloud — I think it's important to remember that the Creative Cloud is not just for individuals," he tells the media. *"We recently announced the Creative Cloud for teams, we think that the collaboration features that you have, with Creative Cloud for teams is the better opportunity even for teams, and for enterprises, when you think of the combination of what we're doing with the Creative Cloud and the Marketing Cloud."*

"I think the message that I'm trying to send all of you, is that the Creative Cloud's the future of creative," Narayen adds.

It's a garbled and unclear message which simply does not resonate with the media — or Australian customers. The video of Narayen's shaky performance goes viral on YouTube, and some Australian customers start vowing to abandon the company's products any way they can, to signal their disgust with its commercial habits.

Blocked Access

A few hundred kilometres south in Canberra, there's a second issue making headlines, with another multinational company strictly controlling customer access to another valuable asset.

But this time the issue is not about software — it's about television.

The United States Embassy to Australia is a beautiful, classical American facility. Built from predominantly Australian materials but with an architecture based on a Georgian style which had been popular in the southern states of the United States in the colonial period, the building located in the Canberra diplomatic suburb of Yarralumla is a landmark monument.

Its well-sculptured gardens are peaceful and serene, and the entire facility evokes a feeling of confidence and power. Just the sort of impression which the United States no doubt likes to make wherever it has influence.

Australia and the United States have long been close allies and even friends. The close positioning of the US Embassy in Canberra to Australian Parliament House is emblematic of this relationship.

But today the mood of the current US Ambassador to Australia, Jeffrey Bleich, is perhaps more reminiscent of the hardened steel fence — complete with spikes to deter anyone seeking to climb over — that surrounds the embassy, than the serene gardens found within.

It's April 2013, and Bleich is hot under the collar. The subject of his frustration? Nothing less than naughty Australian Internet pirates.

In a statement published on his Facebook page at the time[191] Bleich notes that, like hundreds of millions of others, he and his family had just started watching the latest Season 3 of the popular Game of Thrones television series developed at great expense by US cable network HBO.

It's a great series — chock full of gritty dramatic goodness, with all of the sex, violence and political intrigue that a modern audience could love. But Bleich is not concerned about the plot or character development.

Bleich's gripe is that Australians are pirating the show in record numbers — in a much higher percentage per capita than other countries are. This, he believes, is depriving HBO of its rightful revenue from developing such a landmark work of art.

In his post, Bleich takes pains to remind Australians that the people behind the show have to earn a living from their efforts.

"... stealing is stealing," he writes. *"Buying a book in a store costs more and takes longer than stealing it from your neighbor's house, but we all know it is the right thing to do and it allows authors to make a living and write more books. So please celebrate UN World Book and Copyright Day by doing the right thing – Tyrion Lannister will thank you for it."*

Bleich — and the US content industry that he is representing with his complaint — is not the first to have publicly criticised the level of Internet piracy associated with Game of Thrones in Australia.

In point of fact, since the release of its first season in 2011, the show has become a focal point for a rapidly evolving and highly contentious debate in Australia about the issue.

The most obvious reason is that Game of Thrones is one of the most popular television shows globally. Like every popular show, as soon as it airs on commercial television stations or is distributed through cable networks, it is illegally copied and uploaded so that millions of freeloaders can download and watch it without paying a cent for the privilege — or even watching any advertisements embedded in the programming.

But there is another reason that the unauthorised distribution of Game of Thrones has become so contentious in Australia.

This is because Games of Thrones has evolved to be the most visible example of how corporations are harshly controlling the distribution of content in Australia.

There are only certain, highly specific ways in which Australians can watch Game of Thrones legally. And all of those avenues come with compromises which are objectionable to many consumers.

The only way to legally watch the show as it airs — week by week — is to subscribe to a monthly plan through Australian pay TV network Foxtel. The company was able to successfully outbid all of its competitors, especially Australia's ailing commercial free to air television networks, for access to Game of Thrones, when HBO started canvassing distribution options down under.

This means that to watch Game of Thrones on a week by week basis, Australians have to commit to subscribe to a monthly cable or satellite television plan from Foxtel, or at the very least one of its Internet-delivered monthly plans.

The pay TV giant's plans are nothing if not confusing — a casual visitor to Foxtel's website is hard-pressed to determine what they actually cost — but they usually start at around $50 per month and range up much higher than that. And they don't just deliver consumers Game of Thrones — they deliver much more. Each individual plan will offer dozens of shows which a consumer may have no intention of watching.

The only alternative ways of accessing Game of Thrones — buying the DVDs of the show, for example, or downloading episodes via Apple iTunes — don't deliver new episodes on a timely basis. Fans would have to wait months and months to watch the content which US consumers have had in their hands

— via a cable subscription to HBO or merely be subscribing to the company's online streaming service — instantly.

Australian access to Game of Thrones is such a fraught issue that it has attracted global attention. In February 2014, the notorious piracy site EZTV issued a statement noting that it stood *"ready"* to help out Australians with access to the show.

"Even for those who are happy to pay, we provide more flexibility and a better viewing experience," an EZTV spokesperson told Internet piracy news site TorrentFreak at the time[192], referring to the fact that, even for those who have already paid to access a monthly subscription plan to access Game of Thrones through Foxtel, the BitTorrent distribution route may be attractive, as it allows high-quality TV content to be viewed on any platform and without an Internet connection.

Foxtel's viewing platform is also available on many console, television, set-top and mobile platforms, but not all, and it also requires an Internet connection to stream TV series such as Game of Thrones. EZTV's downloads are not subject to digital rights management and can be watched anywhere and at any time.

The result of all this is that Australians have continually refused to access the show on commercial terms; instead choosing en masse to download Game of Thrones online. TorrentFreak and others have been highlighting our country's disproportionately high piracy rates for years.

This isn't a criminal act — but it is a case of breaching civil liability.

There is no doubt that HBO and Foxtel have noticed what's happening. And the they — and Bleich, representing the US Government — are not happy about the situation.

Making out like bandits

These two issues are big ones. They dominated the Australian technology media at the time they aired, creating thousands of headlines, hundreds of thousands of comments and constant debate.

But they're not the only story around.

At almost the exact same time that Shantanu Narayen is struggling to defend his company's price hikes to Adobe's Australian customers and Jeffrey Bleich is taking a hard line on content piracy, there's another debate going on across town.

This debate, at least on the surface, appears to be about something completely different: Taxation.

And the key focus is another major technology company: Apple.

The company founded by Steve Jobs and Steve Wozniak in a garage in Cupertino in the early 1980's has been doing pretty well lately — in fact, incredibly well.

It had a terrible time throughout the latter years of the 1990's, but based firstly on Apple's success with the iPod from 2001, and then later on with a series of follow-up products including the iPhone, the iPad, revised Macintosh computers and various ancillary products, Apple's revenue has been growing rapidly.

And that includes Australia.

According to its spartan annual filings with the Australian Securities and Investments Commission — representing virtually the only financial disclosure which Apple makes to the public each year about the state of its local finances — Apple Australia's revenue skyrocketed over the years from 2006 through 2012. In 2006, Apple pulled in only $720 million in Australian revenues. By 2015, that figure multiplied more than ten-fold to about $7.8 billion[193].

Ordinarily, this should be a cause for celebration, with everyone winning through Apple's success. Consumers get great products, Apple shareholders make huge piles of cash, and the increased revenue drives increased taxation income for the Government.

However, throughout this decade, one stakeholder group missed out on benefiting much at all.

Despite its ten-fold Australian revenue increase, throughout this period Apple kept on ratcheting up its claimed local expenses, meaning its Australian taxable profits rose only slightly in response.

For example, in 2015 Apple Australia paid only an extra $4.5 million of corporate income tax that year — despite the fact that it made $1.8 billion more revenue compared with the year before, to a total of $7.8 billion.

There are many — completely legal — mechanisms which Apple was using to cut their corporate tax rate. Structures such as offshore billing mechanisms and complex internal pricing controls were rife.

Another factor was that the Australian Taxation Office was just not keeping up.

Neither was Apple alone in this practice of what can only be described as legalised tax avoidance.

That same year, search giant Google revealed it expected to pay just $74,000 in corporate income tax for the 2011 calendar year, off Australian revenue which it claimed was just $201 million. The figure flew in the face of industry estimates pegging Google's Australian income at closer to $1 billion.

In its financial statements that year[194], Google Australia did not list its activities as being the provision of advertising and software services, both of which it charges Australian customers for.

Instead, it noted that it has agreements with its US parent, Google Inc, and a company called Walkway Technologies for the provision of research and development services, and with Google Ireland and Google Asia-Pacific for the provision of sales and marketing services. Consequently, almost all of

Google Australia's revenues were listed as being for services thus rendered to those companies.

"The company's service revenues are generated under service agreements with Google Inc, a company incorporated in the United States of America, Google Ireland Ltd and Google Asia-Pacific Pte. Ltd, all of which have Google Inc as their ultimate parent company," Google wrote in its ASIC filing. *"As a consequence, the company is dependent on the operational support of Google Inc, for future revenues and profit under the agreement."*

Google Australia's financial statements were audited by accounting firm Ernst & Young, which certifies in the documents that the financial report of Google Australia *"gave a true and fair view of the company's financial position as at 31 December 2011"*, and that it complies with applicable laws.

This may be so; yet it still felt as though the company — like Apple — was using the law to escape paying its 'fair go' share of tax in Australia.

Three Sides of the Same Coin

On the face of it, these three issues are separate.

What, after all, does the cost to consumers of technology goods and services sold in Australia have to do with how the companies who sell them are taxed?

What does the fact that some extremely popular forms of content are strictly limited in terms of their availability to Australian consumers have with either?

However, when you dig a bit deeper into the companies concerned, what really becomes obvious is all of these issues are essentially about the same issue: Money. And not just a little bit of money — massive whopping piles of cash.

In two of these issues, what we see is a clear case of giant corporations using their total control of a limited asset — be it software or a highly desirable form of content — to leverage the systematic extraction of huge sums of money from the Australian public.

In ordinary circumstances, this would not be an issue.

Nobody, after all, is forcing Australian consumers to licence Photoshop from Adobe. And there are many forms of entertainment available. Nobody is forcing Australians to pay Foxtel substantial sums of money to watch Game of Thrones in a timely manner, as each episode is released.

However, if you dig a little deeper into each situation, what is apparent is that there is a power dynamic at work which is extremely difficult for ordinary Australian consumers to resist; and difficult for the Federal Government to control.

Take, for example, the alternatives to Photoshop.

There is no doubt that cheaper alternatives such as Affinity Photo or even free options such as the GIMP application offer similar functionality to Adobe's market-leading product.

But when your daily livelihood becomes dependent upon compatibility with Adobe file formats, and support for Adobe process flows, it becomes increasingly likely that you will avoid the inconvenience of using a different process flow from the rest of the industry, and merely go for the default option.

Similarly, there is a huge amount of social pressure associated with choosing the appropriate form of entertainment.

The interest in the most popular television shows is pervasive across Australia — ranging from Game of Thrones to Masterchef and the Biggest Loser.

When everyone at your workplace and within your social group is following the same content, week by week, and having the same discussion about it, to not have access to that content means being left out of a cultural milieu.

It's a first world problem, to be sure — but it's a real one.

The taxation situation represents the other side of this coin.

On one side, giant multinational technology and media companies such as Apple, Adobe, Google and HBO make a habit out of creating incredibly valuable software, hardware and media products, and making them available to Australian consumers at significantly enhanced costs compared with prices in their home US market.

On the other side, those same companies are taking advantage of favourable taxation regulations to maximise the costs that they are forced to disclose within the Australian jurisdiction; and thus minimise their local tax burden.

Confluence

In mid-2012, all three of these seemingly unrelated factors came together in an explosive political nexus.

It started with the issue of price hikes on technology software and hardware products and video, music and gaming content; better known as the 'Australia Tax'.

One of the leading voices concerned about the price hikes being levied against Australians over time by technology and content companies was Labor MP Ed Husic.

Husic — the Member for the Western Sydney electorate of Chifley since 2010 — was not quite a 'digital native', but he was one of a handful of younger politicians who had joined Federal Parliament after a background dealing with the technology sector. Before joining Parliament, Husic had held a number of senior roles with the Communications, Electrical and Plumbing Union of Australia (CEPU) throughout the 1990's and early 2000's, culminating in a position as its national president.

Because of this, the Labor MP had a great deal of experience battling with telco giant Telstra on a daily basis for better rights for unionised workers.

With this kind of background, it wasn't a giant leap for Husic to start making war on major technology multinationals for better — or even basically fair — prices for Australian consumers who, in many cases, were essentially forced to use their products.

Since early 2011, just months after his elevation to the Parliament, Husic had been trying to get answers from companies like Adobe, Microsoft, Apple and Lenovo as to why they wouldn't engage with the government on this issue.

At the time, Husic had warned Adobe and its fellow technology vendors that they could not *"ride out"* consumer acrimony about the so-called "Australia tax" levied on basic technology products. The issue was simply not going to go away until it was resolved.

In 2012, having laid a significant lobbying background, Husic successfully persuaded then-Communications Minister Stephen Conroy and other senior Labor figures that the then-Labor Federal Government should take a closer look at the issue. A Federal Parliamentary committee was tasked with examining the topic, with Husic himself placed in a pivotal role.

Husic and his fellow parliamentarians made a point of inviting a whole bevy of technology and content companies to make submissions to the committee.

But this invitation was immediately met with a cold reaction from some of the technology giants.

Adobe in particular wasn't happy.

Initially, the company merely ignored the inquiry.

Then, after a wave of consumer and political pressure hit Adobe, the company deigned to notice it, noting that it would not give evidence to the inquiry, but would send an observer to keep an eye on it.

Meanwhile, the committee was fielding hundreds of submissions from concerned consumers frustrated by the issue. Some pointed out that they could literally fly to the United States, buy a copy of Photoshop from a US retailer in US dollars and fly back — all for the same price that it cost to buy Photoshop in Australia.

Adobe's reticence to face its accusers did not escape the notice of the politicians on the committee.

Committee chair Nick Campion stood up in the House of Representatives in October 2012 to note that some companies were *"treating the Parliament with contempt"*. The statement was clearly aimed at the major technology multinationals.

"... to one degree or another, there has been a real unwillingness to submit evidence in public or to appear before the committee on the part of both industry associations and major companies in the area of IT," he told the House of Representatives[195].

He added: *"The committee detects a deep reluctance and resistance on the part of the relevant companies to discuss in public the issues that the committee is considering or to publicly defend their business models and pricing structures ... the industry seems to employ the tactic of giving either little or limited cooperation to the committee, particularly in public testimony."*

Campion said this behaviour stood in stark contrast to what had happened in other inquiries which had investigated areas of commercial sensitivity – for example, the retail sector inquiry in 1999, in which Woolworths appeared twice and included its chief executive and five other senior managers.

"If it is good enough for an Australian company such as Woolworths to give public evidence on matters of commercial interest to them, it should be good enough for Apple and others to appear and do the same," Campion thundered in the chamber.

"It is not good enough for the industry to simply stonewall the inquiry—or, for that matter, to ignore interested consumers who have a legitimate public interest in IT pricing."

And it wasn't just Labor that was irritated by the behaviour of the companies concerned.

Nationals MP and deputy committee chair Paul Neville stood up and noted that he supported Campion's irritation.

"We feel that we have come to a point where there is obstruction, avoidance and evasion," Neville told the House of Representatives at the time.

The recalcitrant vendors would eventually be subpoena'd by the House of Representatives Standing Committee on Infrastructure and Communications; forced to send executives to appear in front of its members; and most eventually did make submissions to the inquiry in an attempt to explain their pricing behaviour with respect to their products.

But by the time that each vendor was drawn into these straits, it was almost unnecessary for them to testify.

The vendors' unwillingness to explain their pricing behaviour told its own story.

The sheer fact of the matter — which the IT price hike inquiry made clear — is that many giant multinationals had been exploiting favourable regulatory conditions in the Australian market for years; selling Australian consumers the exact same products at a large markup— often digital downloads — compared with cheaper prices in their home markets.

The justifications which the vendors presented before the IT price hike committee only reinforced this fact.

Take the submission which Adobe's Australia and New Zealand managing director Paul Robson made to the committee. In it, Robson openly acknowledges the wave of complaints the Committee had collected regarding Adobe's Australian prices[196].

"The Committee has received a number of submissions that refer to 'Adobe's prices'," he noted. *"... these are mostly references to prices of software that are available in our online store."*

As Adobe had previously done a number of times, Robson justified the local costs by referencing Adobe's local distribution partners.

"It is important for Adobe to make its products available to customers online , but this is only one channel to market available to our customers," he added. *"Direct sales and sales through our channel partners are also very important for effectively supplying and servicing our Australian customer base and ensuring the success of the Australian business."*

"Since we conduct most of our business through our 500 - plus local channel partners, the majority of the costs of the ecosystem as a whole are incurred locally and in local currency. The cost of doing business in Australia is higher than in North America , as has been noted by many companies, as well as the Productivity Commission's Retail Inquiry which reported in 2011."

There is some truth to Robson's comments — the Adobe ecosystem is indeed important to the Australian economy, employing thousands of Australians and supporting many small businesses.

But his comments also did not directly address the fact that Adobe also has a substantial number of customers who would simply prefer to buy its products directly from Adobe itself — without going through a local distributor. The company allows customers to do that — but also burdens them with increased costs to do so, which the company's US customers do not pay.

As the IT price hike inquiry found in its final report:

"Based on the evidence received over a 12 month inquiry, the Committee has concluded that in many cases, the price differences for IT products cannot be explained by the cost of doing business in Australia."

Taxation

At around the same time, Federal Parliament had opened up another front in what was rapidly becoming a battle — if not a war — against many of the very same global technology giants who had been dragged kicking and screaming into the IT price hike inquiry.

Across town, Malcolm Turnbull — then merely the Shadow Communications Minister and member for the seat of Wentworth — was starting to look into the other side of the technology giants' finances.

It was the constant consumer complaints about the high prices being levied by the global technology giants — a classic case of unfairness which Labor loves to attack — which had initially attracted Husic to investigate the likes of Adobe, Apple and Microsoft.

But Turnbull — often considered to be a potential future Treasurer — was more interested in the tax avoidance practices of the big IT giants, due to the potential that the issue had to impact on Federal Government revenues.

At the time, it was rapidly becoming apparent that multinationals such as Apple, Microsoft and Google were shifting corporate profits offshore in a major way, by claiming huge local costs for their local businesses that allowed them to create a situation in which their claimed Australian taxable profits were extremely minimal.

By 2012, Turnbull and a number of other senior figures within government circles had started to note this fact. There was no suggestion of illegality, but was the Commonwealth receiving its fair due, they wondered? Probably not.

In an article published on his website at the time[197], Turnbull said an important long-term issue in terms of Australian public policy was *"the erosion of our tax base due to the growing significant of online commerce and offshore-domiciled service providers in many sectors and markets"*.

"Many transactions which previously generated economic activity and tax revenue in Australia no longer do so," the Liberal MP wrote.

No kidding.

Husic also swung into action, raising the issue publicly in the strongest possible terms, and even injecting the topic into his parliamentary inquiry into the price of technology goods and services.

"It's simply staggering to see Apple make more money but manage to pay less tax in Australia," the Labor MP told the Financial Review in early 2013[198].

"When you consider the massive overcharging that has occurred with some of their products, it seems both Australian consumers and taxpayers are shouldering a heavy load to fund Apple's bottom line."

Here it was Apple in particular that came in for censure from the committee.

In attempting to justify its taxation habits, Apple focused on the argument that its Australian office was structurally separated from its US headquarters, and thus paid something close to full price for products which it on-sold locally.

"Apple Pty Ltd purchases its hardware and software products predominantly from its affiliates overseas at an arm's length price, resulting in profits commensurate with the value of Apple Pty Ltd's sales and marketing efforts undertaken in Australia," the company told the committee.

Apple went to lengths to hose down the public commentary on its financial affairs. The managing director of its Australian division, Tony King, who had been conspicuously absent from the public eye for many years despite Apple's massive financial presence in Australia, made an unusual appearance before Husic's IT price hike inquiry.

At the time, King told the inquiry that Apple had a very good relationship with the tax man.

"I am happy to talk in generalities around the components of our tax return and the process that we go through with the Australian tax office every year," said King.

"That process is very open, rigorous and transparent. We report to the ATO all the revenue that we derive in the Australian market. We report to the ATO all the costs of doing business in the Australian market, from product costs to all of our operating expenses. That brings us down to a net profit number. That net profit number is a number that we are very open about with the Australian tax office."

Yet again — as with the issue regarding the cost of IT products sold in Australia — Apple's argument regarding its taxes largely appeared to fall on death ears. It felt at the time as though the company's financial approach — and that of a number of its fellow technology vendors — while legal, had failed the notorious 'pub' sniff test. It just felt wrong.

Small business owners across Australia, after all, could hardly be expected to simply grin and bear the amount of corporate tax they were paying the ATO, when that sum appeared to be less than the amount massive technology multinationals like Google were chipping in, and when Apple's tax burden was such a tiny proportion of its rapidly ballooning revenues.

There was some basis to Apple's justification for its taxation approach, known amongst accountants as utilising 'transfer pricing'. In formal terms, Apple Australia is indeed a separate company than Apple as it is constituted in the United States; and it must indeed maintain some mechanism for determining the transfer of value between these companies — even if, in effect, its US headquartered company owns 100 percent of its Australian operation.

But it's also true that this justification doesn't tell the whole truth about Apple's taxation approach.

As the company's revenues and profit margins have risen markedly over the past decade, Apple's Australian tax burden has not risen in a congruent fashion. The company's transfer pricing approach has instead allowed it to (legally) minimise its taxation burden in Australia; despite the fact that this revenue was earned down under.

(Apple did eventually emerge relatively well from the taxation issue. In August 2017, for example, the company noted that it had avoided any penalty from its transfer pricing approach, working through the issue during a five year audit by the Australian Taxation Office.

"We have confirmation from the ATO that all our corporate taxes are up to date and we continue to engage only with the ATO as to our current and future taxes," Tony King told a parliamentary committee at the time[199] The company did however, disclose in January 2018 that its tax bill with the ATO had substantially risen[200].)

As always, it was about the money. The giant multinational companies could get away with profit-taking in Australia; so they did so the absolute maximum that they could. That's just good capitalism. There was no suggestion of illegality, just that matters as they stood may not have represented a *"fair go"* for Australia.

In doing so, companies like Apple, Google, Microsoft, Adobe and many others were able to essentially hit the Australian hip pocket in several places at the same time: At the cash register, where large markups ensured we paid more than we could have; and through the hit to taxation revenue, which ensured that our government didn't collect the tax revenue it could have.

This approach was applied when Australians bought software from companies such as Microsoft and Adobe; hardware from companies such as Apple; and video games on platforms such as Steam or Sony's PlayStation Network.

And it even applied to the popular television shows that we would like to watch; with companies such as HBO making huge revenue from exclusively licensing content to Australian pay TV companies like Foxtel; who then, in turn, controlled

Australian customers' entertainment options by locking that content up and forcing Australians to buy bundles of unwanted content to access single shows in a timely manner.

All of this effort represented a systematic effort to do one thing: Make as much money as possible.

Of course, this wouldn't be such a big deal if the companies concerned took this approach across the board.

What rankles so much is the unfairness of the fact that they don't take the same approach to their home countries. Adobe charges much more for the products it sells in Australia — even if they are software downloads — than it does when it sells them in the US.

And Apple, although it does invest in Australia through creating jobs in its retail stores and head office administration, certainly does not invest locally to the same extent that it does in its home country of the US, where it is conspicuously building huge manufacturing factories in order to ensure the politicians in Washington DC aren't too displeased with its offshoring practices.

What can be done about it

The first thing to realise about the events detailed in this chapter is that none of the companies concerned — Apple, Microsoft, Adobe, Google or even HBO and Foxtel — were inherently doing anything wrong under the law in pursuing the activities this chapter describes.

These corporations have an inherent responsibility to make a return on their shareholders' investments — maximising profits through increasing revenues and minimising their costs.

They also have a legal responsibility to do so within the law. And in all the cases discussed in this chapter, the companies concerned did so.

The problem with their actions is not that they undertook them. The problem is that they were able to in the first place because appropriate regulatory controls were not set by the Federal Government to stop situations significantly unfavourable to consumers and taxpayers from occurring.

In short, companies such as the multinational technology giants I've mentioned are able to do what they do because of the playing field which the Federal Government has set for them. When that playing field is not level; when it is not fair; when it allows giant corporations to get away with actions that the rest of us consider to be beyond the pale; it is the Government's fault — not the fault of the corporations concerned, who must merely act according to their own interest within the regulatory controls set.

Take the case of Adobe, for instance.

It is clearly unfair for the company to charge Australian consumers significantly more than the company is charging their colleagues based in the United States.

But the problem is not Adobe's specific pricing. Adobe is only able to levy this pricing because, many people believe, Australia's laws are not fine-grained enough to deal effectively with this kind of situation.

Adobe surely has competitors; but those competitors are not strong enough to stop Adobe leveraging its control over the image editing market to charge consumers whatever it likes. And Australia's Government has not taken action to restrain the company in this situation.

The same situation applies to Microsoft (whose Office suite is also in a dominant market position); and HBO's repeated deals with Foxtel — which leave the Australian consumer no choice but to deal with the pay TV giant's unreasonable terms for accessing the most popular form of content in the world.

The same lack of appropriate regulatory controls applies to the taxation situation which these companies find themselves in.

The continued refusal of consecutive Federal Governments — Labor or Coalition — over the past decade to correctly set taxation controls designed to rein in the sophisticated financial strategies utilised by technology giants such as Apple and Google has created a situation where such companies are able to shift massive amounts of profit offshore, without the burden of having those profits taxed to an appropriate level in the country where they were earned.

The Solution

There is no quick fix total solution to many of these issues.

The ability to break down the effective product monopolies created by technology and content multinationals is necessarily predicated upon the existence of real competitors; software and content that is as good as the products which already dominate the market.

This is not a situation that government at any level can easily create.

And taxation of multinationals is a similarly fraught issue. Much of the ability of any individual government to deal with this problem rests on their ability to collaborate with other jurisdictions — especially the home jurisdiction of the companies concerned. This is a complex problem further complicated by intense, multi-jurisdictional lobbying efforts conducted by multinationals.

Some might refer to this issue as *"herding cats"*.

But we should not give up hope. There are indeed many common sense tweaks which the Federal Government could have long ago made around the edges of its industry policies in order to deal with these kinds of pricing and taxation issues.

As the IT price hike inquiry pointed out in its eventual multi-partisan report, competition could be substantially boosted by lifting parallel import restrictions to allow a flood of alternative goods to be imported into Australia and provide competition to the multinationals' own distribution efforts. This approach would be likely to be as effective across industries ranging from book publishing, to video games, software and beyond.

The Government could also do more to ensure that Australian consumers were able to legally avoid geographically-based circumvention mechanisms to accessing certain forms of content. This measure alone has the potential to unlock a huge swathe of access to content currently only available through strict and expensive terms in the Australian market.

Other useful measures could include the creation of a 'right of resale' for digital products — stopping vendors from forcing every consumer to licence a new copy of their products, even when there are many consumers who no longer need a copy they own and would be willing to sell.

And the Federal Government itself could also better leverage its purchasing power to buy more technology products and services in bulk, so as to be able to leverage the maximum possible discount from major technology vendors.

When it comes to the taxation situation, successive Federal Governments have, over the past several years, taken a number of measures to deal with the issue and reinforce the notion of a 'level playing field' for all companies. Some of the stimulus for this issue has come from the IT price hike inquiry, and a similar inquiry held by the Senate.

In February 2016, for example, the Turnbull Liberal Government introduced legislation to Parliament that would force foreign providers of digital content, such as Netflix, to pay goods and services tax (GST) in Australia[201].

In January of that same year, Australia was one of 31 countries to sign a multilateral agreement in Paris to share tax information on the activities of multinational companies[202] .

These two measures came hot on the heels of the *Tax Laws Amendment (Combating Multinational Tax Avoidance) Bill,* which passed in December 2015 and aims to ensure tax is paid by major international companies that operate in Australia but book profits offshore[203].

"Passage of this legislation sends a clear message that Australia has no tolerance for tax avoiders," said Treasurer Scott Morrison at the time. Transfer pricing rules have also been tightened.

In addition, the Australian Taxation Office itself has joined the crackdown on tax avoidance practice.

In November 2017 the ATO revealed it would initiate what it described as *"joint forensic audits"* with other countries' tax authorities, in an escalation of the agency's ongoing investigation of tech multinationals' taxation habits[204].

The agency's existing push on the issue has already netted about $5 billion in revenue for the Federal Government, since the ATO began actively investigating the area 18 months ago.

The measures are already forcing the multinationals to change their approach.

Microsoft, for example, had maintained a low Australian revenue base by billing Australian clients for many of its products and services from Singapore. The company has now reached a settlement with the ATO which will see more revenue accounted for directly in Australia.

Others appear to be pushing back against the Government to a certain extent. For example, some of Google's most recent financial accounts state that the company is lodging an objection to *"amended income statements"* issued it by the ATO.

Lessons

The key lesson which can be learnt from the 'Australia Tax' situation is that it highlights the necessity of governments ensuring that legislation and regulatory measures stay congruent with market conditions.

The 'Australia Tax' situation — in which tech multinationals have been charging Australians substantially higher prices than they do consumers in their home countries — is not a new issue. Neither is the issue of content companies locking up access to their content in Australia.

And certainly the issue of taxing multinationals appropriately is not new at all. This is a problem which successive Federal Governments have grappled with across multiple industries over a protracted period.

These issues had been kicking around Canberra for years, with various stakeholder groups and journalists raising them continually. They were even raised in various committees and other parliamentary forums at various times, before they came to the forefront of the public's attention.

And yet, it was evident that it took many years before they were addressed.

What this indicates is a weakness of the current policy development process found within Federal Parliament and the Federal Government. That process all too often seems to be based on addressing the needs of those who 'scream loudest' — in short, those who are getting the most attention.

But a truly effective policy development process would have picked up on the Australia Tax and tech multinational taxation issues as they were happening — and folded them into existing processes designed to ensure legislation and regulatory measures keep track with the market.

This is the only way to ensure that a level playing field exists continually for all enterprises operating in Australia — for it to be continually monitored and tweaked.

And this issue goes beyond the cost of paying for goods, or fairly taxing companies.

As the IT price hike inquiry wrote in its report:

"The importance of IT products to every sector of Australian society can hardly be overstated. IT products are woven into the fabric of our economy and society, and have driven rapid change in the way Australians communicate, the way we work, and the way we live."

"Given the ever-increasing importance of IT products to Australian society and the economy – in driving innovation, reducing isolation in regional and rural Australia, or improving the lives of Australians with a disability – it is essential that Australians get a fair deal."

SUMMARY

Policy Details

Over the past decade, a number of major multinational technology and content firms — generally based in the US — have charged Australians substantially more for access to their products than they charge consumers in their home markets.

This pricing approach came to be known as 'the Australia Tax'.

At the same time, some content firms have strictly locked down access by Australians to content such as high profile television shows, leading to high rates of piracy. Many of these same firms have used complex financial mechanisms to avoid paying significant taxes in Australia, despite their revenues having increased substantially at the same time.

What Went Wrong

The companies concerned have taken advantage of the lack of attention which successive Federal Governments have paid to the technology and content sectors.

This has meant that they have been able to get away with overcharging consumers at one end of the spectrum, and locking up access to premium content, while transferring their substantial local profits offshore.

At the heart of this issue was a fundamental lack of understanding on the part of Federal politicians and policymakers relating to the dynamics of the technology industry.

Avoiding This Situation in Future

Governments must ensure legislation and regulatory measures stay congruent with market conditions. This approach must go beyond addressing the needs of those who 'scream loudest' and take a more objective approach.

CHAPTER 7

Unicorns

"I don't think Australian startups have a loud enough voice in government yet, in fact the plumbers' union is probably better organised than the startup community in terms of lobbying government ..."

—Atlassian co-founder Scott Farquhar

It's the week before Christmas 2010, and the rooftop above the office of Sydney startup accelerator Pollenizer is jumping. As the deep blue of a glorious Sydney summer day fades into the reds and oranges of a stunning sunset over the city's breathtaking harbour, the who's who of Sydney's startup scene is getting down to boogie.

Pollenizer's office is located in the hip Sydney suburb of Surry Hills, and the attendees at the party are the coolest of the cool — managing companies which are the hottest of the hot.

In one corner of the roof, well-known Australian futurist Ross Dawson is swapping notes with a gentleman wearing a Soylent Green t-shirt. In another, serial entrepreneur Bart

Jellema is conferring with friends over the huge quantities of pizza which Pollenizer has ordered for the occasion.

Sporting a pair of bright red reindeer ears, Nikki Durkin of hyped startup 99dresses is holding court, while a few metres away a number of Pollenizer staff are handing out beers left, right and centre.

The party is filled with a mix of millionaires and paupers; playboys and serious financiers; venture capitalists and software engineers who've recently dropped out of top jobs at Google to start companies which they hope will grow as large.

There are graphic artists, web coders, dharma bum accountants. They're all from different backgrounds and they all have different stories to tell. But they're all interested in one thing: Money.

Everyone in the room is trying to create — or fund — the next big technology startup to come out of Australia.

Just as the evening hits a crescendo and the sun dips behind the horizon, the two celebrated founders of Pollenizer, Phil Morle and Mick Liubinskas, emerge onto the balcony overlooking the roof. A wave of laughter greets the room as everyone realises Mick is wearing a beautiful red dress which shows off his hairy legs to great effect.

"May I present to you," laughs Morle, *"Michael Liubinskas!"*

The masculine Liubinskas makes a leg at the audience and somehow manages to keep his balance while juggling two heavy cartons of "Pure Blonde" beer.

"Nobody share this photo, please," he laughs. I chuckle as I shift my high definition video camera to get a better view of the action. It'll be uploaded to YouTube first thing in the morning … after a double espresso wipes away the cobwebs from the night before.

"Thank you all for coming, it's been an amazing year!" Liubinskas beams. *"And just because I'm wearing a dress,"* he warns the audience, *"none of you guys can flirt with me!"*

The audience laughs, cheers and goes back to their partying and networking. It feels like the two are very much the same thing.

Liubinskas wanders down the stairs and starts handing out more beers. Later he claimed on Twitter that software entrepreneur Scott Farquhar — who in a short half-decade will become one of Australia's youngest billionaires courtesy of the IPO of Australian technology unicorn Atlassian — had tried to hide the Pollenizer co-founder's normal clothes[205] as a further joke.

Positioned strategically behind Liubinskas, beaming widely, is Durkin. The entrepreneur can claim credit for the Pollenizer founder's Christmas attire. Earlier in the year, Liubinskas bet Durkin that she couldn't sell 1,000 dresses that year through her 99dresses site. But Durkin delivered on her end of the bargain. In return, Liubinskas had to wear a dress himself.

A recovering industry

The Pollenizer Christmas party of 2010 was not extraordinary because it was a party. That night in 2010, there were a thousand other parties of different varieties going on in Surry Hills alone. You could feel the heightened atmosphere in Sydney's famed hipster district floating on the air.

It was extraordinary because it was a party held by Australia's technology startup sector.

It was extraordinary because suddenly ... Australia actually had a technology startup sector.

There is no doubt that Australia had seen high-flying technology startups before. When the famed dot com boom hit Silicon Valley in the late 1990's and early 2000's, Australia had its own share of fame and fortune. Companies like Sausage

Software, Ecorp, LookSmart and a bevy of others rose to dizzying heights during those heady few years. One might even count high-flying — and fast-falling — upstart telco One.Tel amongst that list.

However, most eventually crashed down to earth as investors and consumers globally realised that most of the large tranche of dot com startups formed during the period were set to fail.

There was a week in mid-April 2000, particularly, where the US Nasdaq entered complete free fall. Many American companies simply slipped out of the bottom of the market at that point.

The crash richocheted around the world and hit Australia particularly hard. For most of the next decade very few investors, either in Australia or globally, were willing to throw money at a sector which had proven so astonishingly volatile. Very few technology startups of any kind were formed in Australia in the years after 2000. Any financier worth their salt didn't see any attraction to throwing more of their good money after the bad.

But as the mid 2000's turned to the late 2000's, a curious thing began to occur.

In the US, nascent technology blog TechCrunch, formed by maverick entrepreneur and publisher Michael Arrington in his bedroom, had started to chronicle a new dot com boom.

A handful of companies led by search giant Google and online retailer Amazon had survived the dot com crash and had started to grow — really grow. They were now large enough and old enough that they were started to spout veteran coders and businesspeople smart enough and hungry enough to want to create their own technology powerhouses.

I distinctly remember when Arrington broke the news in October 2006 that Google was in talks to buy YouTube[206]. The deal (for US$1.65 billion in stock) seemed preposterous at the time, given that the video sharing site had launched less than a year previously.

But it also effectively signalled the global second coming of the Dot Com Boom that had so shaken up things in the late 1990's. Once again, large piles of cash money and incredibly driven entrepreneurs had started to connect with each other in the rapidly growing tech startup sector.

The trend was also beginning to be felt in Australia.

There wasn't much money around town at that time, and there weren't many entrepreneurs. But there was enough of both for some energy to be felt in the scene, and most of that energy had started to circulate around Pollenizer in Sydney.

A center of gravity

Pollenizer itself was typical of the wave of companies coming out of Silicon Valley. Like many of those firms, it was formed by veterans of the first dot com boom. Phil Morle and Mick Liubinskas had both worked for Sharman Networks in the early 2000's. The nominally Australia-based company achieved global notoriety in its time for creating the early file-sharing software Kazaa, which allowed millions of consumers globally to swap copyrighted files such as music and movies with complete disregard for the rule of law and the interests of the content industry.

Eventually Sharman faded away, but Morle and Liubinskas survived, formed a fast friendship and went on to much greater things.

It was a classic technology startup partnership.

Morle was the technologist of the pair — he was Sharman's chief technology officer — while Liubinskas handled marketing and business development. But over time their skills mingled and they came to focus on a larger task involving many different skills — assisting others to grow startups of their own.

Pollenizer was formed to provide consulting, operations, production, commercial and technical support — really, anything a startup could want — to Australia's growing cadre of technology startups.

When there's a gold rush going on, often the best thing to do is to sell shovels. So Liubinskas and Morle got busy pitching to anyone who would listen.

The pair's rapid success was testament to their hard work, and soon they were involved in a cluster of interesting companies. If you examine their resumes, you'll see the names of Australian technology startups like Tangler, Spreets, Wooboard, Flightfox, Omnidrive, Dealised, LawPath and many more.

Often these companies were based on models that were proving successful overseas.

Wollongong-based Omnidrive, for example, eventually failed in its mission to deliver cheap online cloud storage[207]. However, it could have easily become the next Dropbox, which went on to become a billion dollar behemoth. Flightfox tapped into the global trend for providing an aggregation platform for consumers to access cheap and convenient plane flights, and for airlines to monetise every last inch of their capacity.

The common denominator across companies like these is that they were founded by individuals who wanted to both challenge existing titans of the various industries they were competing in, as well as launch their own personal fortunes in a way that surviving the daily grind to earn a monthly salary never could.

They figured if they could peel off only a small percentage of the revenues enjoyed by an industry titan, then they would make themselves millionaires.

Pollenizer's unique model meant that it not only provided direct operational support to help such companies build and launch products and set up their own back office, but also often invested directly in them financially.

This meant that Pollenizer itself had a vested interest in seeing its growing brood succeed.

As the company's Christmas party in 2010 highlighted — amongst many other similar occasions — by 2010 Pollenizer had become a center of gravity for the Australian technology startup scene. Anyone who was anyone in the scene in Sydney in that time knew of the company, and most were peripherally involved in it in one way or another. To be involved with Pollenizer was to be part of a giant melting pot of talent, energy, youth and ambition.

Of course, there wasn't truly much money involved in the whole shebang.

Until Spreets.

Spreets

It's a little hard to recall in 2018, given that the online retail marketplace has changed so radically in just the past few years. But as the decade turned around 2010, Internet retail 'aggregators' which leveraged the mass buying potential of consumers to drive heavily discounted deals were just getting up to full speed.

At the time, such aggregators were just about the most hyped websites to be found anywhere.

In a sense, the hype was justified.

Each aggregation website initially specialised in just one daily deal per day. This 'deal' would be a heavily discounted offer from a single online retailer. The retailer benefited because the aggregator drove so many buyers to its site that it made a huge amount of revenue in one day.

The profit margin on this revenue would be small, because the deals were heavily discounted; and of course the aggregators took their cut off the top as well. But the retailers still made out like bandits because of the total volume of revenue. Everyone benefited all through the chain — from consumers to aggregators to retailers.

The poster child for this trend globally was Groupon, which was making out like a bandit in the US. At one point, the company was on track to make $1 billion in sales faster than any business had done so — ever.

But Groupon had not yet launched in Australia and would not do so until February 2011.

In the meantime, a number of local companies appeared to be trying to emulate Groupon's success through directly copying its model. One of the leaders in the pack was Spreets.

Spreets was founded in 2009 by a couple of Australians. One of those was a veteran of the first dot com boom. From 1999 through 2001 — right through the middle of the first boom — Dean McEvoy was business manager for Hothouse Interactive[208], one of Australia's pioneering web development agencies.

After a series of other semi-successful ventures, McEvoy eventually hit pay dirt with Spreets, which appeared to emulate Groupon's buying model right from its launch in December 2009. His co-founder was Justus Hammer, a younger entrepreneur who had nevertheless developed a strong ability to help startups grow rapidly through the application of modern online marketing techniques tied to data analytics. This is a talent which he applied extremely effectively at Spreets.

It didn't take Spreets long to accumulate a couple of hundred thousand subscribers all thirsting for its daily deals, and just two and a half years after it launched, the company was the subject of a lucrative deal with ailing local web property Yahoo!7 that would see its founders and investors take a cool $40 million off the table in one hit.

It was another Pollenizer Christmas party which had gotten Spreets started in the first place.

McEvoy had been involved with Pollenizer dating back several years, when the company agreed to help support his previous startup, Booking Angel. This led to a continuing relationship.

"... at Christmas drinks in 2009, I worked up the courage to pitch another idea to Phil," McEvoy told Business Insider following the Yahoo!7 deal[209].

"I was filling up his wine as much as I could before I was like: 'I saw this pretty cool thing in Silicon Valley, it's this group buying thing, we should have a look at it, you know. I know there are these devs you have not doing much, with not many projects lined up, what are you going to do with them anyway?'"

"Thankfully I got them drunk enough and they agreed," he joked.

It's an amusing anecdote; but it also goes some way to demonstrating the potential that existed in a melting pot like Pollenizer; where creativity, technical acumen and business analysis collided head-on with cashed up venture capitalists.

In the end, Spreets ended up being only of middling value to Yahoo!7. The company's founders, it turned out, had sold out at the height of the hype wave. In the years to come, retailers would realise that aggregators could not fully deliver the rivers of gold that they had promised. They had their place, but that was all - a place.

But in the meantime, the deal filled Pollenizer's sails full of a strong gust of financial air, allowing the company to expand and assist with funding many other companies.

As the company rose, so the whole Australian technology startup ecosystem rose with it.

Of course, Pollenizer might have been the center of gravity for the technology startup ecosystem in Sydney, but meanwhile other pools of energy were accumulating elsewhere.

Melbourne had its York Butter Factory and a separate pool of investors, while Brisbane's Fortitude Valley was starting to find its own place in the national startup ecosystem. Other technology startup accelerators were also arising in capital cities such as Perth, Adelaide and Canberra. Pollenizer was not the only golden foam rising with the wave of technology startup rejuvenation hitting Australia.

But it certainly was on the bleeding edge.

Unicorns

Over the next several years, a number of Australian technology startups would escape the early stage startup death cycle (90 percent of small businesses fail within the first several years) and start to grow into legitimate companies.

Some of these companies have essentially become household names in the technology sector, and at least one (Atlassian) has achieved the Holy Grail of Silicon Valley: Becoming a billion dollar company ... a *'unicorn'*.

Envato, founded in 2006, would eventually grow to a size of about 260 staff through its model of operating a number of online marketplaces for web designers, with themes, code snippets and plugins, graphics, video, audio and photography all on offer. The company is headquartered in Melbourne.

Sydney's Campaign Monitor became a large global company specialising in providing hosting services allowing businesses to easily design and send email newsletters of all kinds.

Canva, also from Melbourne, offers online design tools. 99designs was another marketplace providing online access to thousands of freelance designers. Redbubble provided a way for artists to monetise their artworks online.

Nitro achieved global success with its innovative PDF software, while Tyro started to make inroads into the Australian payments scene. Aconex provided a popular software as a service platform for construction firms.

And the list went on and on.

Of course, for every company that succeeded and went on to grow, many more failed.

Each startup launched with great fanfare, issuing media releases left and right, holding ritzy launch events or merely seeding social media with enticing lures for their products and services — whatever those might be. Each took severe umbrage at the notion that they weren't going to conquer the world — even if they didn't yet have any kind of concrete business model.

And yet most rapidly failed, running out of steam in less than a year and quietly fading away; domain names left to expire and their assets distributed to investors.

The glorious thing, however, was that this failure didn't seem to faze most of the founders involved. After a few months, they were back up and running again — either in a new startup with new partners, or helping a more established company grow more rapidly. Despite the huge and rapid company churn that was obviously happening in Australia's still-nascent technology startup sector, it seemed they were was plenty of work for anyone interested.

Atlassian

By late 2010, it was clear that Australia's technology startup scene was fully in the grip of its second boom.

The clear signal at the time was a huge investment round taken by the software firm that had emerged as the poster child for that boom: Atlassian.

The company was famously founded in 2002 by two software engineers who had met while studying at the University of New South Wales in Sydney. The pair maxed out a $10,000 credit card to get things started.

It didn't take long before Atlassian released its first product, Jira — a project and issue tracker that provided an easy to use tool for software-driven projects to track their work. Before long, the company had picked up a number of clients and started launching more products to expand its suite, such as Confluence, a team collaboration platform.

As the global software development industry went through a transition from traditional, 'waterfall', methods of software development to embrace the new, 'agile' way of working, often using cloud computing platforms, they went looking for innovative products to support that change. And Atlassian was right there with its many customers on that journey.

Like Pollenizer, Atlassian was selling shovels in the midst of a gold rush.

By July 2010, it had become apparent to Atlassian's founders, Mike Cannon-Brookes and Scott Farquhar, that they had an extremely hot product on their hands — a company which had the potential to expand globally, joining the ranks of industry titans like Microsoft, Oracle and Amazon.

This led the pair to knocking on many doors in the famed US tech hub of Silicon Valley, where they found ideal partners in venture capital firm Access Partners. Atlassian outlined its plans to eventually go public on a US exchange such as the tech-focused Nasdaq; and Accel provided the perfect support — $60 million in investment capital and access to its expertise[210] — considered amongst the best globally for fast-growing technology firms.

The investment should have been purely good news — and it was a success story which Cannon-Brookes and Farquhar were keen to talk up to the media as an example of how great Australian companies could conquer the world. They hoped their success would show the way for others to follow in their footsteps.

And yet, the funding round also created a substantial debate.

Diverging paths

The problem with the Accel investment in Atlassian was that it created a bittersweet situation for some in Australia's technology sector.

Most in the industry were honestly happy for Atlassian and its success, but there was also some surprise that the company had not considered taking investment from Australian financial sources. The nature of the Accel investment effectively meant that US investors — not Australians — would reap a substantial chunk of the rewards from the rapid growth of an Australian software enterprise.

Atlassian perhaps accelerated this debate by utilising the high profile media opportunity of its investment news to take a swipe at the Australian scene, and the regulatory environment underpinning it.

The company's co-founder, Mike Cannon-Brookes said at the time that some internationally saw the Australian business climate as *"a bit sketchy"*.

Issues such as the (Labor) Federal Government's infamous mining tax, he said, *"scare people"*. And the nation's high taxation rate could also scare off investors. *"We had to work through some of those issues,"* he said[211].

Cannon-Brookes noted that there were a number of solid Australian venture capital firms operating locally ... but he also claimed that the amount of money and management expertise that Accel offered would be hard to find in Australia.

"The Australian market for technology companies is pretty anaemic," he said at the time.

There was also the fact that Atlassian's eventual stated aim was to list on the US-based NASDAQ exchange.

This would place Atlassian in premium company alongside many other giant technology multinationals, and gift the company with a huge amount of global exposure. But again, it necessarily involved the company eschewing Australian investment to focus on the US heavyweights.

Emotions ran high during the eventual debate which ensued from this investment. And not everyone spoke purely with words.

Another high-profile entrepreneur, Matt Barrie, took note of the Atlassian experience at the time. And later on, when his own phenomenally successful company, online marketplace Freelancer.com, was the subject of a $400 million offer from a Japanese firm, Barrie made his own highly visible statement in response to the debate about foreign investment in Australian technology startups.

Barrie turned down the offer and listed his company on the Australian Stock Exchange instead, stating that it had been his opinion for years that it was *"a national imperative"* to build the technology industry up in Australia[212].

Barrie added at the time: *"We need to build the ASX up for technology like we have for resources. We have been spectacularly good at that – more money has been raised on the ASX in the last five years than NASDAQ."*[213]

The Freelancer founder wasn't trying to tweak the noses of the celebrated Atlassian founders. But there was no doubt that his approach and personal views on how to build a great Australian tech startup sector ran directly contrary to theirs.

Barrie's actions went on to have a significant impact on Australia's technology sector, with many dozens more early stage technology concerns going on over the succeeding several years to list on the local bourse.

The net effect has been a substantial education campaign that has brought Australian investors up to speed with the differing nature of rapidly growing technology companies; including how to judge their financial success and plan investments in them. Australian investors are now much more comfortable with — even enthusiastic about — ploughing money into hyped

Australian tech startups. Barrie can personally claim a great deal of credit for this situation.

As a side note, it has also resulted in a number of fascinating outlier situations.

Take, for example, the Australian cryptocurrency mining ventures that conducted reverse listing procedures on the ASX, essentially gaining a back door onto the stock market by acquiring failed mining companies. This created the very futuristic situation of companies which had made their income mining for physical assets giving way to those who mine for virtual gold — usually using the 'Bitcoin' standard.

This trend, in turn, spurred further investment in the technology sector.

Over the next several years, tens of millions of dollars started pouring into the venture capital scene, directly targeted at early stage investment in the Australian technology sector. Companies like BlackBird Ventures and others launched[214] , backed by many of the same Australian technology entrepreneurs who had already seen their companies succeed beyond their wildest dreams.

By 2015, even Australia's conservative and slow moving superannuation funds had started to get in on the action[215] ; realising that it was just common sense to invest a tiny proportion of their investment capital in fast-growing technology companies which might occasionally drive an outsized return.

A greater truth

It's a good story.

But The Frustrated State is not about good stories being told about Australia's technology industry. If it is about anything, it is exploring how there could be many more good stories — and of a greater magnitude — had our political sector maintained a little more nous about this highest growth of all growth industries.

In hindsight, there are two truths which became readily apparent from the differing paths which the most successful technology startups to come out of Australia over the past decade have taken.

Firstly, it is clear that each approach is valid.

The approach taken by Atlassian and followers such as BigCommerce by taking US investment capital and potentially listing overseas is valid and can lead to growth and financial return, as well as the possibility for strong reinvestment in the Australian technology startup ecosystem.

The different approach taken by Freelancer to list locally, in addition to others such as online retailer Kogan, is also valid and similarly helps to boost the Australian technology ecosystem and unlock further investment through investor education.

There is room for both.

But the greater, all-encompassing truth which the debate over the divergent investment approaches exposed was that the industry was surviving — and, in fact, thriving — without much in the way of government support at all.

What the debate between the differing approaches taken by Atlassian and Freelancer exposed was that there was a fundamental lack of vision from the Federal Government on the issue of growing Australia's technology industry.

There was no support from Government to bolster the underlying innovation and funding ecosystems either way — either through attracting foreign investment or educating local financiers. Without such support and guidance — without any obvious path at all — the industry had been left to choose its own direction.

Sometimes this worked out well, as in the case of the ASX listings of Freelancer and many other firms, and in Atlassian's global success.

But just as often it had negative consequences such as high-flying technology entrepreneurs leaving Australian shores to set up shop overseas due to a lack of local support; or the fact that investment returns from the success of Australia-based tech startups sometimes also went overseas, instead of remaining in local hands and possibly being reinvested. In many cases, successful Australian tech startups no longer saw any point to being headquartered Down Under on a permanent basis, and either left or sold out to foreign buyers.

Any objective analysis would have to conclude that Australia was not taking full advantage of the wins that we did have in the tech startup sector. As a nation, we were not leveraging that success to the hilt, the way some other countries were. Policy was not aligned with the direction of the industry; not supporting its success; and was in fact even hindering it.

It took Australia's tech startup sector a while to fully realise these facts, and the Government's almost complete lack of interest in making redress. After all, the sector had only just gotten up onto its feet after the first dot com crash.

But eventually the sector did wake up somewhat, and started engaging with Federal, State and Local Governments around the country.

Lobbying

The most visible group to form for the purpose of representing Australia's tech startups to government dubbed itself StartupAUS.

Formed in Sydney in 2013 by a veritable 'who's who' list of successful technology entrepreneurs and venture capitalists — including many of those who had featured so prominently at Pollenizer's parties — StartupAUS started making political noise, especially in Canberra.

The group was led by its outspoken chief executive Peter Bradd, who had shot to public attention after helping found the Sydney co-working space Fishburners. The space would go on to become home to over 150 tech startups, and form a second center of gravity for the sector in Sydney.

StartupAUS' first major lobbying effort arrived in force in 2014. The organisation produced what it billed as the first comprehensive plan to boost Australia's technology startup ecosystem; a report which it distributed widely to the media and to politicians directly.

It also served as a blueprint detailing what had gone wrong in the sector over the past decade, through the lack of government attention.

The report highlighted a number of key issues facing Australia, including the fact that Australia's startup sector was maturing at a slower rate than many other nations; that high-growth tech companies had the potential to contribute 4 percent of the nation's GDP by 2033, compared to just 0.2 percent today (adding 540,000 jobs to the economy); and that in 2013, Australia invested just $4.5 per capita in venture vapital for start-ups, compared to $120 in Israel, $85 in the US, $20 in South Korea and $15 in the UK.

If that wasn't enough, the report also found in general that Australia's startup ecosystem was lagging behind those of many other developed nations, and faced several profound challenges that were hampering its growth and the nation's ability to transition to a knowledge-intensive economy.

The Crossroads report noted that the conditions for a successful startup system had not yet been successfully established, primarily due to market failures in areas such as education, expertise, access to capital and regulatory support.

And the picture ahead was not looking rosy.

The report found that up to 70 percent of Australia's total economic activity was services-based, and subject to digital disruption, due to the wave of technology-led change that had already started to sweep across other countries.

Put simply: Australia was missing out on the potential to capitalise on the new wave of knowledge industries which the second dot com boom was helping to create.

Our tech startup sector had gotten back to its knees after the first dot com crash. But it would struggle to get further without underlying supporting structures that could only be set by government.

And at the same time, many of our existing, legacy industries were under direct threat by that very same technological innovation.

"The consequences of action or inaction will be plain to see and because of the exponential nature of technology-driven change, Australia has the potential to pass a point of no return and be permanently relegated to a derivative economy," warned the report's author, Adrian Turner.

Turner was himself an entrepreneur who had created several companies, and written a whole book on the topic of digital disruption — *Blue Sky Mining: Creating Australia's Next Billion Dollar Industries.*

Again, it was many of the same entrepreneurs and investors who had been orbiting around Pollenizer years ago that were instrumental in creating this landmark report.

Bradd, local venture capitalist Bill Bartee, Cannon-Brookes, 99designs founding investor Leni Mayo, Blue Chilli chief growth hacker Alan Jones, Liubinskas, and Niki Scevak, who had gone to university with the Atlassian boys and went on to become a significant entrepreneur and investor in his own right, were all involved.

The report made a series of simple recommendations to help fix the mess.

Some were focused on driving immediate benefits, such as relaxing visa and 457 working regulations for entrepreneurs and workers with ICT skills; changing the tax treatment for Employee Share Ownership programs to incentivise workers to join and stay with startups; funding trade missions to locations such as Silicon Valley; and setting up a landing pad in Silicon Valley for startups expanding overseas.

Others were designed to have an impact over the medium- to long-term, such as investing in universities and incubators to support skills and business development, removing disincentives for experienced Australian entrepreneurs to repatriate from overseas, and supporting local investment through direct matched government investment and establishing government-backed seed funds.

Implementing legislative changes to enable the increasingly popular crowd-sourced equity funding model was also on the medium-term wishlist, as was creating a capital gains tax exemption and/or tax deduction for angel investments.

And there were even foundational improvements such as ensuring that computer science was taught in every primary and high school in Australia.

The point was made repeatedly in the StartupAUS Crossroads report that these were not initiatives which should be difficult for the Federal Government to progress. Many of them had already been enacted in a number of savvy countries overseas, and many were expected to actually make the Government a long-term sizeable return, either through direct investment returns or increased taxation income.

The only problem was that the report fell on death ears.

Problems with both sides

The problem that StartupAUS and other likeminded groups faced — even with the ammunition provided by the Crossroads report and other similar material — was that, like other digitally native industries such as the video game development sector, they found it hard to get a hearing at all from Australia's top politicians and political parties.

At the time the Crossroads report was delivered — May 2014 — Tony Abbott was firmly entrenched as Australia's 28th Prime Minister.

The Member for Warringah had come to power after many years of publicly highlighting his lack of interest in — and at times, antipathy to — policies which would actively support Australia's technology sector.

During the 2010 Federal Election, Abbott had pronounced himself *"no Bill Gates"*, during an infamous interview with Kerry O'Brien on the 7:30 Report[216], and he had followed up with a series of similar statements regarding what he saw as the pointless nature of major projects such as the NBN, which Abbott purported to see as little more than an entertainment platform, suitable for distributing television content and supporting the nation's youth to waste their time playing video games.

"The man is a luddite," said Communications Minister Stephen Conroy in 2010[217]. And it appeared much of the nation agreed.

Perhaps because of the PM's lack of interest in the technology sector, in Abbott's administration there was no Federal Minister dedicated to handling innovation policy. There was a Minister for Industry and Science, but the holder of that title, Ian Macfarlane, appeared more interested in supporting the interests of the mining industry than talking to technology entrepreneurs.

Abbott appeared to confirm his antipathy for the tech sector in general when asked a question by Opposition Leader

Bill Shorten in May 2015 about the Government's support for teaching coding in schools.

Most first-world countries view this simple educational framework as a key plank of their ability to build lucrative knowledge industries and improve living standards. But Australia's 28th Prime Minister replied[218]:

"Let's just understand exactly what the Leader of the Opposition has asked. He said that he wants primary school kids to be taught coding so they can get the jobs of the future. Does he want to send them all out to work at the age of 11? Is that what he wants to do? Seriously? Seriously?"

Labor was proving a more receptive target. Right around the country, Labor State Government administrations had started actively ploughing money into supporting the technology startup sector.

Annastacia Palaszczuk's Labor Government in Queensland, for example, revealed plans in July 2015 to throw $24 million at the state's rapidly expanding startup sector, as part of a much wider $180 million package of reforms aimed at creating *"jobs of the future"[219]*.

In Victoria, Minister for Trade and Investment Philip Dalidakis — a former protege of Stephen Conroy — was doing a roaring trade enticing tech multinationals to set up their local headquarters in Melbourne. And even the NSW Liberal Government was getting into the act.

But Labor had its own problems with the technology sector to deal with.

Back in 2009, the then-Labor Federal Government had damaged the tech startup sector's Australian interests by passing tax law changes that sought to rein in the ability of some employees to achieve better rates of taxation by placing some of their remuneration in company stock.

As anyone who's been employed by early stage startups will attest, they don't usually pay wages and salaries at market rates - but instead attract talent by offering workers stock options that could prove extremely lucrative, should the startup achieve financial success.

Labor's legal changes had largely removed this tool from Australian startups' toolbox, making it hard for them to attract the best talent. And the party's ongoing changes to immigration legislation — designed to protect Australian workers from cheap overseas labor — didn't precisely endear the party to entrepreneurs either.

In short, the cost of hiring, paying and firing skilled workers in Australia … was just too damn high — due to many Labor policies which had been designed to protect workforces, not stimulate industry growth.

The share issue had become so contentious by February 2014 that even consulting giant Deloitte was producing whitepapers arguing for a change[220]. The Coalition had promised to take a look at the issue … but again, it didn't precisely move very far under Abbott's Prime Ministership.

And that wasn't the only thing that was being sat on.

During the previous Labor administration, the Parliament had undertaken a review into the capital financing requirements of IT startups. Evidence had been taken, experts had been consulted, and recommendations had been tabled as to how the situation could be improved in Australia. Again, common sense suggestions were on the table.

But successive Labor administrations — Gillard's, Rudd's, and then Abbott's, had done nothing with the report.

Under these three Prime Ministers, innovation policy in general was squarely on the backburner.

It would take a fundamental change of political leadership to break this circuit.

Enter Turnbull

Malcolm Turnbull has, at many points, had a bad rap within the pages of The Frustrated State.

There is much to criticise about the Member for Wentworth's handling of technology policy. On a number of issues — notably the National Broadband Network — many believe that Turnbull has mishandled technology policy, leading to outcomes for Australians that could be described as unfavourable.

However, when it comes to innovation policy — the policy that supports the development of technology startups — it must be said that Australia's 29th Prime Minister was precisely the breath of fresh air that the nation needed.

Upon ascending to the Prime Ministership in mid-2015, Turnbull wasted no time rectifying the mistakes of the past.

In his very first press conference after taking the throne from Abbott, Turnbull took the time to publicly note that Australians were facing disruption from technology, and that the Government needed to work to take advantage of that trend, rather than rejecting it.

In his first comments to a brief media conference in Parliament House in Canberra[221], Turnbull emphasised that he wanted the Australia of the future to be *"agile, innovative and creative"*.

At the time, the Member for Wentworth said that Australia needed to recognise that the disruption that was occuring driven by technological change was *"our friend"*, if the nation was agile and smart enough to take advantage of it. *"There has never been a more exciting time to be alive than today,"* the PM-elect said. *"There has never been a more exciting time to be an Australian."*

If we look back to Chapter Three of the Frustrated State, we demonstrated that Turnbull has primarily viewed technology as a tool for business.

This view did not serve Turnbull well during his time as a Liberal MP, Shadow Minister and then Communications

Minister in Tony Abbott's Coalition administration. It led to poor outcomes for the National Broadband Network, which must necessarily be seen as a public good, far beyond its business utility.

But if you apply Turnbull's beliefs to the tech startup sector, what is apparent is that they did serve him well in that area.

It took only a few short months holding the Prime Ministership for Turnbull to radically change the Federal Government's approach to the tech sector.

In early December 2015 — a little over three months after taking the reins of leadership — Turnbull released his flagship innovation policy.

Dubbed the National Science and Innovation Agenda, the policy could have been written by the tech startup sector itself, so closely did it mirror its wishes. Virtually every area mentioned by the scores of reports into Australian innovation which had come before — including StartupAUS' Crossroads report — was addressed[222].

Early stage investors were gifted taxation concessions, as were Australia's venture capitalists. New rules governed how companies could treat intellectual property for depreciation purposes. The CSIRO — Australia's science flagship — received $200 million for an early stage innovation fund and a further $20 million for an accelerator program.

Incubators and accelerators such as Pollenizer won $8 million, and bankruptcy laws which have allowed many US companies to come back from the brink of failure were also to be legislated. The controversial Employee Share Scheme problem was to be knocked on the head with new legislation, and there was plenty of new funding for research infrastructure, university grants, and innovation 'landing pads' in tech-savvy locations such as Silicon Valley and Tel Aviv.

The list of policy initiatives outed by Turnbull in December 2015 seemed almost limitless; a slam dunk for the nation's tech sector. Here, finally, was the government support that the industry had been needing for a decade.

It felt like manna from heaven.

Learnings

This was obviously good news for Australia's tech startups. It was a once in a generation policy initiative that represented a watershed moment for all of their hopes. And of course, it was broadly received as such, garnering strong praise from many in the industry. Some, of course, thought the new policy didn't go far enough, and many others would never forgive the new Prime Minister for his controversial reshaping of the NBN, no matter what other good he did.

But the arrival of this all-encompassing vision — representing a huge grab-bag of everything tech startups could ever have asked for — only ultimately brought more questions for the underlying process.

How is it possible, for instance, that Australia's national innovation policy could have swung 100 percent — from complete ignorance to complete acceptance — through merely changing the Prime Minister? When that change happened within the same party?

How is it possible that successive Government administrations on both the Labor and Coalition side of the political fence could have ignored innovation policy for the past decade?

Why did it take the actions of one interested individual — one Prime Minister — Malcolm Turnbull — to swing the situation around 180 degrees, in just a few short months of taking the leadership?

In short, why is the policy formation process around this highly important industry — an industry which will remain critical to Australia's future economic success — so goddamned fickle?

What is apparent from the failure of innovation policy in Australia over the past 15 years since the first dot com crash is that all of the existing structures for policy development failed the sector in that time.

Successive Federal Government administrations ignored many reports from Parliamentary committees recommending common sense innovation reforms. They ignored industry and media pressure for reform. For many years, they ignored their own backbenchers (Wyatt Roy from the LNP and Ed Husic from Labor being notable examples who have spent years of effort advocating for startup issues behind the scenes in their party rooms).

State Governments came to the party sooner — driven, perhaps, by the need to remain competitive in the war for corporate talent and economic development against other states. But even State Governments started supporting Australia's tech startup sector perhaps five years after it would have been prudent for them to do so.

It is also apparent that the personal motivations and actions of just one man — if they be Prime Minister — is enough to change the strategy of a whole government.

Solutions

If we are being honest, at this point, there are no easy solutions to the quandary which this chapter poses the reader.

It's easy to argue that the solution to the ignorance which Australia's Federal Government has shown the nation's tech startup sector over most of the past 15 years could be solved by closer integration of the political sector with industry. But this does not explain the intimate relationship which some industries — such as resources or agriculture — have long enjoyed with politicians, while others are left out in the cold.

It's also easy to argue that the power over policy development and industry regulatory reviews should be taken out of the hands of the few, and systematised. But this already happens — through the Parliamentary Committee process and in many other forums.

In truth, the answer to this issue lies somewhere in between process, the personal and political.

It is incumbent upon industries seeing support to do everything they can to ethically lobby government and other groups such as the media for that support. It is incumbent upon politicians to keep an open mind and an open door during this process, while still keeping in mind broader community expectations. And it is incumbent upon all players in the democratic process to take the process of parliamentary investigation and review more seriously — so that the scores of reports emanating from Parliamentary and Government Committees do not go ignored.

In this fraught political nexus lies great opportunity for Australia's promising industries to receive the support they need.

We can only hope the lesson of the tech startup sector's second coming is not forgotten, the next time a high-growth industry comes around with a good story to tell.

As for Australia's tech startup sector, one gets the feeling that it is only just now getting started.

Many of the attendees at Pollenizer's parties a decade ago are now in positions of influence and are still pushing for change.

Scott Farquhar, who allegedly tried to hide Mick Liubinskas' normal clothes on the night of the Christmas party that he wore a spectacular red dress for, is now one of Australia's richest tech billionaires. In November 2017 — as this book was in the final stages of getting ready for publication — he warned changes to the visa immigration system could stunt the growth of local tech companies[223].

"I don't think Australian startups have a loud enough voice in government yet," he said. *"In fact the plumbers' union is probably better organised than the startup community in terms of lobbying government ..."*

SUMMARY

Policy Details

Over much of the past decade, there has been a fundamental lack of vision from the Federal Government on the issue of growing Australia's technology industry. This was understandable following the dot com crash in the late 1990's and early 2000's. However, the industry has substantially revived since that time.

Despite this, over this period there has been little support from Government to bolster the underlying innovation and funding ecosystems. Without such support and guidance — without any obvious path at all — the industry had been left to choose its own direction.

What Went Wrong

Successive Federal Governments had failed to heed the recommendations of its own Parliamentary committees in setting appropriate industry policy regarding the tech sector.

In addition, policymakers did not appear to be keeping a close enough eye on the industry to realise that investment in tech startups, and the number of Australian tech startups being formed, had recovered since the first dot com crash.

Avoiding This Situation in Future

Government should heed committee recommendations — particularly where bipartisan reports exist — in setting industry policy, in addition to backbenchers with specialised knowledge.

In addition, Governments should be wary of letting individuals guide the entire policy landscape. The polar opposite approaches taken by successive Prime Ministers Tony Abbott and Malcolm Turnbull demonstrate how just one man — if they be Prime Minister — can act as a strong enabling or disabling force, affecting the interests of entire sectors.

CHAPTER 8

Interception

*"Nobody could say this has
been a rushed process."*

—Attorney-General George Brandis

The hour is very late, and George Brandis is getting irritated. The Liberal Senator from Queensland is, despite the unfavourable epithets often flung his way by political opponents, genuinely a patient and highly considered man.

He did not rise through the ranks of the Queensland legal profession to the lofty position of Queen's Counsel over the past several decades by accident. He did it through hard work, long hours, and an eye for the subtle niceties of the law which has earned him a strong reputation amongst his peers.

Neither did he arrive at the position of Attorney-General of the Commonwealth of Australia by accident. Brandis applied the same patience, diligence and tenacity to his political life as he did his profession; and with the same results.

There is no doubt that his tendency to make black and white pronouncements sometimes places him at odds with his colleagues in Malcolm Turnbull's Cabinet; and sometimes the public. To George Brandis, sometimes tradition and his own strongly cast view of how the world should be dictate that the correct outcome of an issue appears obvious to him; but not to others.

And yet none would doubt the Senator's ability, when the chips are down.

However, tonight Brandis is facing many of those same qualities in his opponents across the Senate Chamber floor.

On one side of the Chamber sits the Greens Senator Scott Ludlam; a politician known as much for his tenacious ability to draw details from faceless bureaucrats during marathon Senate Estimates Committee hearings as he is for the stunningly flamboyant hair which has set hearts fluttering across the continent.

Ludlam and Brandis have been locking horns for years, on a wide variety of issues. They're intellectual equals, but there is an emotional mutual contempt between the pair that is often palpable when they're in the same room. Ludlam most likely sees Brandis as a conservative fuddy duddy, locked in a past that never existed and with an outmoded vision of the future that will never come to pass; Brandis probably views Ludlam as an ill-informed left-wing radical that he'd be happy to see the back of.

They're both smart people. But they just don't like each other.

In the middle sits one of Australia's most cunning masters of the political arts; the maverick independent Senator Nick Xenophon, whose talent for completely shameless self-deprecating humour is matched only by his knack for political opportunism. Both have won him favour with his South Australian constituency. And like Brandis, he's a lawyer and a stickler for the niceties of the law.

You never really get the feeling that Xenophon doesn't like anyone in particular; he seems to get along with the leaders of every political persuasion.

However, like Ludlam, he often locks horns with Brandis.

The occasion is the Senate debate over the controversial *Telecommunications (Interception and Access) Amendment (Data Retention) Bill 2015.*

The hour is getting late indeed; and George Brandis is getting irritated.

Senator Xenophon has been discussing the legal situation regarding telephone tapping and email logging in the US. It's a subject the South Australian maverick has researched thoroughly; and he makes his points about the issue clearly. But his efforts win him little ground with Brandis.

"You are wrong!" Brandis tells his fellow Senator in a confident tone. And he goes on, to explain, at length, why he believes this to be the case. Then, after having made his argument, he addresses his Ministerial Advisor, Justin Bassi, who is sitting close to him in the Senate chairs set aside for political aides[224].

"Is that right, Mr Bassi?" Brandis asks. *"My advisor, Mr Justin Bassi here ... is extremely well informed about these matters, about the American system. Indeed I notice he is even wearing his CIA cufflinks today in honour of the occasion — just to feed the paranoia of Senator Ludlam over there."*

Xenophon — always ready with a humorous comeback — is ready with a witticism to respond to the Attorney-General.

"I do not have a set of CIA cufflinks, unlike Mr Bassi," the South Australian Senator tells Brandis. *"I do not want a set; it's okay."*

"I say this to your advisers; to your team: I have a great regard for them. You have a pretty exceptional team, although some of them did take me to task quoting Taylor Swift rather than Britney Spears.

I think we are both missing out on cultural references, Attorney, in respect of that!"

Labor Senator Jacinta Collins accuses Xenophon of needing to *"get out more"*. *"That is right!"* he responds. *"I do not have a life, not in this place!"*

Xenophon — as is his political knack — has defused much of the tension in the Senate Chamber with humour. But there is an underlying fact here which is a little troubling.

In most countries, in most Parliamentary chambers, in most political debates, it would be an extraordinary act for the name of the CIA to be invoked. The foreign intelligence agency of the United States is a hugely influential force globally; and one that has close links with many of its counterparts internationally, including in Australia. One does not invoke its name lightly; one does so only in a very considered manner.

But this is not precisely a highly considered situation.

The year is 2015. It's Australia, and this is the fraught and explosive debate which our Federal Parliament is having over highly contested data retention legislation. Mention of CIA cufflinks is perhaps only one of the minor extraordinary items on this year's agenda.

Welcome to ground zero in Australia's data retention war.

Reality

I want to start this chapter by noting right up front that this section of The Frustrated State is not about the question of whether some form of data retention powers — the ability of law enforcement and intelligence officials to legally access telephone, SMS and email call logs — are necessary.

In fact, most participants in Australia's extremely long-running debate about the issue of data retention would acknowledge that they are, at least in some form.

After all, we live in dangerous times.

Hyperbole aside, the risks to public safety posed by factors such as terrorism and violent criminal activity — not to mention the kind of petty crime and violence which are common in major metropolitan areas — are obvious and widespread. At the same time, the resources allocated to our law enforcement and intelligence agencies are never quite what they should be.

We also live in a time in which the criminal element has access to greater resources than ever for keeping their activities secret.

Technologies such as encryption, the remote hacking of computers, mobile phones and computer networks, sophisticated counterfeiting techniques and even the ability to 3D print a handgun in the privacy of your own home are now extremely commonplace and widespread. They are demonstrably being used by criminals and terrorists — in Australia and in every other country — to mask their activities.

To have any hope at all of keeping up with the bad guys — let alone stopping some forms of extremely dangerous crime before it is committed — our police officers and intelligence agencies need access to powers which criminals and terrorists do not have — such as the ability to request logs from telecommunications companies of who called who — and from where. Or the ability to see who may have emailed dangerous secret documents to who, and when.

It is also commonly agreed that clear limits should be placed on these powers to ensure they are not abused.

In this context then, almost all of the debate in the data retention space relates to the question of how much power should be granted to law enforcement and intelligence agencies; and precisely how that power should be limited and governed. It's not the black and white strokes which are important here — but the grey zone in between the extremes.

This chapter is not about that debate about where the lines should lie. It's an important topic, but a bigger one than we could examine in these pages — fit for a whole separate book of its own.

In this context, and congruent with the overall theme of the Frustrated State — Government mismanagement of technology policy — this chapter is about the mismanagement of the implementation of a data retention regime in Australia, rather than the question of whether one is needed or not.

In the beginning

As stated earlier in this chapter, there is a broad consensus in the Australian community that some level of legal data retention powers are necessary for effective law enforcement and intelligence work; but that limits and controls should be placed upon this access.

These dual concepts have, for many decades, underpinned the telecommunications regulatory environment that most Australians grew up in.

There were predecessors to it, but most of our modern understanding of this type of access regime in Australia comes from legislation passed decades ago; the *Telecommunications (Interception and Access) Act 1979*.

The TIA Act has long prohibited the interception of communications passing over a telecommunications system, as well as prohibiting access to 'stored communications' (i.e. email, SMS and voice mail messages stored on a carrier's equipment), except where authorised in specified circumstances.

The primary exception to these rules is to enable law enforcement agencies to lawfully intercept or access telecommunications in certain circumstances, pursuant to an interception warrant or a stored communications warrant issued under the TIA Act. A small number of other exceptions are specified for particular purposes, including tracing the location of callers in emergencies, and the fundamental operation and maintenance of telecommunications systems.

The thing to understand about the *Telecommunications (Interception And Access) Act 1979* is that for a long time, it was effective at allowing law enforcement to access the information they needed to get the job done.

As the Australian Federal Police wrote in its March 2014 submission to an inquiry set up by Senator Ludlam into the potential to comprehensively revise the TIA Act[225]:

"The provisions that allow the AFP to intercept, access and receive information relating to communications have proven essential in assisting the AFP to meet the mandate set for it by Government to enforce the criminal law of the Commonwealth and protect Australia from threats to national security."

There were two reasons for this success.

The first was that until the early 1990's, when the first tranche of deregulation took place across Australia's telecommunications industry, introducing some level of competition for the first time, data retention essentially meant that one Government agency — usually state or Federal Police, or an intelligence agency such as the Australian Security Intelligence Organisation (ASIO) — merely needed to request the data it required from another - the Australian Telecommunications Commission.

The ATC was commonly known as Telecom — and then 'Telstra', from 1993.

And it wasn't until 1997, when a second wave of reforms hit the industry duopoly (with Telstra primarily owning and operating Australia's fixed line infrastructure and Optus doing the same for satellite) that substantial numbers of other players started entering the industry.

This move, and the associated first tranche of privatisation of Telstra (T1) meant that suddenly law enforcement and intelligence agencies had to start dealing with a range of private corporations to get access to what had essentially previously been government-owned data.

The other reason was that the basic nature of the technology involved in communications in Australia changed.

Until the Internet started to take off in Australia in the 1990's — with all of its features supporting anonymity of communication — communications essentially meant placing calls or faxes via a telephone network. The fact that Telstra and every other telco was logging all of the data associated with these calls was self-evident by virtue of the fact that a complete, itemised list showed up on your monthly bill.

With these changes — to industry structure and to technology — came a corresponding need for the associated legislation to be updated.

As the AFP told Senator Ludlam's inquiry:

"Reform is not a bid for more powers but an attempt to maintain existing capability in an increasingly complex environment. In 1979 when Telecom was the only telecommunications provider, and fixed land-line telephony was the only means to communicate over a network, the AFP had a comprehensive ability to identify and attribute services back to individuals, and to then lawfully obtain any telephone based communications."

In its submission, the AFP went on to discuss the issue of whether the TIA Act continued to be effective in light of ongoing technological changes.

"The experience of the AFP is that it does not," the agency wrote.

"Even with periodic amendments to the TIA Act, the ability of agencies to effectively intercept, access and identify communications has not kept pace with the: Diversity of the evolving telecommunications and digital landscape; Increasing use of sophisticated forms of encryption; Emergence of new categories of industry participants; and changing criminal use of communications."

Enter OzLog

With this extensive history of the TIA Act in mind, updating the *Telecommunications (Interception and Access) Act 1979* to take into account the changed industry structure and technological developments should not have been that much of a complicated exercise.

And in fact, by the mid 2000's, when the need for an update became apparent, a number of other other jurisdictions had already made similar moves.

The most notable of these legislative shifts was the Data Retention Directive[226] passed by the European Parliament in March 2006. The directive forced EU member states to store the telecommunications data of their citizens for between 6 and 24 months. Police and other security agencies would be able to request access to details such as IP addresses, time and date information relating to phone calls, emails and text messages.

Critically, access to the data would be regulated by a court.

The EU Data Retention Directive had a structural flaw, in that it lacked specific protections for a wide range of individuals that require professional privacy under the law — including physicians, journalists, lawyers and so on.

In addition, some privacy advocates felt that it represented an overreach law that did not provide the fine-grained controls which such a powerful measure should.

But at its heart, it contained a great deal of common sense. It was the kind of law that would be expected to be passed in the digital age. It dealt with changing technology; yet simultaneously avoided the worst excesses of data retention, in that it did not log people's web browsing history; and it regulated access to the retained data via a court.

Yet when the concept of updating Australia's own data retention regime suddenly came to the forefront of Australia's national security policy discussion in June 2010, many of these lessons appeared to have been lost on government policy makers.

For starters, the fact that there actually was live policy discussion around updating the TIA Act only came to light as the result of an article published by tech media outlet ZDNet[227].

That article initially stated that the Government — which was at that point reeling from Julia Gillard's leadership coup only a month before — was looking to retain Australians' web browsing history, in addition to telephone, SMS and email logs.

The web browsing angle was quickly hosed down, as the Attorney-General's Department, which was leading the proposed legislative reforms, pointed the shocked media at the EU Data Retention Directive and its court-controlled access to metadata.

But in Senate hearings in October that year — after allowing months of frenzied speculation as to what was actually going on — a set of AGD public servants (who appeared to be discomfited by the need to discuss the data retention issue in public at all) admitted relevant policy discussions had been going on for years[228], involving both industry and law enforcement organisations .

One senior AGD public servant admitted they could not precisely remember when discussions around the issue commenced.

"Can I say it's been around for a very long time — I can't remember how it started," they said.

Under sustained pressure from Ludlam, the public servants revealed the origins of the project related to the way that law enforcement authorities and certain branches of government such as AGD had been working with the telecommunications industry for years on the issue of telecommunications interception to aid in crime-fighting.

What developed from that point onward was what appeared to be a very complex and prolonged cat and mouse game between the media, crossbench politicians such as Ludlam, and the Government, which appeared to be at pains throughout much of the process to block the public from knowing what specific policy options it was considering, and who it was discussing them with.

Throughout this process, one question kept on coming up again and again.

The need to update the TIA Act was relatively obvious, even if there was substantial debate about the specific details which would make up those reforms. So why was the Government trying so hard to keep its plans under wraps?

The heart of the matter

As the issue progressed over a number of years from 2010, it rapidly became apparent that there were a number of factors in play which were shaping the situation.

The first was that the Attorney-General's Department itself appeared to be demonstrating a degree of naivety about the process which would be required to actually impement the data retention concept being proposed.

In February 2013, the Pirate Party — which holds no seats in any Australian Parliament — used Freedom of Information laws to force the Department to release a treasure trove of documents pertaining to its data retention efforts.

A close examination of the documents appeared to imply that the Department might not have had a firm grasp on the technical, operational and commercial underpinnings which would be required to make an enhanced data retention regime work in Australia[229].

In short, it could be possible that the Government was unwilling to discuss the issue of data retention in detail publicly because — despite having had years to develop a coherent policy — its own understanding of the topic had not yet fully matured.

It is certainly possible that the Government did, indeed, have a nuanced view of data retention behind the scenes. It had the resources, after all, of the law enforcement and intelligence agencies to draw upon. But if it did have this nuanced view, it did not appear to be displaying it in a way that would drive public confidence in the proposals.

The second factor was the reticence of major ISPs to get involved in the process.

Telstra and Optus — with their origins in government — were used to acquiescing to surveillance requests. They had concerns about the proposed new data retention regime — especially who would shoulder its obvious costs — but ultimately saw it as a cost of doing business.

But the newer telcos — players such as iiNet, Internode, TPG and more — did not have the same background. These were companies which had grown up during the deregulated era post-1997, and had never had the kind of onerous regulatory controls levied upon them that Telstra and Optus had. So they fought back against what they saw as burdensome regulation[230].

In 2010, an iiNet spokesperson admitted the telco had been briefed about the data retention proposal as early as 2009. But the company — and a number of other major Internet service providers — had privacy and cost concerns about the proposal.

"... our estimate is that complying with such a scheme would require a large datacentre storing possibly 20 thousand terabytes of data at a cost of around $60 million," iiNet told Ludlam's Senate inquiry in 2014. *"There is no indication that the government would pay these costs."*

Others objected to the ideal on principle.

"My personal view is that it is an insanely difficult and expensive process to implement that serves exactly no purpose whatsoever — in other words nanny state gone totally insane one more time by the current government," said Exetel chief executive John Linton[231].

In short, the Government had not been able to get the whole of the telecommunications industry on-side for its date retention proposal.

The third factor was the nature of the public service itself.

At this stage of the Federal political cycle, the Attorney-General's chair had become something of a revolving door.

When the data retention reforms were first being discussed within the Attorney-General's Department, Labor's Robert Mc-Clelland was the Attorney-General, a post he held throughout the Rudd and Gillard administrations until December 2011.

But from that point on, a succession of qualified lawyers stepped in to take the reins — firstly Nicola Roxon in the Gillard years, then Mark Dreyfus, who remained in the post until Kevin Rudd lost the 2013 Federal Election to Tony Abbott. Brandis took the post from that point and remained in it through the Abbott and Turnbull administrations, before eventually resigning from the Senate in February 2018 to take a position as Australia's High Commissioner to the United Kingdom.

And yet, despite this regular changeover at the political level, AGD itself kept on progressing the Data Retention reforms without significant policy changes. This led to an impression that it was the department itself — backed by law enforcement and intelligence agencies — that was driving the data retention agenda, rather than the political organisation leading the Government — be that Labor or the Coalition.

Prominent network engineer and commentator Mark Newton — who had also been a highly visible commentator regarding the similarly controversial Internet filter policy which The Frustrated State explored in Chapter One — summed up the mood of some of the more radical elements of the anti-data retention movement, when he claimed in September 2012, relating to a Data Retention discussion paper released by Roxon[232]:

"The document is a wish-list of proposals that have been floating around police forces and Attorney-General's Department bureaucrats for years. Indeed, the Data Retention proposal discussed herein dates back to the Howard Government."

Newton wrote that every now and then, departmental bureaucrats would float these kind of data retention and surveillance reforms *"up like trial balloons"*.

Usually, he added. *"their proposers judge that the winds aren't blowing in the right direction, and they pop down again until the next opportunity to try them on. It's almost as if the proposals' owners float them every time we swear-in a new Attorney General, just to see if he or she is credulous enough to give them a permissive hearing."*

Ludlam had previously blasted the AGD public servants developing the data retention reforms, noting at the time that to get any information about the reforms, a Senate inquiry had to be initiated, and the media had to put in freedom of information requests[233].

"Rumours flourish in a vacuum, and you've created a vacuum," he said. *"If you don't trust us to tell us what it is you're doing,"* he added, *"why should we trust you to do it?"*

What all of this contributed to is an impression by the public that the Government of the day — no matter whether it was Labor or Coalition — was letting the public service take the wheel when it came to the proposed data retention reforms.

Further, the Government did not appear to be presenting a fully mature view of what would be required from a technical, commercial or operational front to progress the reforms, and did not have large portions of the Internet industry on side.

And worse, it appeared to be trying to hide this situation.

Because it had not explained its intentions in a transparent and convincing manner, industry itself was up in revolt. And the whole issue kept on blowing up in the Parliament and in public.

Behind the scenes it was causing even more trouble.

Internal dissent

It took some time after AGD's confirmation in mid-2010 that it was investigating data retention reforms for the various sides of politics to fully digest what was happening.

This isn't unusual when it comes to technology policy. Very few of the major players in the Federal arena — and only a handful of the minors — have a solid enough grasp of technology to understand the full context of what is happening in terms of new developments in this space.

But by late 2012, things had started to move behind the scenes.

The first signs that the Federal Coalition — in particular, the Liberal Party backbench — may not completely OK with the proposed reforms broke late at night on the ABC's Lateline program.

Host Emma Alberici had, by this time, herself become slightly notorious for her knowledge of the technology policy world. The host's in-depth knowledge on topics ranging from the National Broadband Network to the Internet filter and yes, Data Retention, was — at that stage — as rare amongst mainstream journalists as that same knowledge was amongst Federal parliamentarians.

Her guest on this night was Liberal backbencher Steve Ciobo. And, contrary to the carefully considered positions taken by his Liberal brethren so far on the data retention proposal, Ciobo did not hold back — unleashing on the Labor government over the issue.

"I think that this proposal is akin, frankly, to tactics that we would have seen utilised by the Gestapo or groups like that," Ciobo told Alberici[234].

Challenged about the statement on Twitter after the Lateline session, Ciobo elaborated: *"What's obscene about that statement?"* he asked. *"The only obscene thing is a proposal to monitor and record the entire population!"*

On one level, Ciobo's comments could easily be brushed off. After all, in late 2012, with Julia Gillard riding high as Prime Minister, who cared about the opinions of one lone Opposition backbencher?

But on the other hand, the MP did have a certain credibility to comment on the issue.

Ciobo is known for having an interest in technology as well as security. After being elected to the House of Representatives in 2001, the Liberal MP sat on the House of Representatives Standing Committee for Communications, Information Technology and the Arts from 2002 through 2004.

In addition, he sat on the Parliamentary Joint Committee on Intelligence and Security — the same Parliamentary committee examining the Government's Data Retention proposal — from 2005 until 2007.

Worse for those on the Coalition side who were in favour of data retention, Ciobo's comments appeared to run directly contrary to a speech made by Labor Attorney-General Nicola Roxon at around the same time.

"As you will be aware, there has been a lot of press coverage about one component of the reforms – and that is data retention," were the words that Roxon used to a speech in Canberra[235].

Roxon went on to make the case for the Data Retention reforms by referencing the 1994 murder of Cabramatta MP John Newman in Sydney.

"Call charge records and cell tower information were instrumental in the investigation and subsequent conviction on Phuong Ngo," Roxon said. *"These records allowed police to reconstruct the crime scene. Many investigations require law enforcement to build a picture of criminal activity over a period of time. Without data retention, this capability will be lost."*

It was a valid argument, and one which most of the Coalition most likely supported, despite it coming from a Labor Minister.

Yet just days later, a report from The Australian newspaper showed that Ciobo wasn't the only Coalition backbencher concerned, and that Roxon's message about the necessity of the proposed data retention reforms was falling on some deaf ears. The newspaper reported upon a veritable revolt within the Federal Coalition Party room[236]:

"A dozen Coalition MPs warned against the proposal as a restriction on civil liberties in an important signal of support for a growing online campaign against the changes."

It didn't help that the Institute of Public Affairs — a powerful conservative and free market think tank influential in Coalition politics — had damned the whole data retention idea as systematically breaching Australians' right to privacy.

Much of the IPA's concerns revolved around process, as the think tank did not believe the Government had yet made the case for its data retention proposals to go ahead.

"Significant new powers require significant justification. Yet the (Government's) discussion paper makes only a very weak attempt at explaining the rationale for the proposals," the IPA said at the time[237].

"The discussion paper makes reference to a general threat of cyber-terrorism, failing to adequately engage in the question of how these expansive powers are required to face real threats to Australia's national security."

The Coalition wasn't the only political party concerned about the proposed reforms. Labor, too, had its own problems.

It would take some time for the issue to crystallise within Labor ranks. While there was some dissent during the period of the Rudd and Gillard administrations, there was also a great deal of political discipline with Labor ranks at that time.

Nevertheless, the issue was controversial enough that then-Labor Attorney-General Mark Dreyfus took the decision in mid-2013 to shelve the introduction of the legislation until it could be more fully developed, and its issues addressed.

The move came after Federal Parliament's powerful Parliamentary Joint Committee on Intelligence and Security (PJCIS) was unable to reach a verdict on the data retention proposal as it was at that point.

During that process, the committee's chair, Anthony Byrne — a hawkish Labor MP known for his focus on national security issues — himself took the time to criticise the Attorney-General's Department over its secrecy on the Data Retention issue. He said[238]:

"The Committee was very disconcerted to find, once it commenced its Inquiry, that the Attorney-General's Department (AGD) had much more detailed information on the topic of data retention. Departmental work, including discussions with stakeholders, had been undertaken previously."

"Details of this work had to be drawn from witnesses representing the AGD. In fact, it took until the 7th November 2012 for the Committee to be provided with a formal complete definition of which data was to be retained under the data retention regime proposed by the AGD."

After the storm

The process of passing the Data Retention legislation, in the form of the *Telecommunications (Interception and Access) Amendment (Data Retention) Act 2015* was torturous. The legislation had to be reviewed by the Parliamentary Joint Committee on Intelligence and Security; dozens of amendments were filed in the Senate in an attempt to moderate the bill and provide oversight mechanisms and protection for professionals such as doctors and lawyers.

Those amendments were unsuccessful, but Labor did successfully negotiate with the Government for some key oversight mechanisms and exemptions to be included in the bill.

At the time of the bill's passage, Brandis, praised his colleagues senators for *"a very civil and intelligent debate"* about the legislation. The Attorney-General added: *"Nobody could say this has been a rushed process."* Yet in the months after the bill's passage, dissent regarding the bill would not cease.

Labor — despite having passed the bill — was still torn about the issue of Data Retention. At no less a venue than Labor's National Conference in July 2015, a motion was passed that committed the party to formally reviewing the Data Retention legislation.

At the conference, NSW Labor MP Jo Haylen — a former director of administration for Julia Gillard and former deputy chief of staff for Anthony Albanese — made the following statement[239]:

"The challenge for law-makers is to strike the right balance: balance between privacy and security, between transparency and strength, and between the power of government and the rights of citizens. The Government's data retention laws do not strike the right balance and neither does Labor's support of these laws."

And in the months to follow, it would become apparent that the model being followed by the Attorney-General's Department in implementing the new Data Retention regime was far from flawless.

Part of the package of Data Retention reforms involved a funding allocation to be paid to Australian telcos and Internet service providers, to assist them with the process of implementing the Data Retention regime.

But five months after the bill passed, the funding package was still being finalised.

By the time October rolled around, the telecommunications industry was in virtual revolt, with industry group the Communications Alliance releasing data from its members showing that almost none had had their funding applications approved.

As a result, about 82 percent of the 63 companies which responded to a survey issued by the group were not compliant with the Data Retention legislation when it came into force … despite having six months to have gotten their act together[240].

Even Telstra — a former government department — was not able to comply at that stage with the legislation's requirements.

And that's not all of the problems which the new Data Retention regime faced.

One of the central selling points of the scheme was that it would strongly curtail the amount of government agencies — Federal, state and local — which had access to access to Australians' metadata without a warrant, forcing some government authorities to go through law enforcement agencies such as the Australian Federal Police for access.

But almost immediately after the legislation passed, state and Federal agencies right around Australia started petitioning the office of the Attorney-General to have their metadata access returned.

One of the standouts was the Victorian Racing Integrity Commissioner. On Melbourne Cup Day in November 2015, it emerged that the agency — which oversees the Cup and other races — was seeking metadata access[241].

It took only three days before it was revealed that all of the other racing integrity agencies nationally wanted the same access. And they weren't alone, with a bevy of other minor agencies seeking the same.

By late 2016, many of the issues had been resolved. A substantial portion of the funding allocation was flowing through to telcos and ISPs, and it appeared that the scheme had started to work somewhat effectively for law enforcement.

But other issues had started to raise their ugly heads. The Australian Federal Police admitted that it had inadvertently accessed the sensitive data of a journalist[242] (one of the few categories of professionals to receive some protection under the Data Retention regime) without a warrant.

And some agencies had started circumventing the scheme, in an attempt to gain access to the valuable metadata it focused on. *"Australia's data retention scheme is still a mess,"* claimed tech media outlet iTnews[243]. This sensationalist headline wasn't completely true. Most of the Data Retention scheme had started to operate as planned, and the public outcry was dying down as the scheme settled into ongoing operation.

But it wasn't completely false either.

Lessons

The process of reforming the *Telecommunications (Interception and Access) Act 1979* to support modern Data Retention powers should have been a relatively smooth journey.

It is clear that there was always a strong case to introduce such powers in Australia, as long as the case was supported by key law enforcement agencies, oversight and governance controls, and as long as the process for introducing the legislation associated with a new Data Retention regime was transparent, inclusive and bipartisan.

Unfortunately, a number of these key elements were missing from the attempts by successive Federal administrations — both Labor and Liberal — to introduce a new Data Retention regime in Australia.

There were three key problems with the process which both Labor and the Coalition progressed in order to introduce a new Data Retention regime.

Firstly, the initial consultations regarding the need for such a regime were conducted behind closed doors and in a secretive fashion. While this is common practice amongst policymakers within Federal Government departments with regard to early stage policy proposals, certain issues are too controversial to be kept secret for long.

Data Retention was one of these issues. The existence of this consultation process was always bound to leak — and leak early.

This meant that the Federal Government was caught on the back foot from the first stages of the development of the Data Retention regime. The secretive nature of its initial policy development efforts meant that those efforts became suspect in the eyes of the public; as journalists expended a disproportionate amount of effort in an attempt to determine what was really happening behind the scenes.

If the Data Retention policy development process had been conducted out in the open right from the start, this would have defused much of this controversy.

The fact that this secrecy at times extended to powerful groups such as the Parliamentary Joint Committee on Intelligence and Security severely bedevilled the process of getting the Data Retention legislation through the Parliament. These groups should have been on board with the development of this legislation right from the start.

The fact that they were not appears to show that the Attorney-General's Department, at least to some extent, misunderstood the controversial nature of the reforms being proposed, or perhaps misplayed its approach.

The second issue which the new Data Retention regime appeared to face was a lack of expertise.

From the earliest stages of the policy development process, the Attorney-General's Department did not appear to display the technical, operational and commercial knowledge which it required in order to seamlessly progress the implementation of the new regime.

This apparent lack has had consequences for the regime, which has taken several years to bed down, following the passage of enabling legislation.

It appears that the Department attempted to rely too heavily on the support of industry in providing information that would allow it to successfully develop a workable model for implementation.

This created two negative outcomes for the new regime: Firstly, it caused a degree of uncertainty when the stakeholders involved — ranging from ISPs and telcos to the Department itself — attempted to implement it. Secondly, it created the impression that the Government's legislative approach was not fully mature.

The final mistake made by policymakers during the process of enacting the Data Retention reforms was not garnering the support of industry.

Throughout the policy development process, it was apparent that the Attorney-General's Department viewed its primary stakeholders during the policy formation process as being law enforcement and intelligence agencies such as the Australian Federal Police.

This, in and of itself, is not a bad thing. Such agencies were key stakeholders in this process.

But the Department appears to have neglected a full understanding that the major ISPs and telcos would also necessarily be equal partners during the process of policy development and implementation.

It was inevitable that a number of these companies would oppose the whole process on ideological grounds. But most were pragmatic about it — they just wanted to get the process of implementing Data Retention over with, so they could continue operating their businesses, relying on certainty in terms of the regulation with which they were required to comply.

There was a lot which successive administrations could have done to engage early, deeply and transparently with industry on the issue of Data Retention. This was particularly important, given that industry would be responsible for enacting the reforms.

Looking back and looking forward

The process of modernising the *Telecommunications (Interception and Access) Act 1979* was never going to be a completely painless exercise.

Success in this policy area relies on finding the correct balance between the demands of civil libertarians on the one hand, and law enforcement organisations on the other. Both have their supporters within Australia's parliaments and in civil society.

And so the enactment of any reforms in this area is always going to become a contest between two extremes. Policymakers must strive to find the balance.

It is debatable whether the *Telecommunications (Interception and Access) Amendment (Data Retention) Bill 2015* found that balance.

The truth is that this type of legislation will continue to evolve; as technology and the needs of civil society also evolve.

What is not debatable, however, is that successive Federal administrations did not cope as well as they could have with the need to introduce these reforms.

The key issues include an unnecessary and unhelpful focus on secrecy during the policy development process; a perceived lack of technical, operational and commercial expertise in this specific policy development field, and a failure to engage effectively with industry as a key stakeholder in the process.

There is no doubt that many future Australian Governments will need to update the national telecommunications access regime in future.

We can only hope that they learn from the lessons of the past when doing so — and avoid many of the headaches that have plagued policymakers in this field in the past.

SUMMARY

Policy Details

In the years from 2013 through 2015, successive Federal Governments attempted to introduce a Data Retention regime, which would require Australia's ISPs to store key details about Australians' telecommunications activities.

Ultimately, this legislation largely represented a necessary reform of the *Telecommunications (Interception and Access) Act 1979*, in that it would maintain the ability of law enforcement and intelligence agencies to access telecommunications data they already had access to. However, it also expanded that access in some controversial areas.

What Went Wrong

The Government made the mistake of attempting to withhold key pieces of information about the reforms, including the fact that it was considering them at all. In addition, it appeared that the Government had not retained the full expertise which it required, in order to inform the development of the policy. It also was not successful in getting industry on-side to assist with the process.

Avoiding This Situation in Future

Some policy topics are too controversial to be kept behind closed doors for long, and would benefit from public consultation from an early a stage as possible.

Government departments must retain expert technical, operational and commercial expertise which can reliably and accurately inform policy development

Industry will be a key stakeholder in any policy reform process which relies substantially on its assistance.

CHAPTER 9

Defending the Fortress

"The question of competition came up and I showed him a picture of then Cabcharge CEO Reg Kermode, looking super-grumpy at a parliamentary inquiry. I said 'There's this taxi tsar, widely understood to have complete control over the industry."

–Uber Australia General Manager
David Rorsheim

The date is 19 August 2014, and David Morris is on his way to the Como Hotel in South Yarra.

Morris isn't in any particular rush, but he organises a hire car to get him where he's going anyway. He has previously downloaded the Uber application to his smartphone and entered his credit card details for automatic payment.

Uber is extremely easy to use; so hailing a hire car from the app is a cinch. Morris simply opens the app and hits a button to summon a car. His location and destination are instantly transmitted to Uber's central servers and seconds later, a shining, clean Chrysler 300 is on its way to pick him up.

The driver of the Chrysler 300 — a gentleman named David Brenner — has no trouble finding Morris. He also has the Uber app open on his smartphone, which is attached to his dashboard. The app passes him Morris' details, and minutes later Brenner pulls up next to Morris' location.

Morris gets into the passenger seat of the Chrysler 300, and his colleague, a Mr Robinson, gets in the back.

It's just like catching a taxi, but quite a bit easier, as all of Morris' details have already been entered into the app. And the big Chrysler — a gorgeous tank of a car — doesn't have any taxi markings. It looks like just another private vehicle. It's a pretty nice car, though — a lot nicer than the markedly more inexpensive models which usually make up most cities' taxi cab fleets.

When the trio arrive at the Como Hotel — a relatively modest yet comfortable facility well-liked by business travellers — Morris asks Brenner to confirm the bill. *"Nine dollars,"* the driver responds.

Following the confirmation of the transaction on Morris' credit card — already registered in the Uber app — Morris receives a receipt via the same application. And Uber sends an email to Morris with the header 'Your morning trip with Uber'. The email displays the route taken, the times involves and the fare calculation. Brenner's name and photo are also included in the email.

It's all very civilised.

It should have been a mundane trip in an ordinary hire car. After all, hundreds of thousands of Australians undertake the same process every day. They book a car through a smartphone app, it arrives, and away they go to their destination.

But there was one simple reason that this trip was an extraordinary one. And it's the same reason we know all about it in so much detail.

David Morris and his colleague did not get in David Brenner's car with the intent of making a trip to the Como Hotel in South Yarra, although that is where they ended up.

David Morris and his colleague were undercover compliance officers working for the Victorian Taxi Services Commission. They got into Nathan Brenner's car with the intent of catching Brenner — and Uber as well   in the act of breaking the law.

The reason we know about this trip in so much detail is because it ended up in court — in fact, in several courts. Courts where David Brenner was forced to hire legal counsel to defend his right to charge customers for trips in his Chrysler 300, as part of his work as a private car operator providing the 'UberX' service for Uber.

This trip to the Como Hotel was, in short, a sting. And Nathan Brenner got stung.

Stung

Nathan Brenner got stung good.

It took a while for the case to wind its way through the courts. But eventually (in December 2015) the Victorian Taxi Services Commission was successful in its bid to convince the Melbourne Magistrates Court that Brenner was acting as a commercial car driver without the accreditation required under Victorian law — and that Uber was assisting in this criminal activity.

The Court fined Brenner $900 — a hundred-fold increase on the cost of the trip which Morris and his colleague Robinson had taken to the Como Hotel in South Yarra in Brenner's Chrysler 300.

But there was a much larger amount in the offing as well, with the Court finding that Brenner would also have to pay the legal costs of the Victorian Taxi Services Commission — an amount which would easily run into thousands of dollars more.

The TSC was jubilant. *"Today's decision vindicates the actions taken by the TSC to enforce the law as it currently stands,"* its chair Graeme Samuels said in a statement[244]. And the agency warned Uber and its fellow app-based hire care services that it would continue to enforce that law.

The broader context and implications of the court case also appeared to be self-evident.

Founded in early 2009 in the tech mega-hub of San Francisco, Uber is one of a clutch of companies that have used innovative smartphone apps tied to clever back-end systems to start to carve off chunks of the lucrative personal transportation industry, which has long been dominated by taxi cab companies.

The company started providing its services in San Francisco in 2010. It then went on to expand internationally, adding cities such as Vancouver and Toronto in Canada and Paris in France.

All of this has been great for consumers. Uber has made a point of providing services to ordinary hire care users that are better than those offered by the taxi industry in every way — cheaper, more convenient, and its cars have been cleaner and better maintained than most cabs.

But the company has also run into one major problem expanding its operations: Government regulation in a very strongly controlled industry.

In several cities, Uber has been accused of breaching local taxi regulations, and has been forced to fight a series of running battles with city administration in order to continue operating.

For example, in Washington in January of the same year Uber launched in Australia, an Uber driver's cab was impounded as part of a sting operation by the city's taxicab regulator[245], which had alleged Uber was operating an unlicensed taxi service. Similar issues have been raised in San Francisco, Massachusetts, Chicago and more.

Nathan Brenner's case in Melbourne was just the latest example of this specific brand of legal trouble. The case showed that this issue had landed in Australia.

It's true that in many ways, Uber has not helped its own case.

At the end of his trip with Nathan Brenner, David Morris explained to the driver that he was a compliance officer with the Taxi Services Commission. It appears that Brenner subsequently relayed the facts of the trip to Uber's local representatives, as you would expect him to.

The day after the trip, Uber sent an email to Morris claiming that the journey to the Como Hotel did not actually take place, with the words *"did not ride"* noted[246]. It was a cheap trick ... and one that did not impress the courts.

Rapid growth

It's true that regulations in a number of states may not have been on Uber's side.

According to the laws and regulations which structured the Australian taxi industry at this time — which organisations such as the Victorian Taxi Services Commission and counterparts in every state were responsible for enforcing — Uber was very much operating an illegal and uncompliant car hire service across Australia.

But while organisations such as the Victorian Taxi Services Commission were conducting stings on its drivers, Uber was certainly not sitting around resting on its laurels.

Uber Australia general manager, David Rorsheim, had spent a substantial amount of time and effort convincing the company's global chief executive, Travis Kalanick, that it would be worth Uber's time and effort to expand into Australia early in its corporate life.

Right from the get-go, Rorsheim — an Australian engineer with a Masters in Business Administration who had made the pilgrimage to live and work in Silicon Valley — had used the lucrative nature of the Australian taxi industry as a motivating factor to get Uber into Australia.

"He's an intense guy, but I'd done my homework," Rohrsheim told the Financial Review newspaper in December 2015, recalling this pitch to Kalanick[247].

"The question of competition came up and I showed him a picture of then Cabcharge CEO Reg Kermode, looking super-grumpy at a parliamentary inquiry. I said 'There's this taxi tsar, widely understood to have complete control over the industry." Cabcharge is a company which provides card payment services to Australia's taxi industry.

Kalanick had understood right at the start of the creation of Uber that the company's revenue would come at the expense of the global taxi industry and that that industry would not hesitate to use red tape to fight back against the incursion.

After only two years in operation in Australia, Rorsheim's team had already created a huge dent in that local industry, signing up 15,000 drivers to connect to its network and ferry consumers around every major city; and counting over one million Australians as its customers nationally.

Analysis published by blog Pocketbook and Gizmodo in January 2015 found that Uber's market share had grown an astonishing 700 percent over the preceding 12 months[248]. The company had reportedly captured some 22 percent of electronic taxi payments in December 2014 alone.

At the heart of the growth was Uber's simple proposition, which the company had imported into Australia.

The company's smartphone app, which instantly located a user's precise location via GPS and then allocated the most appropriate local car to pick them up, made it significantly easier for users to organise personal transport. There was none of the usual complex telephone calls to book a taxi or even waiting around by the side of the road to hail one.

The fact that a users' payment details — a credit card — were already pre-entered into the app — made the process of payment (often cumbersome and a source of tension in a taxi) seamless. Receipts were distributed seamlessly via email following the trip.

Uber had initially launched with its own hire cars and even continues to work with taxi operators themselves.

But it was the company's UberX model — in which any individual can use their own personal car to pick up passengers, in a kind of 'peer to peer' model, which produced most of the company's growth.

In most states in Australia, the local state government charged taxi operators a substantial fee to operate a taxi. This would normally take the form of allocating a licence, which could cost as much as $300,000 to $400,000. Control over these licences meant control over an exclusive ability to provide taxi-like services in major cities, essentially guaranteeing the licensor a revenue stream to back their investment.

Under this existing model, everyone appeared to win. The State Governments outsourced personal transport and got huge licensing fees in return, while taxi organisations were able to make huge piles of cash. Individual drivers could earn more if they worked harder and were smarter about the locations where they tried to pick up passengers.

But Uber's model was revolutionary because it enfranchised two groups of people: Drivers who could not afford to pay hundreds of thousands of dollars for their own taxi licence, or who simply wanted to work for themselves and not the giant taxi oligopolies, and customers, who wanted a cleaner, faster, cheaper and more efficient hire care model.

Who likes to spend time on the side of the road trying to hail a cab, only to find it filthy inside, and the car run down? Not Uber customers, that's for sure.

Uber's model challenged the very foundations of the taxi industry.

And consumers responded.

A Choice investigation in August 2017[249] found that the UberX service was cheaper than an equivalent taxi 90 percent of the time, with taxis being 40 percent more expensive than UberX, on average. UberX's surge pricing feature — where users pay more in high demand situations — caused price spikes, but only very rarely.

Taxis did show up to pick up their customers quicker, but this was only because they could be hailed from the street — when booked, taxis were uniformly slower to arrive than an UberX. In general, users gave an average rating of 8.3 out of 10 for the UberX experience — compared with a much lower 6.7 for their experience with a taxi.

Unstung

Ultimately Nathan Brenner would succeed in his bid to have the $900 fine (plus the legal costs of the Victorian Taxi Services Commission) overturned.

In mid-May 2016 — six months after the initial judgement — County Court Judge Chettle heard the case and found in Brenner's favour — throwing the charges out.

Chettle's rationale for doing so was complex. He accepted most of the arguments made by the prosecution — the Victorian Taxi Services Commission — but noted that there was a clause in the law that provided a historical defence against these arguments. Chettle essentially appears to have reinterpreted that clause, with the aim of allowing individual hire care drivers in Victoria some legal relief against prosecution.

"It may be an unintended anachronism, but I cannot ignore it," he said of the obscure legal clause[250]. *"It is no part of my function to amend or repeal sections of legislation. It is my task to give meaning to legislation."*

The taxi industry — represented by the Victorian Taxi Association — immediately complained about the judgement, slamming the decision as *"a comedy of errors"* and arguing that Uber's actions and the legal judgement fundamentally undermined the law regarding car hire services in the state[251].

The Victorian Taxi Services Commission was predictably irritated as well, while Uber was predictably happy with the judgement.

But it was the response of the Victorian State Government — which is, as Judge Chettle had highlighted — ultimately responsible for setting laws in the state — that was the most interesting.

"It highlights the complexity of this issue, which we continue to give the detailed consideration it needs in the interest of Victorian passengers," said Public Transport Minister Jacinta Allan at the time[252].

It appeared at the time that the Victorian Government had started to realise what hundreds of thousands of consumers in the state already knew: Uber was a service that people wanted to use.

The company's Australian growth had already made it a household name. It was not the Victorian TSC's job to recognise that, or the demand for Uber's services — it was the TSC's job to enforce the law. And it was not the role of the Australian taxi industry to recognise Uber's growth either — the industry had a responsibility to its key members to ensure their existing business models were supported and maintained.

But the Victorian Government did have a responsibility — to Victorian taxpayers, who had overwhelmingly already voted with their feet in validating the fitness of Uber's service for use. The outcry that would arise if the service was simply banned outright — as the initial court action against Brenner seemed to suggest — would have been more than any government could have borne.

In short, it was time to start adapting to change.

Change

The lesson which it was possible to take from the case of Brenner v Taxi Services Commissioner in Victoria was that it was clear that change was in the air. The case ultimately proved to be a victory for Uber and the new generation of personal transport apps, although that victory was based on a technicality which could be easily resolved through a tiny amendment to the legislation.

However, the bigger point was that the case made policymakers within the Victorian Government sit up and take notice that the law was clearly out of step with technological reality — a reality which was hotly in demand by hundreds of thousands of Victorian consumers.

The game had changed; now regulation would need to try and keep up with it.

As the Maddocks law firm wrote in October 2016[253]:

"Chettle J's decision in Brenner v Taxi Services Commissioner highlights the fact that the laws governing the operation of commercial passenger vehicles in Victoria are (to some degree) outdated and in need of change."

However, it would take that change a while to fully appear in Australia. Before it could occur, a few more rounds of regulatory pain would need to be experienced.

Almost overnight, as Uber's massive and extremely rapid success became painfully obvious to policymakers, consumers and the legacy taxi industry alike, a string of government actions nationally made it clear that Uber could not just slink into town and change the whole taxi business model from under the feet of state governments and industry alike.

As the Victorian Government had already realised, it was simply not possible for any jurisdiction to simply ignore the hundreds of thousands of consumers already using Ubers' services. After all … those consumers were also usually voters. And politicians are nothing if not concerned about the worries of voters.

But those same politicians were also keenly aware that each State Government was bringing in many millions of dollars each year in revenue from selling taxi licences. And the taxi industry itself had powerful friends in high places.

This placed State Governments in a substantial quandary. In short, they were torn between the interests of their constituents, and the interests of big business and the lure of valuable revenue that fuelled investment in other things constituents also wanted — such as schools, hospitals, well-funded police forces — and yes, roads for all those hire car services to drive upon.

Most jurisdictions would eventually completely legalise the use of Uber and other apps. But along the way, there would be were many bumps in the road.

In September 2015, for example, the NSW Roads and Maritime Services agency week suspended some forty owners of vehicles involved in UberX-style ride-sharing services, ruling the use of vehicles for this purpose as illegal[254], despite the fact that the NSW State Government was at that time currently conducting a review into the future of the related taxi industry.

The move was something of a low blow for the NSW Government — publicly it had stated that it was reviewing the personal transport industry, but meanwhile it was having its enforcers go to town on UberX ridesharers.

The Queensland Government instigated a cease and desist order against Uber in 2015 in an attempt to stop the company and its drivers from operating in the state at all[255].

But the move didn't really stop Uber. The company had learnt from its Victorian experience with compliance officers, and started actively blocking the Queensland Government's own inspectors from booking its services and thus being able to fine its drivers. The Brisbane Times reported at the time that:

The acting director of the Department of Transport and Main Roads for taxis and limousines Noela Cerutti had told a committee … *"They now can, with their technology, recognise not only a sim card, but the handset … "So we've gone through hundreds of phones trying to catch the next driver in doing the wrong thing."*[256]

By this stage, the legacy taxi industry itself had started to fight back. One initiative in October 2015 saw the industry launch a centralised app for booking taxis nationwide, dubbed 'hail'.

The app was to initially operate in major metropolitan and regional centres across Australia and some cities overseas, providing passengers with a single taxi booking platform and access to the closest available taxi in their area from participating networks, regardless of which taxi network the driver belongs to.

However, the national collaboration ironically attracted the attention of the Australian Competition and Consumer Commission, which took a dim view of the proposal.

"ihail will achieve a potentially dominant position from launch – not through competition, but because of the larger fleet of taxis its ownership structure delivers," said the competition regulator's chair, Rod Sims[257]. The app was temporarily blocked.

Meanwhile, Uber was facing its own new wave of Australia-based competition. Smelling money in the air — and on the roads — a number of Australian entrepreneurs were achieving early success with local apps Ingogo and GoCatch, which took a middle of the road approach to personal transport. Each app leveraged the existing taxi system, but attracted drivers by distributing new jobs directly through a mobile phone app.

It was a more moderated approach than Uber's take no prisoners style — and resonated wth many Australian consumers who weren't quite ready to start hopping into cars to engage in ride sharing activities completely unregulated by the law.

What the entrance of Uber into the Australian market had created was essentially regulatory chaos.

Adoption of the company's services from either a consumer or provider perspective was almost instantaneous. All anyone who wanted to call an Uber had to do was spend less than a minute installing its application on their smartphone.

And becoming one of the company's drivers was only slightly more complicated. Once the paperwork was out of the way, the company's app — attached to your car's dashboard — started sending you job offers to pick up customers and deliver them to their destinations. All you had to do was keep driving.

This whole dynamic caused chaos for the carefully constructed and regulated dynamic between the powerful taxi industry and State Governments around Australia, who were pulling in substantial revenue figures from that industry. Somewhere along the line, the consumer had been left on the side of the road in terms of the support they were getting from either party.

Uber rectified that imbalance.

Public Transport Turmoil

The underlying trend which the Uber situation highlighted was that there was a distinct tension for policymakers between the need to support the development of a new industry which was directly supported by, and benefited consumers — and the interests of an entrenched, established situation which was, in and of itself, already providing substantial direct benefits to Government.

In the past 15 years, this trend has repeated itself many times in Australia.

The public transport example itself can be found in fields far beyond Uber.

For example, in 2009, the NSW Government-owned corporation Railcorp — which operates the train network throughout the greater Sydney region — took sharp action to defend what it saw as its own interests through threatening a Sydney software developer with legal action[258].

At the time, the developer had launched a train timetable application that had been so successful that it had become the second-most popular application within the transport application in Apple's App Store for the iOS smartphone platform.

The application scraped data from Railcorp's public site in order to display upcoming train information in a format similar to that displayed on Railcorp's own monitors within Sydney train stations.

The reason it was so successful was that Railcorp itself was not providing this information — despite the fact that it was highly in demand and extremely useful to train passengers — through its own smartphone platforms.

Yet Railcorp's reaction was to issue the developer with a cease and desist notice, in an attempt to force the developer to remove the app from public view.

One would have thought that the NSW Government would have learnt its lesson from the Railcorp case. Eventually the situation was resolved, with the state opting to invite all developers to use its publicly available data to build more apps.

But in 2011 the situation was repeated.

Another local developer had his app — this time dealing with bus timetabling — forcibly put on ice, after the NSW Government abruptly decided to withdraw the transport data it had made available publicly ... with the precise intention of fuelling the development of apps such as the developer had built[259].

"The system is not yet able to provide a reliable or sustainable feed," a spokesperson for the NSW Government's Transport Department said at the time.

Network Nasties

The issue of dealing with entrenched industries has also been a substantial one for Australia's telecommunications industry.

In 2010, the nascent National Broadband Network Company was engaged in a series of complex negotiations with the national competition regulator — the Australian Competition and Consumer Commission — to set the number of points at which NBN Co's customers — Retail Service Providers (RSPs) such as Telstra and Optus, as well as smaller competitors such as iiNet, TPG and Internode — were able to connect to its network.

NBN Co and a number of smaller telcos like Internode had preferred a minimalist version supporting just 14 such points around Australia, while larger telcos had wanted more — at least 200.

A smaller number of points of interconnect would facilitate a heightened level of competition in Australia's telecommunications market, as even smaller companies such as Internode — a fraction of the size of a dominant telco such as Telstra — would be able to afford to provide services nationally.

But a larger number of PoIs would strongly favour the entrenched players such as Telstra and Optus, because these two companies already had existing network infrastructure located around Australia which they could use to connect to a greater number of PoIs.

At the time, Internode managing director Simon Hackett pointed out that the disparity in equity to the NBN network was clearly a black and white situation.

"The clear choice of NBNCo (and smaller retail service providers) is for there to be a small number of POI's (circa 14) located in capital cities," he wrote in a blog post[260]. *"A small number of PoI's in capital city locations means dramatically lower economic and technical barriers to entry and participation for all RSPs. It will lead to a larger number of more diverse service providers (and services) on the network."*

"The opposite view is held by the very largest RSP's (Telstra and Optus especially), who have been lobbying for there to be a much larger number of PoI's (circa 200). This is not surprising, as these are the players who own their own extensive fibre backbone networks that will let them plug into 200 POI's without significant investment."

Hackett warned that there would be consequences if the large PoI model was followed.

"This large number of Points of Interconnect will ... drive the industry toward having a smaller number of bigger players, rather than a larger number of smaller players, as the overheads of operating (and ramping up to survive all the way to that terminal size) in 120 PoIs may be too much for very small players to afford," the executive wrote.

It was a prediction which the ACCC ignored; settling on a model of 121 PoIs.

But it was a prediction which came to pass.

As the industry rapidly consolidated in the years after 2010, with Internode and many other ISPs being bought up by iiNet, and iiNet in its turn being bought up by TPG (leaving only a handful of competitors left in Australia's broadband industry, including the unscathed majors Telstra and Optus), the ACCC remained unrepentant about its decision.

"While the ACCC was concerned that the acquisition of iiNet by TPG may lessen competition in the retail fixed broadband market, particularly in the short term, the ACCC concluded that this would not reach the threshold of a 'substantial' lessening of competition as required under section 50 of the Competition and Consumer Act," ACCC Chairman Rod Sims said at the time[261].

But it didn't take long for the reality to set in that, at least in part due to the ACCC's flawed PoI decision — which overly supported the major telcos, to the detriment of the minor ones — Australia had lost the majority of its competition in the retail broadband market. Market competition now boiled down to just a handful of major players — with little real differentiation between their offerings.

Restraining the cloud

Yet another similar situation arose around the years from 2010 through 2015 with respect to the burgeoning class of cloud computing technologies which were slowly taking over the global market for outsourced IT services for big businesses.

Major organisations such as Australia's largest banks, retail giants, telecommunications companies and government departments and agencies had for many years been forced to operate their own huge data centres, to provide a home for the tens of thousands of computer servers which they used to operate their businesses and provide services to customers.

It had become common for such organisations to outsource the management and even ownership of such facilities to major enterprise IT services players such as IBM, HP, Fujitsu and CSC. But ultimately, the servers and the physical infrastructure (space, power and cooling) that constituted these massive business platforms remained owned by the companies which utilised them.

But by the early 2010's, companies such as Amazon Web Services, Microsoft, Google and Salesforce.com had begun to provide credible alternatives that were hosted in their own data centres. These 'cloud computing' platforms were more scalable, more reliable, more secure, cheaper and more easily accessible than the existing large platforms.

So it wasn't hard to see why major Australian organisations started to adopt them — en-mass. Suddenly, fixed capital expenditure could be turned into a regular, scalable operational expense. Suddenly, huge, inflexible, depreciating assets could be removed from the corporate balance sheet. Even end user consumers benefited from the low costs these businesses were paying to provide them with services.

Yet again, the only group not happy was the Government.

In November 2010, Australia's banking regulator, the Australian Prudential Regulatory Authority, issued a blunt general warning to the entire financial services sector regarding cloud computing services, warning that the *"innocuous"* nature of such services could mask hidden concerns about offshoring.

"While these applications may seem innocuous, the reality is they may form an integral part of an institution's core business processes, including both approval and decision-making, and can be material and critical to the ongoing operations of the institution," Puay Sim, the regulator's general manager of its supervisory support division, wrote[262].

Sim added that the institutions it regulated *"do not always recognise the significance of cloud computing initiatives"* and *"fail to acknowledge the outsourcing and/or offshoring elements in them"* — which could be a risk.

"As a consequence, the initiatives are not being subjected to the usual rigour of existing outsourcing and risk management frameworks, and the board and senior management are not fully informed and engaged," the public servant said.

It took a while, but the fallout from this pronouncement was significant. In 2012, for example, ANZ Bank dumped Salesforce.com's customer relationship management system to satisfy regulatory requirements globally[263].

ANZ had been using the platform — which had become ubiquitous within Australian sales departments — in its life insurance business. The bank's chief information officer Anne Weatherston had previously described the Salesforce.com platform as *"a fantastic product"*. Still, ANZ considered the platform to be a red flag for regulators — even though it stored no customer data on Salesforce.com's servers.

This avoidance of cloud computing platforms popular in the broader (less heavily regulated) private sector also became a feature of government IT service provision.

In July 2013, for example, the then-Labor Federal Government administration issued a new cloud computing security and privacy directive which required departments and agencies to explicitly acquire the approval of the Attorney-General and the relevant portfolio minister before government data containing private information can be stored in offshore facilities.

The new policy was issued in the name of the then-Attorney-General, Mark Dreyfus, and the Minister Assisting for the Digital Economy, Kate Lundy. And it attracted instant criticism.

"The new policy from AG to have any public cloud with personal info approved by Minister & Attorney-General is a real barrier to use

public cloud," wrote Steven Stolk, the chief information officer of the Australian Sports Commission on his Twitter account[264].

"The flow chart shows all flow that has personal info going to the Minister!" And then, the CIO added: *"The process just seems too risk averse. Privacy risk outways security, which can be assessed at the agency level."*

The cloud providers themselves also objected.

In a submission to the Department of Communications' Public Consultation on Deregulation Initiatives in the Communications Sector[265], Microsoft's local managing director Pip Marlow wrote:

"We understand that the Federal Government, quite rightly, has a requirement for strong protective security policies and practices, particularly in relationship to sensitive and classified information assets. We do, however, also feel that agencies should be able to leverage security guidance to make their own risk-based assessments on whether to utilise cloud services."

Microsoft wrote that the Attorney-General's cloud guidelines had *"added an additional hurdle for agencies' consideration of cloud computing services."*

"This guidance has not only added a procedural barrier into the consideration of offshore-hosted cloud services for non-security classified data; it has created confusion around the privacy requirements of agencies and putting the Federal Government's internal guidance on cloud at odds with the more constructive guidance of the Office of the Australian Information Commissioner," Microsoft wrote.

And even the US Government — home to most of the major cloud companies — weighed in on the Australian Government's antagonism to the cloud.

"Like people who once thought keeping their money hidden under the mattress was better than having it in a bank, some voices across the region, and even in Australia, have called for limiting the flow of data across borders, and requiring firms to install local data

centres in each market to ensure local "control"," US Ambassador to Australia Jeffrey Bleich wrote in late 2012[266].

"This "beggar thy neighbour" protectionism would be just as self-defeating in the digital economy as in every other sector."

Common factors

There is a common journey which ties all of these seemingly disparate cases together.

In each case, what we see is a situation in which a new company has arisen and is providing services which consumers — be they individuals looking to make short trips within their own city or giant companies looking to buy millions of dollars' worth of enterprise IT services — want to buy.

These new products and services are often based on or facilitated by advances in technology that unlock functionality making existing products and services cheaper, more efficient or more effective. Or they may create a whole new category of goods and services.

Usually this service is able to operate for a short to intermediate window of time — from months to years — before it achieves a level of growth which means it starts to challenge the viability or at least gross profit level of existing industries.

It is at this point that policymakers usually become interested in the burgeoning new industry. This interest is almost always spurred by lobbying and 'education' efforts by entrenched existing industries, which have a vested interest in stopping, or at least slowing, the development of innovative new market competitors in their sector.

Sometimes — as in the case of cloud computing adoption in Australia's public sector (and highly regulated private industries such as banking), this interest can be spurred by other reasons, such as a desire by oversight and governance structures to ensure security controls around sensitive data remain intact.

But whatever the case, they have the same effect: Cruelling the adoption of new technologies, new products, and new services; despite the fact that this adoption may have a long-term beneficial impact on government, end user customers, and even the economy as a whole.

Complicating this issue even further is the fact that the new industries often do not have the resources to focus on engaging with Government in order to support the development of beneficial regulation or wider reforms to support their market entrance — or even, at a basic level, to restrain the overwhelming market power of incumbents.

This is the power of entrenched industries — and it's not going away any time soon.

Learnings

It is possible to glean two key lessons which policymakers can take away from this chapter, and its focus on entrenched industries.

The first is the timelines on which this kind of regulatory change occurs.

The key technological improvement which facilitated the creation of Uber was the launch of the Apple iPhone, which first debuted in the United States in June 2007, and then launched in Australia the following year. This product singlehandedly revolutionised a number of completely separate industries, through its fusion of communications functionality and user interface innovation.

The success of the iPhone spurred the launch of Uber in March 2009, two years later.

Uber launched in Australia three years later in November 2012, picking Sydney for its first market. After only two years, the company's operations had created a substantial dent in the revenues of the existing taxi industry. Uber can be seen as a more efficient version of an existing industry — not a whole new service — so it didn't expand the whole pie — it just cut into it.

Shortly after this, regulatory agencies such as the TSC — spurred, no doubt, by political lobbying efforts by the existing taxi industry — started to fully enforce local regulations designed to sanitise — but effectively protecting — the existing industry.

And after another several years of chaos, the situation has now effectively been normalised. Jurisdictions such as the ACT have led the way, and some others, such as the Northern Territory are still lagging. But by and large, it is now legal to operate an UberX service — and to catch one — under certain conditions and in most places in Australia.

This is a four to five year journey to legitimacy. Similar timelines have been seen in other areas mentioned in this chapter, such as the acceptance of public transport apps supported by government-owned data, or adoption of cloud computing technologies in sensitive industries and government (which, like Uber, is now legal and commonplace).

What this situation illustrates is that policymakers across a number of key areas need to keep a keen eye on foundational technological improvements.

It is understandable that the launch of the iPhone by itself would not cause a revolution in policy development circles in Australia.

Yet the rapid and early success of Uber in key United States markets from March 2009 should have been a warning signal to Australian policymakers that they should be preparing for the launch of similar services in Australia. It was clear from a very early point in Uber's corporate lifecycle that the company would expand rapidly in first world markets — and that Australia, with its entrenched taxi industry, would be a likely candidate for expansion.

Given the common lag time between US success and international expansion by innovative companies, Australian policymakers should have had responses pre-prepared for the launch of Uber in Australia.

That's just common sense.

The second factor is the issue of how to deal with entrenched industries.

If you haven't been directly involved in politics (or been directly lobbied), it may seem strange that entrenched industries such as the taxi industry are able to gain as much influence as they have with policymakers. The question comes up again and again — why don't newcomers such as Uber get the same say that entrenched players do?

There is an easy answer. Entrenched players are able to leverage significantly greater resources towards engaging with the political process.

Not only do can they hire government relations specialists and firms to engage with politicians on their behalf, but they are also usually contributors to and actively involved with industry association groups, which lobby on behalf of entire industries. These groups enjoy tremendous access in the halls of power in Canberra — because politicians want to ensure that these groups won't actively oppose them during the electoral cycle.

It would appear, then that the lesson, here, for politicians and policymakers is not to listen to entrenched industries as much — and to smaller, more innovative players more.

But the truth is that politicians and policymakers should listen to both less.

The true indication of where the national interest lies is more likely to come from ordinary consumers than it is the companies who represent them. If politicians and policymakers were able to keep their ear to the ground in the cases detailed in this chapter — listening constantly to the needs of consumers of all types of products and services — they would have quickly realised where the direction of policy should lie.

They would have realised quickly that Uber wasn't just a fly by night startup — and adjusted policy quickly to deal with it. They would have more rapidly adapted government platforms to take advantage of the new cloud computing paradigm — and allowed banks to do the same; which is precisely what chief information officers wanted for their organisations.

They would have facilitated the rise of government open data platforms so that innovative applications could have provided access to transport data.

And they wouldn't have allowed Telstra and Optus to effectively re-monopolise the broadband market in the new NBN paradigm.

Aligning themselves with the needs of the people — who buy goods and services and also vote for or against them — also directly serves the needs of politicians themselves — to be re-elected and win Government. They ignore the people at their peril.

This lesson will serve policymakers well, as they grapple with the extraordinary realisation that the process of setting policy never ends — and that Uber itself may not be the end goal. As the Canberra Times wrote in an editorial in September 2017[267]:

"It's worth asking why the ACT government appeared to rush its approval of a ride-sharing market in 2015. To its credit, its decision showed it recognised that Canberrans wanted an alternative to the troubled taxi market, and that there was little point impeding a newer, better product."

"Yet there were alternatives. The ACT government never explicitly handed Uber a monopoly; it was careful to say it was welcoming ride-sharing rather than a single business.

"... Perhaps it's time to think about how to build Australia's best ride-sharing market, rather than simply the first."

SUMMARY

Policy Details

State Government policymakers and transport Ministers had failed to reform legislation and regulatory controls in order to deal with the introduction of ride-sharing services such as Uber.

What Went Wrong

It was clear very soon after the launch of Uber in 2009 in the United State that its model represented a strong challenge to the existing taxi industry, and that it was inevitable that that model would be introduced to other first-world countries such as Australia within the next several years.

Despite this, Australian policymakers appeared to have been blindsided by Uber's rapid success in Australia, leading to a series of tense standoffs and even court cases involving the taxi industry, state governments, Uber, and even individual drivers, who often got caught in the controversy.

Avoiding This Situation in Future

Policymakers across a number of key areas need to maintain an awareness of the implications of fundamental technological change.

Policymakers must also maintain an awareness of industry change in key international markets such as the United States and UK, because that change will be likely to be reflected in Australia.

Policymakers must seek out the views of both entrenched industry players and challengers. But ultimately they should listen to the views of ordinary consumers first and foremost, because these will provide the most reliable.

CHAPTER 10

A Note About Energy

"Climate change is the great moral challenge of our generation."

—Opposition Leader Kevin Rudd

If you were one of the original backers of The Frustrated State on the Kickstarter crowd-funding plaform, you may have realised that there is a notable absence from the book as it has been published.

When I first came up with the idea for The Frustrated State, I had planned to include a chapter on technological change in the energy sector.

At that stage, I had planned to examine events over the past decade in this sector, initially through the lens of Malcolm

Turnbull's ill-fated support for Kevin Rudd's Emissions Trading Scheme.

I then planned to progress through to the current day situation, where there is still sharp disagreement about the policy direction the Government should with respect to the growth of renewable energy.

There is no doubt that this topic is very much still a live one.

As I write the final words of The Frustrated State in April 2018, the future of Australia's energy sector continues to be one of the most contested spaces in Federal and State politics.

Debate over the future of Australia's power generation industry — especially our heavily polluting coal-fired power plans — rages every day.

The contention over our place as a leading exporter of fossil fuels — again, with coal taking pride of place — is almost as strong.

And even seemingly fringe issues such as the potential for Australia to build nuclear power stations — as unlikely as that future seems — have their place in our parliamentary debates.

At the same time as this debate is occurring, technological change is also occurring at a rapid clip.

As I drove through Canberra this afternoon, I caught a glimpse of one of Elon Musk's new Tesla Model S sedans gliding down the highway — entirely silent, and entirely powered by its on-board battery … with no petroleum required to give it motive power.

Those same batteries — grouped together in a huge bank in rural South Australia — are also already doing much to assist that state's residents in surviving the peaks and troughs of energy demand, in summer weather that demands huge amounts of air conditioning to keep residents alive.

Providing for the future of Australia's energy needs may seem like an issue specific to the resources or energy sectors.

But when it really comes down to it, this issue, like all of the other issues in the book, is essentially a matter of technology policy.

Once the ideology has been set aside, it fundamentally revolves around the nuances — and there are many — of how Australia transitions from legacy technology platforms to more sustainable renewable systems.

And yet, as I got very deep into writing The Frustrated State, I realised that I was not the right person to tell this particular story.

When I started my career as a journalist — around the year 2000 — energy technology was certainly not considered part of the remit of most technology journalists. We covered personal computing, enterprise software, telecommunications — really most technology — but power stations were not considered *"technology"*. Neither, for that matter, were cars.

It took the launch of Musk's Tesla company, with its ambitions to revolutionise the motor vehicle industry with battery technology, to get tech journos as excited about battery megawatts as they were about hard disk gigabytes.

In 2018, it is common to read energy stories in the pages of technology media outlets.

But I didn't personally live through the many debates that have occurred in Australia on this topic over the past decade.

I wasn't there for the press conferences, I didn't interview the key players, and I don't know the ins and outs of how this story played out.

So I chose to replace that chapter with a story I did know in detail — that of Australia's adoption of Data Retention reforms.

With that said, however, I did think that I would take this opportunity to note a few similarities between Australia's energy issue and other tech policy topics.

It's clear, for instance, that Australia's small cadre of renewable energy players face much the same problem as do innovative ride-sharing services like Uber: Huge, entrenched monopolistic players blocking their path to growth.

They're slowly coming on board, but huge energy utilities have been loathe for many years to progress off highly polluting coal-fired power stations.

As with Australia's tech startup and video game development sectors, it is extremely clear that our renewable energy sector will continually boom for some time. The changing nature of the technology alone ensures this.

And yet, Governments are often fighting this rising tide — rather than supporting it.

Then too, Governments also face a similar infrastructure challenge with the rise of renewable energy as they did with the National Broadband Network issue.

Should the Government invest directly? Restructure the industry to support a more efficient market? And how will it deal with the inevitable shrinking of demand for baseload power from energy utilities, when the placing of solar panels on rooftops becomes completely normalised?

The launch of Tesla's Powerwall battery particularly comes to mind as an influential factor here, ideally positioned as this product is to help many millions of Australians remove their dependence on our national energy grid.

Governments need to make some very rapid choices about how to deal with these issues … or risk market chaos as regulatory controls fail to keep up — to say nothing of risking Australia's competitive position globally.

I don't personally have the answers to these issues.

But it's not hard to see them constantly coming up in Australia's national energy debate.

I only hope that our politicians are more prepared to deal with the energy issue, than they have proven themselves at dealing with other technology issues over the past decade.

CHAPTER 11

Despair and Hope

During my time as a journalist observing Australia's technology policy environment, I have experienced many moments of despair.

I felt despair in November 2007 when the new Rudd Labor Government confirmed it would enact mandatory filtering of Australia's Internet.

I felt despair in 2011 when it became clear that Australia's video game development industry was facing complete obliteration ... and the Government was doing little to halt the trend.

And I felt despair when the new Abbott Coalition Government introduced its 'Multi-Technology Mix' model for the National Broadband Network in December 2013.

If you've read sizeable chunks of The Frustrated State, I have no doubt that you, too, have felt despair about the future of technology policy in Australia.

How, after all, can our great nation move forward and take a global leadership role in the technology field, when our politicians and policymakers get so many things completely wrong?

It's true: There is reason for great concern.

The Frustrated State provides an absolute wealth of evidence that Australia's political sector is systematically mismanaging technological change and crushing hopes that the nation will ever take its rightful place globally as a digital powerhouse and home of innovation.

And yet, there is also reason for hope. Consider, if you will, the following facts.

- Labor's Internet filter plans were eventually withdrawn and replaced with a significantly more limited approach.

- The Rudd Labor administration successfully pivoted from the failure of its first FTTN NBN plan into a greatly expanded, universal fibre approach.

- Despite the Coalition's intervention, the NBN project is still progressing forward and providing better broadband across Australia.

- Many government departments and agencies are making progress on adopting cloud computing, centralised IT purchasing, strong project management and governance frameworks, transparency measures and agile methodologies.

- Australia's video game development sector has recently enjoyed a string of successes in the mobile gaming space.

- The Coalition Federal Government has legislated to address the taxation of multinational corporations, and the Australian Taxation Office has moved to assist.

- Malcolm Turnbull's late-2015 National Innovation and Science Agenda addressed many of the concerns of Australia's tech startups.

- A number of controls and governance oversight were included in the Government's reform of the *Telecommunications (Interception and Access) Act 1979*.

- Uber and other ridesharing services have largely been legalised in Australia, with appropriate legislative controls.

When I was considering what title to give this book, I hit upon the term 'frustrated' because it does much to indicate the current state of technology policy in Australia.

What this book illustrates is that bad technology decisions are holding Australia back from reaching its true potential.

That potential is *frustrated*. And Australians are *frustrated* about that lack of progress.

But the examples given in this book do not mean that no forward progress at all is being made.

At a basic level, Australia's chaotic, messy, inefficient and often unproductive political system does work.

The Frustrated State does not dwell on success stories; that is not its purpose. But if you examine the current state of the nine major policy issues examined in its pages, what is apparent is that progress is being slowly made.

Bad ideas such as Labor's mandatory Internet filter do eventually get rejected by the system. And good ideas such as support for fast-growing technology startups do eventually get adopted.

It often takes a while. But change does usually eventually occur in a positive fashion.

If there is one message which The Frustrated State exists to push, it is the following: *It doesn't have to be this slow.*

If politicians and policymakers take the time to learn from the mistakes of the past and understand the broader context which their decisions take place in, then they will be able to accelerate Australia's progress in these areas.

The evidence from comparable countries overseas who have improved their ability to deal successfully with technology policy shows that this will have a strongly beneficial impact.

The good thing is that many of the lessons which are enshrined in the pages of The Frustrated State are not terribly difficult to implement. They just take a bit of time and effort, with the right mindset.

The best policy is developed when politicians and policymakers take the change to step back from the political blast furnace and take a long, hard, objective look at the issues they are dealing with, transparently considering ideas from all key interest groups, from across the political spectrum and success stories from other jurisdictions.

Great policy can often turn into real-world success when best practice from highly competitive private industry is brought into a public setting.

And yes, along the way, Governments should indeed pick winners. It should be apparent right now that the national interest will not be best served if Government maintains a focus on existing industries in areas such as resources and agriculture. The industries of the future must also be a part of the bigger picture.

It's true that we're asking a lot from our busy politicians to keep all of this in mind, alongside the demands of dealing with their electorates and campaigning to win elections.

Our political leaders don't always have the hours or the resources to do the deep research and take the time to get policy right.

But it's also true that Australians have paid a high cost for their mistakes.

If our politicians take the time to understand technology policy, learn the lessons of the past and change their approach in future, this will benefit us all — from corporations to individuals and the public interest as a whole.

But if they do not heed the warnings of this book, then many of us will continue to experience many moments of despair; and many more of us will continue to feel very … frustrated.

References

1   https://en.wikipedia.org/wiki/File:Parliament_House_Canberra_Dusk_Panorama.jpg

2   https://creativecommons.org/licenses/by-sa/3.0/deed.en

3   https://pixabay.com/en/matrix-matrix-code-control-1274888/

4   https://creativecommons.org/publicdomain/zero/1.0/deed.en

5   http://www.abc.net.au/7.30/scott-morrison-on-todays-economic-growth-figures/8316538

6   https://www.smh.com.au/politics/federal/labor-resists-pressure-for-900-million-loan-adani-coal-mine-should-stand-on-its-own-two-feet-20170412-gvj4qh.html

7   https://en.wikipedia.org/wiki/Carmichael_coal_mine

8   https://www.smh.com.au/politics/federal/adani-loan-too-much-of-a-risk-for-taxpayers-according-to-independent-study-20170731-gxmarj.html

9   https://theconversation.com/the-future-of-australian-coal-an-unbankable-deposit-77021

10   https://www.bloomberg.com/news/articles/2017-06-02/trump-s-paris-exit-dims-prospects-for-indian-solar-power

11   http://australiabulletin.com/2017/05/03/the-future-of-australian-coal-an-unbankable-deposit/

12   https://qz.com/871907/2016-was-the-year-solar-panels-finally-became-cheaper-than-fossil-fuels-just-wait-for-2017/

13   https://www.bloomberg.com/news/arti
cles/2017-01-03/for-cheapest-power-on-earth-look-
skyward-as-coal-falls-to-solar

14   https://qz.com/1098375/wind-power-is-now-cheap
er-than-thermal-and-nuclear-power-in-india/

15   https://theconversation.com/toyota-names-
2017-end-australian-car-making-to-cease-
experts-react-23037

16   https://www.zerohedge.com/news/2016-10-11/
aussie-property-bubble-scale-no-other

17   http://www.chiefscientist.gov.au/2017/09/article-
the-australian-financial-review-why-smashed-avoca
do-is-innovation-that-counts/

18   https://www.zerohedge.com/news/2016-10-11/
aussie-property-bubble-scale-no-other

19   https://www.bloomberg.com/news/arti
cles/2017-02-28/central-sydney-now-fuels-quarter-
of-australia-s-economic-growth

20   https://www.smh.com.au/business/the-economy/
the-charts-that-suggest-the-housing-bubble-is-out-
of-control-20160224-gn2b46.html

21   https://www.9now.com.au/60-minutes/2016/clip-
cikw06urf002es3nnfzstdfvl

22   https://tradingeconomics.com/australia/wage-
growth

23   https://www.smh.com.au/politics/federal/australian-
incomes-more-equal-than-a-decade-ago-but-aver
age-household-debts-have-doubled-20170912-gy
g2lr.html

24   https://www.smh.com.au/politics/federal/universities-
set-to-lose-12b-in-funding-under-turnbull-government-

changes-20170805-gxq0ez.html

25   https://www.theaustralian.com.au/business/opinion/
      robert-gottliebsen/unions-only-have-themselves-to-
      blame-for-car-factory-closures/news-story/6730f15e
      875cdfe59652267243255098d

26   http://www.chiefscientist.gov.au/2017/09/article-
      the-australian-financial-review-why-smashed-avoca
      do-is-innovation-that-counts/

27   https://finance.google.com/finance?q=NASDAQ%3A
      AAPL&ei=donkWaj4Gcqc0QTe0J1Y

28   http://www.visualcapitalist.com/countries-econom
      ic-complexity/

29   https://theconversation.com/revisiting-the-banana-
      republic-and-other-familiar-destinations-15088

30   https://www.zdnet.com/article/conroy-charts-national-
      broadband-agenda/

31   https://delimiter.com.au/2010/06/28/oh-dear-conroy-
      watched-the-soccer-during-the-spill/

32   http://delimiter.com.au/2010/06/28/conroy-re-com
      mits-to-filter-slams-lundy-amendments/

33   http://www.abc.net.au/news/2007-12-31/conroy-an
      nounces-mandatory-internet-filters-to/999946

34   https://www.itnews.com.au/news/conroy-brands-efa-
      anti-filter-campaign-a-disgrace-169681

35   https://delimiter.com.au/2013/06/27/vale-stephen-con
      roy-australias-greatest-ever-communications-minister/

36   https://www.theage.com.au/arti
      cles/2003/03/04/1046540188131.html

37   https://www.smh.com.au/arti

cles/2004/06/29/1088392648667.html

38   http://www.abc.net.au/news/2006-06-21/free-internet-filter-half-baked-solution/1783236

39   https://www.theage.com.au/arti
cles/2002/05/13/1021002429844.html

40   http://www.abc.net.au/news/2006-06-21/free-internet-filter-half-baked-solution/1783236

41   http://newsweekly.com.au/article.php?id=2413

42   https://en.wikipedia.org/wiki/Stephen_Conroy

43   https://www.theaustralian.com.au/news/nation/rudds-decision-to-take-holy-communion-at-catholic-mass-causes-debate/news-story/fa9a821764ce71df689601e112
53f835?sv=ff6cce9173b750f7c4928b191e8097ce

44   https://www.smh.com.au/news/national/minister-warned-on-porn-filters/2007/12/31/1198949746454.
html

45   https://www.dailytelegraph.com.au/news/opinion/filter-our-freedom-of-speech-right/news-story/7e7fa024ee597
4ad2c5302a2485c13e5?sv=955c9431805b23c7c0280e608
9dd2fd0

46   https://www.acma.gov.au/theACMA/closed-environ
ment-testing-of-isp-level-internet-content-filtering

47   https://www.news.com.au/news/isp-filtering-gains-momentum/news-story/8483ea4b485e08f37940c5acff60
60bb

48   http://www.abc.net.au/news/2009-03-19/internet-filter-blacklist-leaked-on-web/1623890

49   http://www.abc.net.au/news/2009-03-19/leaked-black
list-irresponsible-inaccurate-conroy/1624118

50 https://www.news.com.au/news/blacklist-looks-like-acmas-conroy/news-story/8bff44321e21ec0de1f4fa738a2eb143

51 https://www.sbs.com.au/news/insight/tvepisode/blocking-net

52 https://www.theage.com.au/news/national/teenager-cracks-government-porn-filter/2007/08/25/1187462562878.html

53 http://delimiter.com.au/2010/08/05/its-dead-opposition-to-block-labors-filter/

54 http://delimiter.com.au/2010/08/09/filter-will-be-exorcised-if-it-returns-says-turnbull/

55 http://delimiter.com.au/2010/07/09/filter-delayed-for-a-year-by-rc-content-review/

56 https://delimiter.com.au/2013/05/16/asic-blocked-numerous-sites-over-9-months/

57 https://www.smh.com.au/news/national/torrid-start-for-trujillos-three-amigos/2005/08/26/1124563033635.html

58 https://www.zdnet.com/article/telstra-keeps-adsl2-under-wraps/

59 https://www.zdnet.com/article/phil-burgess-best-quotes/

60 https://www.zdnet.com/article/more-great-phil-burgess-quotes/

61 https://www.smh.com.au/business/racist-backward-sols-parting-shot-20090526-bl3p.html

62 https://www.zdnet.com/article/telstra-to-slash-tech-costs-under-review/

63 https://www.zdnet.com/article/telstras-3g-schedule-pushed-ericsson/

64 https://www.theage.com.au/news/busi
ness/time-for-coonan-to-make-a-highspeed-deci
sion/2006/04/07/1143916720410.html

65 http://www.abc.net.au/am/content/2008/s2361484.htm

66 https://www.zdnet.com/article/phil-burgess-best-quotes/

67 https://www.zdnet.com/article/phil-burgess-best-quotes/

68 http://www.optus.com.au/portal/site/aboutoptus/
menuitem.813c6f701cee5a14f0419f108c8ac7a0/?vgnexto
id=4b1002c0ed1c6110VgnVCM10000029867c0aRCRD
&vgnextchannel=daf6d7ef03820110VgnVCM100000298
67c0aRCRD

69 https://en.wikipedia.org/wiki/OPEL_Networks

70 http://pandora.nla.gov.au/pan/79983/20091030-1529/
www.pm.gov.au/node/5233.html

71 http://australianpolitics.com/2007/03/21/rudd-launch
es-broadband-policy.html

72 https://www.smh.com.au/politics/federal/preselection-
rumble-over-labor-seat-20130326-2gsde.html

73 http://pandora.nla.gov.au/pan/80090/20130918-1430/
www.minister.dbcde.gov.au/conroy/media/media_re
leases/2007/government_committed_to_fttn_national_
network.html

74 http://pandora.nla.gov.au/pan/80090/20130918-1430/
www.minister.dbcde.gov.au/conroy/media/media_re
leases/2008/007.html

75 http://pandora.nla.gov.au/pan/80090/20130918-1430/

www.minister.dbcde.gov.au/conroy/media/media_re
leases/2008/016.html

76   https://www.smh.com.au/politics/federal/when-the-
pms-biggest-decision-was-up-in-the-air-20090410-a2sd.
html

77   https://www.smh.com.au/politics/federal/when-the-
pms-biggest-decision-was-up-in-the-air-20090410-a2sd.
html

78   https://www.computerworld.com.au/article/632805/
leaked-document-details-rudd-govt-strategy-telstra-nbn-
negotiations/

79   https://delimiter.com.au/2010/09/14/conroys-new-
nemesis-malcolm-turnbull/

80   http://www.dailymail.co.uk/femail/article-3234785/
How-social-media-crush-Malcolm-Turnbull-new-Silver-
Fox-PM.html

81   https://www.arnnet.com.au/article/356195/australia_
doesn_t_want_100mbps_internet_says_turnbull/

82   https://delimiter.com.au/2010/09/25/nbn-opposition-
not-pointless-says-turnbull/

83   https://www.itnews.com.au/news/turnbull-lays-out-
case-for-nbn-cost-benefit-233249

84   https://delimiter.com.au/2010/09/25/nbn-opposition-
not-pointless-says-turnbull/

85   http://delimiter.com.au/2010/09/15/ludlam-warns-
turnbull-dont-be-a-nbn-wrecker/

86   https://delimiter.com.au/2011/01/07/quigley-faces-
down-alcatel-bribery-questions/

87   https://delimiter.com.au/2010/12/31/please-explain-
alcatel-bribes-turnbull-tells-quigley/

88   https://www.zdnet.com/article/mike-quigley-the-back
        ground-check/

89   https://www.theaustralian.com.au/news/investigations/
        rueful-chief-admits-mistakes-on-alcatel-corruption-
        disclosure/news-story/4518f391703e6c24d956ecf659a8d
        92c?sv=4d17106a1e4e8a62637d389f3c8b118c

90   https://www.smh.com.au/national/gillard-dismisses-
        abbott-s-nbn-claims-20110101-19ceu.html

91   https://delimiter.com.au/2012/10/10/turnbull-on-quig
        ley-witch-hunt-says-conroy/

92   https://delimiter.com.au/2013/07/18/poison-words-
        turnbull-nbn-board-go-to-war/

93   https://delimiter.com.au/2013/07/18/poison-words-
        turnbull-nbn-board-go-to-war/

94   https://delimiter.com.au/2010/10/19/turnbull-files-
        private-members-bill-for-nbn-transparency/

95   http://delimiter.com.au/2010/03/17/conroys-nbn-stall
        ing-may-cause-greens-pullout/

96   https://delimiter.com.au/2011/03/11/nbn-korea-kept-
        its-hfc-cable-says-turnbull/

97   https://delimiter.com.au/2011/10/24/coalition-nbn-
        policy-shifts-to-fibre-to-the-node/

98   https://delimiter.com.au/2012/04/30/fttn-a-huge-mis
        take-says-ex-bt-cto/

99   https://delimiter.com.au/2011/01/11/fibre-broadband-
        speeds-pointless-claims-turnbull/

100   https://delimiter.com.au/2010/12/20/many-poi-nbn-
        model-insane-says-hackett/

101   https://delimiter.com.au/2015/08/04/turnbull-revises-

history-on-nbn-satellite-demand/

102 https://delimiter.com.au/2012/08/28/im-no-fttn-zealot-says-malcolm-turnbull/

103 http://www.abc.net.au/technology/articles/2013/02/21/3695094.htm

104 https://twitter.com/turnbullmalcolm/status/2272306609829924865

105 http://www.abc.net.au/technology/articles/2012/11/16/3634499.htm

106 http://www.abc.net.au/pm/content/2012/s3638019.htm

107 https://delimiter.com.au/2012/08/21/turnbull-slams-pro-nbn-zealot-journalists/

108 https://delimiter.com.au/2012/11/16/parochial-turnbull-slams-nbn-cheerleader-media/

109 https://delimiter.com.au/2013/03/08/hands-off-nick-ross-conroy-warns-the-abc-and-the-australian/

110 https://delimiter.com.au/2010/12/20/nbn-abbott-rejects-%E2%80%9Cvideo-entertainment-system%E2%80%9D/

111 http://delimiter.com.au/2011/06/23/abbott-would-dig-nbn-cables-up-says-gillard/

112 https://delimiter.com.au/2011/06/23/gillards-rip-it-out-claims-ludicrous-says-turnbull/

113 https://delimiter.com.au/2013/04/09/coalition-releases-long-awaited-rival-nbn-policy/

114 https://www.malcolmturnbull.com.au/media/transcript-launch-of-the-coalition-broadband-policy

115 https://delimiter.com.au/2013/04/15/coalition-rejected-

78-support-labors-nbn/

116   https://theconversation.com/user-pays-for-fastest-inter
net-access-under-coalition-plan-13328

117   https://delimiter.com.au/2013/08/07/get-fucked-turn
bull-staffer-turns-on-blogger/

118   https://delimiter.com.au/2013/10/03/ziggy-switkowski-
appointed-nbn-co-exec-chair/

119   https://www.smh.com.au/politics/federal/nbn-chief-
quigley-calls-it-quits-20130712-2pu5w.html

120   https://delimiter.com.au/2013/12/12/nbn-co-abandons-
fttn-rollout-hfc-areas/

121   https://delimiter.com.au/2013/10/22/turnbull-wont-
comment-nbn-jobs-boys/

122   https://delimiter.com.au/2013/12/16/turnbull-appoints-
liberal-supporter-ergas-nbn-panel/

123   https://www.news.com.au/technology/online/nbn/
nbn-abandons-the-optus-hfc-network-will-instead-
turn-to-fttdp-technology/news-story/d29e2ebda
5b24e733ec1ed6de01bb0d4

124   https://www.afr.com/technology/web/nbn/fresh-nbn-
leaks-showing-fttn-delays-raise-broadband-policy-ques
tions-20160331-gnv0uz

125   https://www.theaustralian.com.au/news/one-third-of-
nbn-users-wish-it-had-never-happened/news-story/ed
1803c552b4268c83a3e3fd2059102a

126   https://www.smh.com.au/politics/federal/nbn-trials-
cheaper-allfibre-option-20160302-gn8cj3.html

127   https://delimiter.com.au/2015/11/25/were-fixing-
labors-nbn-mess-says-turnbull/

128 https://delimiter.com.au/2015/10/17/nonsensical-farce-nbn-massively-overbuilding-canberras-fttn-with-more-fttn/

129 https://www.theguardian.com/technology/2018/apr/27/nbns-speed-slowed-by-reliance-on-copper-network-its-ceo-admits

130 http://www.abc.net.au/news/2018-03-20/iinet-and-internode-to-compensate-11000-nbn-customers-for-speed/9567410

131 https://delimiter.com.au/2016/06/28/nbn-co-confirms-flooding-kills-fttn-nodes/

132 https://www.lifehacker.com.au/2018/03/heres-what-happens-when-a-car-hits-an-nbn-node/

133 http://www.abc.net.au/news/2018-04-04/nbn-co-boss-bill-morrow-resigns/9617210

134 https://delimiter.com.au/2011/05/25/federal-parliament-warms-to-the-ipad/

135 https://delimiter.com.au/2010/08/09/filter-will-be-exorcised-if-it-returns-says-turnbull/

136 https://www.smh.com.au/national/turnbull-back-to-demolish-nbn-20100914-15aj3.html

137 https://www.smh.com.au/environment/weather/scrap-nbn-to-pay-for-floods-abbott-20110118-19v0z.html

138 https://www.amazon.com/Born-Rule-unauthorised-biography-Turnbull-ebook/dp/B0175VTYQ2

139 https://www.afr.com/leadership/entrepreneur/he-got-it-straight-away-man-who-pitched-ozemail-to-malcolm-turnbull-recalls-his-tech-trendspotting-ability-and-startups-are-heartened-20150915-k9z66

140 https://www.innovation.gov.au/page/agenda

141   https://www.malcolmturnbull.com.au/meet-malcolm/first-speech

142   https://delimiter.com.au/2013/03/14/blackbird-launches-30m-aussie-vc-fund/

143   https://delimiter.com.au/2011/02/16/turnbull-secretly-loves-the-nbn-claims-internode/

144   http://delimiter.com.au/2010/09/16/turnbull-nbn-is-a-business-not-a-public-good/

145   https://delimiter.com.au/2010/08/11/im-no-bill-gates-says-tony-abbott/

146   https://delimiter.com.au/2011/07/19/nbn-helped-coalition-lose-2010-election/

147   http://delimiter.com.au/2010/08/10/coalition-unveils-rival-6bn-broadband-policy/

148   http://www.abc.net.au/news/2013-04-10/kohler-how-malcolm-turnbull-saved-the-nbn/4619868

149   https://www.malcolmturnbull.com.au/assets/Coalition_NBN_policy_-_Background_Paper.pdf

150   https://delimiter.com.au/2013/12/12/nbn-co-abandons-fttn-rollout-hfc-areas/

151   https://www.smh.com.au/politics/federal/brilliant-and-fearless-but-paul-keating-was-right-about-turnbull-20090626-czt7.html

152   https://delimiter.com.au/2012/06/07/abomination-qld-health-payroll-needs-837m-more/

153   https://delimiter.com.au/2012/10/17/criminal-neglect-qld-govt-it-fixes-to-cost-up-to-6-billion/

154   https://delimiter.com.au/2013/06/07/systemic-business-risk-90-of-qld-govts-ict-needs-to-be-replaced-total-cost-

7-4-billion/

155   https://delimiter.com.au/2012/07/27/qld-wrestles-with-winxp-upgrade/

156   https://delimiter.com.au/2011/11/23/vic-government-it-in-flames-1-4-billion-over-budget-all-projects-late-or-failed/

157   https://delimiter.com.au/2012/05/07/it-strategy-to-lead-nsw-from-the-dark-ages/

158   https://delimiter.com.au/2011/07/07/wa-dumps-shared-services-plan/

159   https://delimiter.com.au/2013/12/11/diabolical-mess-scandal-epic-proportions-nt-ict-minister-damns-fujitsu-hell-extraordinary-rant/

160   http://delimiter.com.au/2013/08/28/fujitsusap-project-goes-rails-nt/

161   https://www.zdnet.com/article/customs-blames-users-in-it-debacle/

162   https://www.zdnet.com/article/auditor-slams-customs-it-management/

163   https://delimiter.com.au/2012/06/27/review-brands-atos-change-program-a-success/

164   https://delimiter.com.au/2012/10/22/parliaments-it-systems-a-complete-shambles/

165   http://delimiter.com.au/2010/05/11/border-con trols-340m-it-budget-blowout/

166   http://www.abc.net.au/news/2017-08-28/federal-gov ernments-$10bn-bill-rivals-newstart-cost/8849562

167   https://www.smh.com.au/public-service/government-it-spend-heading-for-10-billion-in-201617-financial-

year-20170324-gv5ipx.html

168   https://delimiter.com.au/2014/04/29/billions-hockey-greenlights-centrelink-core-replacement/

169   https://delimiter.com.au/2011/11/23/vic-government-it-in-flames-1-4-billion-over-budget-all-projects-late-or-failed/

170   https://delimiter.com.au/2010/06/29/woeful-scope-definition-caused-qld-payroll-disaster/

171   https://delimiter.com.au/2013/08/07/anatomy-of-qld-health-it-disaster%E2%80%A8-ibm-should-never-have-been-appointed/

172   https://delimiter.com.au/2012/04/18/at-least-two-web-browsers-for-everyaustralian-desktop-it-should-be-man datory/

173   https://delimiter.com.au/2014/02/14/victoria-police-link-failure-tragic-death/

174   https://delimiter.com.au/2014/03/28/poor-victorian-system-affecting-child-safety/

175   https://www.theguardian.com/australia-news/2017/jan/09/ombudsman-launches-investigation-into-centrelink-debt-recovery-crisis

176   http://www.icac.nsw.gov.au/media-centre/media-releas es/article/4408

177   https://delimiter.com.au/2012/10/24/nepotism-audit-blasts-cenitex-culture/

178   https://delimiter.com.au/2011/12/15/breaking-victorias-it-fail-cycle-first-steps-to-take/

179   https://www.smh.com.au/public-service/departing-pub lic-service-digital-chief-paul-shetler-says-level-of-con tracting-in-aps-is-eye-watering-20161205-gt46y7.html

180   https://www.aph.gov.au/Parliamentary_Business/Com
        mittees/Senate/Environment_and_Communications/
        Video_game_industry

181   https://www.smh.com.au/news/Livewire/Naughty-Dog-
        off-the-leash/2005/01/26/1106415606332.html

182   https://www.kotaku.com.au/2009/11/confirmed-ea-
        closes-pandemic-studios-says-brand-will-live-on/

183   https://www.gamespot.com/articles/ea-cutting-
        1500-jobs-over-a-dozen-games-canceled/1100-6239401/

184   http://www.abc.net.au/news/2011-10-17/australian-
        game-dev-studios-shutting-down/3575196

185   https://delimiter.com.au/2014/05/13/budget-2014-govt-
        dumps-game-dev-funding/

186   https://delimiter.com.au/2010/12/20/nbn-abbott-re
        jects-%E2%80%9Cvideo-entertainment-
        system%E2%80%9D/

187   https://delimiter.com.au/2014/05/15/budget-
        2014-game-devs-bewildered-fund-cut/

188   https://venturebeat.com/2015/02/23/why-you-should-
        start-your-video-game-company-in-canada/

189   https://www.kotaku.com.au/2018/02/developers-and-
        industry-slam-the-federal-governments-response-to-the-
        video-games-inquiry/

190   https://delimiter.com.au/2013/02/14/farce-adobe-ceo-
        flatly-refuses-australian-price-questions-video/

191   https://delimiter.com.au/2013/04/30/us-ambassador-
        begs-australians-stop-pirating-game-of-thrones/

192   https://torrentfreak.com/australia-breeds-pirates-game-
        thrones-140203/

193   https://delimiter.com.au/2016/01/27/apple-australia-
insists-it-pays-all-its-taxes/

194   https://delimiter.com.au/2012/05/03/google-australia-
1bn-in-revenue-74k-in-tax/

195   https://www.theaustralian.com.au/business/technology/
labor-mp-ed-husic-fires-another-missile-at-adobe/news-
story/fff492f0beab2d4c23288be60a175c22?sv=de6b0b2b
67ff79edd7f055c85a95d497

196   https://www.aph.gov.au/parliamentary_business/com
mittees/house_of_representatives_committees?url=ic/
itpricing/report.htm

197   https://delimiter.com.au/2012/05/22/turnbull-con
cerned-by-google-amazon-tax-offshoring/

198   http://www.afr.com/news/politics/national/australian-
government-hits-out-at-apple-tax-bill-20130128-jibuj

199   https://www.itnews.com.au/news/apple-emerges-un
scathed-from-five-year-ato-tax-audit-471421

200   https://www.crn.com.au/news/apple-pays-largest-aus
tralian-tax-bill-in-years-481971

201   https://delimiter.com.au/2016/02/11/federal-govern
ment-introduces-netflix-tax-bill/

202   http://www.oecd.org/tax/a-boost-to-transparency-in-
international-tax-matters-31-countries-sign-tax-co-
operation-agreement.htm

203   https://www.aph.gov.au/Parliamentary_Business/Bills_
Legislation/Bills_Search_Results/Result?bId=r5549

204   https://www.theaustralian.com.au/national-affairs/
treasury/5bn-tax-crackdown-targets-multinational-tech
nology-giants/news-story/0a79e06999e21176eb117fa5c8
5ad626

205 https://twitter.com/renailemay/sta
tus/924954981660102656

206 https://techcrunch.com/2006/10/09/google-has-ac
quired-youtube/

207 https://www.zdnet.com/article/omnidrive-website-van
ishes/

208 https://www.linkedin.com/in/deanmcevoy/

209 https://www.businessinsider.com.au/the-untold-
story-of-spreets-the-aussie-company-yahoo-bought-for-
40-million-2016-3

210 https://delimiter.com.au/2010/07/15/atlassian-
takes-60m-venture-capital-round/

211 https://delimiter.com.au/2010/07/15/atlassian-
takes-60m-venture-capital-round/

212 https://delimiter.com.au/2013/03/21/an-absolute-na
tional-imperative-matt-barries-epic-rant-on-australias-
it-investment/

213 https://delimiter.com.au/2013/09/18/keeping-company-
australia-freelancer-com-turns-400m-buyout-list-asx/

214 https://delimiter.com.au/2013/03/14/blackbird-launch
es-30m-aussie-vc-fund/

215 https://delimiter.com.au/2016/09/14/airtree-rais
es-250m-venture-capital-fund/1

216 https://delimiter.com.au/2010/08/11/im-no-bill-gates-
says-tony-abbott/

217 http://delimiter.com.au/2010/08/10/abbott-is-a-luddite-
says-conroy/

218 https://www.gizmodo.com.au/2015/05/i-dont-think-
the-australian-prime-minister-tony-abbott-understands-

what-teaching-code-in-schools-means/

219   https://delimiter.com.au/2015/07/14/qld-ploughs-24m-into-startups-teaches-coding/

220   https://delimiter.com.au/2014/02/13/deloitte-proposes-concrete-startup-employee-share-changes/

221   https://delimiter.com.au/2015/09/14/turnbull-starts-his-pitch-the-prime-minister-for-innovation/

222   https://delimiter.com.au/2015/12/07/national-innovation-and-science-agenda-turnbull-releases-massive-list-of-new-policies/

223   http://www.afr.com/technology/atlassian-boss-scott-farquhar-warns-visa-rule-changes-risk-stunting-local-tech-growth-20171101-gzd1vv

224   https://delimiter.com.au/2015/11/11/cia-cufflinks-in-the-pms-office-turnbull-hires-data-retention-guru/

225   https://www.aph.gov.au/Parliamentary_Business/Committees/Senate/Legal_and_Constitutional_Affairs/Comprehensive_revision_of_TIA_Act

226   https://en.wikipedia.org/wiki/Data_Retention_Directive

227   https://www.zdnet.com/article/govt-wants-isps-to-record-browsing-history/

228   https://delimiter.com.au/2010/10/29/neuromancing-the-stone-ludlams-ozlog-war/

229   https://delimiter.com.au/2013/02/15/secret-data-retention-docs-display-gross-technical-ineptitude/

230   https://delimiter.com.au/2014/04/02/iinet-opposes-data-retention-web-blocking-plans/

231   https://delimiter.com.au/2010/06/11/data-retention-policy-totally-insane-says-linton/

232 https://delimiter.com.au/2012/09/07/roxon-just-a-front-for-department-says-newton/

233 https://delimiter.com.au/2010/10/29/neuromancing-the-stone-ludlams-ozlog-war/

234 https://delimiter.com.au/2012/09/05/liberal-backbencher-slams-gestapo-data-retention/

235 https://delimiter.com.au/2012/09/05/liberal-backbencher-slams-gestapo-data-retention/

236 https://www.theaustralian.com.au/national-affairs/coalition-mps-hit-out-against-data-retention/news-story/cd282d7b519a38db958f623ee3f3cc3d?sv=d35114ef4cb1c862a0e775f09e5f2a89

237 https://delimiter.com.au/2012/08/31/ipa-damns-extraordinary-data-retention-policy/

238 https://delimiter.com.au/2013/06/24/data-retention-goes-back-to-drawing-board-parliaments-report-criticises-agd-secrecy/

239 https://delimiter.com.au/2015/07/27/labor-pledges-data-retention-policy-review/

240 https://delimiter.com.au/2015/10/12/attorney-generals-dept-proven-comprehensively-unable-to-administer-data-retention-scheme/

241 https://delimiter.com.au/2015/11/03/melbourne-cup-corruption-agency-demands-metadata-access/

242 https://www.theguardian.com/australia-news/2017/apr/28/federal-police-admit-accessing-journalists-metadata-without-a-warrant

243 https://www.itnews.com.au/news/australias-data-retention-scheme-is-still-a-mess-456421

244 https://www.theage.com.au/national/victoria/uber-

driver-nathan-brenner-found-guilty-of-driving-hire-car-without-licence-or-registration-20151204-glfcly.html

245   https://www.washingtonpost.com/blogs/mike-debonis/post/uber-car-impounded-driver-ticketed-in-city-sting/2012/01/13/gIQA4Py3vP_blog.html?utm_term=.79b82db970c0

246   https://www.countycourt.vic.gov.au/sites/default/files/recent-decisions/Brenner%20v%20Taxi%20Services%20Commissioner%20(18%20May%202016)%20Appeal.pdf

247   http://www.afr.com/brand/boss/the-untold-story-of-ubers-arrival-in-australia-20151001-gjyxz4

248   https://getpocketbook.com/blog/the-rise-and-rise-of-uber-in-australia/

249   https://www.choice.com.au/transport/cars/general/articles/uberx-vs-taxi-which-one-is-best

250   https://www.countycourt.vic.gov.au/sites/default/files/recent-decisions/Brenner%20v%20Taxi%20Services%20Commissioner%20(18%20May%202016)%20Appeal.pdf

251   http://www.abc.net.au/news/2016-05-18/melbourne-uber-driver-wins-appeal-for-operating-in-state/7425116

252   http://www.abc.net.au/news/2016-05-18/melbourne-uber-driver-wins-appeal-for-operating-in-state/7425116

253   https://www.maddocks.com.au/uber-australia-whats-changed/

254   http://www.rms.nsw.gov.au/about/news-events/news/roads-and-maritime/2015/150927-ride-sharing-rego-suspensions.html

255   https://www.smh.com.au/technology/brisbane-no-closer-to-uber-app-approval-20140621-zshh6.html

256   https://www.brisbanetimes.com.au/national/queensland/

uber-rules-block-inspectors-from-booking-drivers-to-issue-fines-20151014-gk8viw.html

257   https://www.accc.gov.au/media-release/accc-proposes-to-deny-authorisation-of-ihail-taxi-booking-app

258   https://www.smh.com.au/articles/2009/03/05/1235842537210.html

259   https://delimiter.com.au/2011/06/20/nsw-govt-blocks-another-transport-app/

260   https://delimiter.com.au/2010/12/20/many-poi-nbn-model-insane-says-hackett/

261   https://www.accc.gov.au/media-release/accc-to-not-oppose-acquisition-of-iinet-by-tpg

262   http://delimiter.com.au/2010/11/16/financial-regulator-issues-dire-cloud-warning/

263   https://delimiter.com.au/2012/11/27/regulator-forces-anz-off-salesforce-com/

264   https://delimiter.com.au/2013/07/30/a-real-barrier-sports-commission-cio-speaks-up-on-new-govt-cloud-policy/

265   https://www.communications.gov.au/have-your-say/deregulation-communications-sector

266   https://www.smh.com.au/technology/cloud-agreement-can-bring-blue-skies-20121211-2b77f.html

267   https://www.smh.com.au/national/act/the-act-was-ubers-first-australian-market-but-is-that-market-working-well-20170922-gyn99y.html

www.ingramcontent.com/pod-product-compliance
Lightning Source LLC
Chambersburg PA
CBHW051038250726
48656CB00001B/25